REAL
MAGIC

REAL
MAGIC

ANCIENT WISDOM, MODERN SCIENCE,

AND A GUIDE TO THE

SECRET POWER OF THE UNIVERSE

DEAN RADIN, PHD

HARMONY

BOOKS · NEW YORK

Copyright © 2018 by Dean Radin

Published in the United States by Harmony Books, an imprint of the Crown
Publishing Group, a division of Penguin Random House LLC, New York.
harmonybooks.com

Harmony Books is a registered trademark, and the Circle colophon is a
trademark of Penguin Random House LLC.

Library of Congress Cataloging-in-Publication data is available upon request.

ISBN 978-1-5247-5882-0
Ebook ISBN 978-1-5247-5883-7

Printed in the United States of America

Cover design by Ervin Serrano
Cover images: (eye illustration) polygraphus/iStock/Getty Images; (textures)
Sk_Advance studio/Shutterstock and caesart/Shutterstock; (cover photograph)
plainpicture/Hollandse Hoogte/Richard Brocken

10

First Edition

To my charmed parents, Hilda (1923–2017) and Jerry,
who celebrated their seventy-third wedding anniversary in 2017;
to my enchanting wife, Susie;
and to our two small dogs,
who are spellbound by moving objects, especially cats

CONTENTS

PREFACE

Guest editorial, New Seattle Province, June 1, 2915. A fragment of an ancient digitized file was discovered today during an archeological dig in the region once known as the American Northwest. Precise dating of the fragment is uncertain due to bit corruption, but estimates place it near the beginning of the twenty-third century. It appears to be an editorial from the defunct news service *Galactica Today*. It reads:

It is difficult to appreciate what it must have been like to live at the dawn of the twenty-first century. The climate was spiraling out of control, viral outbreaks were endemic, and the global economy was failing. The population turned to demagogues who promised grandiose, unrealistic futures. As civil order declined, simmering resentments fueled nationalism and then tribalism, which accelerated the pandemonium.

It was not until the mid-twenty-first century, with the crisis in extremis, that hints of a resolution began to appear. Necessity had cracked entrenched scientific dogmas, allowing new ideas to be heard. The resulting brainstorms revealed that the multiple threats were reflections of a single, underlying dilemma—an impasse that new technologies could not solve. The challenge was rooted in humanity's faulty understanding of consciousness, which, as we now know, is the fundamental glue that binds the fabric of reality. This truth was widely scorned in the early twenty-first century because it evoked age-old fears and preconceptions about what scientists of the day naively called *magic*. It took many generations to advance beyond those fears.

Historians today agree that the tide turned around the year 2095, when Hilda Ramirez of Hunan State University first conclusively demonstrated the plasticity of physical reality. Her evidence that the speed of light and other physical constants were mental constructs, not inviolable absolutes, provided a clear path to global harmony.

By the mid-twenty-second century, Olga von Diesel's theory of quasiholography—known today in the vernacular as *neomagic*—firmly placed consciousness on a continuum with matter and energy. The first genetically enhanced magi were soon bred, and even as children they were able to quickly tame extreme weather events. By 2160, the World Federation of Magi was formed and neomagicians throughout the world were tasked with restoring the climate, stabilizing the world economy, and eradicating disease.

What our heroic predecessors failed to appreciate was one of the unintended consequences of the popularization of neomagic, especially among youth. In times past, adolescents expressed their angst by furtively committing acts of rebellious art in public places. Such displays—our ancestors called it *graffiti*—are found throughout the historical record, from crude sketches on the walls of the prehistoric Leang Timpuseng caves in Indonesia to holographic erotica found on the lower decks of the Titan Space Station. This teenage "art" has always been a nuisance, but at least it could be washed away.

Today, with the rise of neomagical graffiti, we face a more serious problem. Juvenile shenanigans, like the latest fad of turning streetlamps into multicolored carnivorous flowers, are no longer mere annoyances. They pose a serious danger to pedestrians. We must put a stop to this childish behavior before it threatens the social order. . . .

After this point the record is unreadable, but the concern expressed is unmistakable. We sympathize with our predecessors because younger magi today find it hard to believe that only a few centuries ago most people were blissfully unaware of the power of consciousness. They lived during dark times when the most educated minds had convinced themselves, despite an enormous body of evidence to the contrary, that reality emerged solely from various forms of energy. Their crude instruments were unable to detect the multidimensional tapestry of consciousness. It took radical advances in theory and the development of the intelligent noosphere to develop a more comprehensive picture of reality.

We now know that the universe is far more flexible than our ancestors could have believed, but we continue to face a troubling conundrum. Rebellious youth persist in carelessly littering the mindscape with seditious thought-forms. Some even warn that these new forms of graffiti may be altering history. An example of that concern involves the famous statue on Liberty Island in New York harbor. There are clues in the chronological record suggesting that our much-beloved statue, the Philodendron of Freedom, was once a large green woman, not the large green plant we've prized for centuries. That we would have honored a statue of a green woman seems preposterous, but if history is being altered, we'd never know for sure. In any case, the consequences of changing history are so dangerous that for the sake of caution we call upon all responsible elder magi to cast binding spells to put an end to these immature pranks before they threaten our very existence.

Chapter 1

BEGINNING

THIS BOOK IS ABOUT MAGIC.

Not the fictional magic of Harry Potter, the feigned magic of Harry Houdini, or the fraudulent magic of con artists. Not blue lightning bolts springing from the fingertips, aerial combat on broomsticks, sleight-of-hand tricks, or any of the other elaborations of artistic license and special effects.

This is about *real* magic.

Occultists sometimes use the Old English spelling *magick* to distinguish fictional and stage magic from the real deal. We'll use the more common term, *magic,* to avoid unnecessary associations with the occult.

Real magic falls into three categories: mental influence of the physical world, perception of events distant in space or time, and interactions with nonphysical entities. The first type I'll call *force of will*; it's associated with spell-casting and other techniques meant to intentionally influence events or actions. The second is *divination*; it's associated with practices such as reading Tarot cards and mirror-gazing. The third is *theurgy*, from the Greek meaning "god-work"; it involves methods for evoking and communicating with spirits.

Unlike books that discuss beliefs about magic from psychological or historical perspectives, or that list recipes for spell-casting, the goal here is to explore real magic from an evidence-based scientific perspective. Why a scientific approach? You wouldn't know it by reading most college textbooks, but there's a vast scientific literature that informs our understanding of real magic. When I was in college, none of my coursework mentioned anything about that literature. But now, after four decades of experimentally studying magic, motivated by scientific curiosity and without a religious background that might have biased me to be overly sympathetic about metaphysical concepts, I've come to two conclusions.

First, there's no doubt that science is the most accurate lens on reality that humanity has developed so far. What we've collectively discovered about the nature of Nature over the last three or four centuries, from the quantum to the cosmological, is an awe-inspiring testament to our creativity and imagination. Technologies based on that knowledge provide proof that our discoveries are valid. So, when considering real magic, it would be foolish to just throw away what we've already learned.

But second, reality viewed through the lens of science is an exceedingly thin slice of the whole shebang. Science is tightly focused on the objective, measurable, physical world. That focus excludes the one and only thing you can ever know for sure— your *consciousness*, that inner spark of sentience that you call "me."

While science as a practice has primarily concentrated on the objective world, scientific *methods* are extremely powerful, so if we wish we can redirect our lens to look inward and explore what consciousness is capable of. When we do that, we are startled to find whole new realms of knowledge. One of the consequences of taking this inner perspective is that the idea of magic transforms from an impossible fantasy into an aspect of Nature that we can begin to study. From this stance, terms such as *paranormal* and *supernatural* are seen as quaint and antediluvian, similar to how modern medicine no longer needs the concept of "bad humors" when discussing the origins of disease.

We'll explore this new realm of knowledge through two major themes. First, based on a substantial body of experimental evidence, we can state with a high degree of confidence that real magic exists. Second, there are rising trends in science suggesting that what was once called magic is poised to evolve into a new scientific discipline, just as medieval astrology and alchemy evolved into today's astronomy and chemistry. The new discipline will be the study of the psychophysical nature of reality, that mysterious, interstitial space shimmering between mind and matter. Understanding how this enigmatic space works in a way that's consistent with the rest of science requires a new worldview—the lens through which we understand reality.

Another theme we'll discuss is that magic didn't miraculously disappear with the rise of the scientific worldview. Magic is still intensely present. Prayer is a form of intentional magic, a mental act intended to affect the world in some way. Wearing a sacred symbol is a form of sympathetic magic, a symbolic correspondence said to transcend time and space. Many religious rituals are forms of ancient ceremonial magic. The abundance of popular books on the power of affirmations and positive thinking are all based on age-old magical principles.

From a conventional scientific perspective, these widespread practices are considered examples of infantile magical thinking, fairy tales. Some scientists even use the word *magic* as a synonym for *nonsense*, because it implies the scientifically appalling idea that some things "just happen" for no discernible or plausible cause. But magic doesn't mean "no cause." It just means that we haven't yet developed scientifically acceptable theories to explain these effects. As we'll see, there are already important hints that may lead to such theories, so it's best to think of real magic not as something impossibly mysterious, but as a forerunner of the future of science.

MAGIC IS EVERYWHERE

The possibility that magic is real can be terribly unsettling to those who'd prefer that it not exist. Consider A. J. Ayer (Sir Alfred Jules Ayer, 1910–1989), a prominent British philosopher who specialized in logical positivism. This is a critical philosophical position that utterly rejects any sort of metaphysical, religious, or magical concepts. As might be expected, Ayer was a hardcore atheist. At age seventy-seven, he died. Fortunately, he was resuscitated, and to everyone's surprise he reported a near-death experience (NDE). He described it as consisting of

> repeated attempts to cross a river and "a red light, exceedingly bright, and also very painful . . . responsible for the government of the universe." Ayer retained his atheism, but declared that the experience had "slightly weakened" his conviction that death "will be the end of me."[1]

That Ayer reported this experience is more astounding than it may seem. Lifelong logical positivists are tough. They don't "slightly weaken" their intellectual positions on anything. The link between magic and Ayer's NDE is theurgy, the third category of magic. NDEs suggest that there may be forms of disembodied awareness, or spirits. For many who've experienced an NDE it's a virtual certainty that such spirits exist.[2] But so far there's no strictly objective way to tell if that's the *only* viable interpretation. We'll revisit this issue in more detail later.

Another example of magic intruding into the mundane world involves William Friedkin, the director of the movie *The Exorcist*. Before he made his famous film, Friedkin hadn't witnessed an exorcism; afterward he decided to do so. He spent time with Father Gabriel Amorth, a Vatican exorcist. His experience with Father Amorth did not overcome his prior agnosticism. But after showing a video of a terrifying exorcism to three prominent neuroscientists and three psychiatrists and *not* getting the blithe dismissal that he expected from those experts, it "scare[d] the Hades out of him."[3]

A third example is provided by historian Michael Shermer, a prominent skeptic of all things paranormal. In Shermer's September 2016 column in *Scientific American*, he asked, "Is it possible to measure supernatural or paranormal phenomena?" His answer was an unambiguous no:

> Where the known meets the unknown we are tempted to inject paranormal and supernatural forces to explain unsolved mysteries. We must resist the temptation because such efforts can never succeed, not even in principle.[4]

"Not even in principle" is reminiscent of a quip attributed to Mark Twain: "It ain't what you don't know that gets you into trouble. It's what you know for sure that just ain't so."[5] Shermer justified his confidence by citing Caltech physicist Sean Carroll, because Carroll concluded that the laws of physics "rule out the possibility of true psychic powers." Why? Because, Shermer continued, "the particles and forces of nature don't allow us to bend spoons, levitate or read minds." Furthermore, according to Carroll,

> we know that there aren't new particles or forces out there yet to be discovered that would support them. Not simply because we haven't found them yet, but because we definitely would have found them if they had the right characteristics to give us the requisite powers.[6]

Sidestepping what history teaches us about going public with such conceits, Shermer nevertheless concluded with certainty that searching for paranormal or supernatural forces "can never succeed." With that, he slammed the door shut.

So far, this is standard skeptical fare. But the peculiar aspect of this story is that two years prior to slamming the door, Shermer encouraged the exact opposite. In his October 2014 column in *Scientific American*, he opened with the following surprising admission:

> Often I am asked if I have ever encountered something that I could not explain. What my interlocutors have in mind are not bewildering enigmas such as consciousness or U.S. foreign policy but anomalous and mystifying events that suggest the existence of the paranormal or supernatural. My answer is: yes, now I have.[7]

He went on to describe an event in June 2014, when he was planning to marry his fiancée, Jennifer Graf. Her grandfather was the closest she had to a father figure, but tragically he died when she was sixteen years old. One of the few heirlooms she kept from her grandfather was a 1978 Philips transistor radio. Shermer tried to get it to work. He put in new batteries, looked for loose connections, and tried smacking it on a hard surface. It still wouldn't work. So he gave up and placed it in the back of a desk drawer in their bedroom. Three months later, Shermer and Graf were married at their home in California. She was feeling sad that her grandfather wasn't there to give her away. After the wedding ceremony, something strange happened. They heard music. They traced it to the desk drawer in the bedroom. It was the grandfather's radio, playing a love song.

They were stunned into silence. Finally Graf whispered, "My grandfather is here with us. I'm not alone." The radio continued to play that evening, fell silent the next day, and never worked again. Shermer's reaction: "I have to admit, it rocked me back on my heels and shook my skepticism to its core." As a result, he wrote, still reeling with awe:

[If] we are to take seriously the scientific credo to keep an open mind and remain agnostic when the evidence is indecisive or the riddle unsolved, we should not shut the doors of perception when they may be opened to us to marvel in the mysterious.

What happened between his modest proposal calling for openness in the face of the mysterious and two years later when he slammed the door shut? I can't speculate about Shermer's change of heart, but one thing we do know is that when one encounters a belief-shattering event it's not uncommon to promptly forget about it, or even to deny that it ever happened. Psychologists use the term *repression* to describe such cases.[8] As magician Peter Carroll once put it, "When people are presented with real magical events they somehow manage not to notice. If they are forced to notice something uncontrovertibly magical they may become terrified, nauseated, and ill."[9]

Shermer's experience suggests that real magic is always present, patiently waiting just below the calm surface of the everyday world. Every so often its tentacles brush our leg, causing shivers to shoot up our spine. It's that electrifying quality that makes magical fiction so captivating, magical stage illusions endlessly entertaining, and magical fraud so easy to perpetrate.

The word *magic* comes from the Greek word *magos*, referring to a member of a learned and priestly class, which in turn derives from the Old Persian word *magush*, meaning to "be able" or "to have power." In the early nineteenth century, the word *magic* also took on the connotation of entertainment, delight, or attraction. *Magic* also implies exotic, alien, or the "other." This subtext is an important reason why magic is persistently alluring. But that allure often manifests in the sense of watching a train wreck—simultaneously attractive and repulsive. *Our* magic, which is a core facet of *our* religious practice, is of course fascinating and perfectly acceptable. But *their* practices are dangerous, outrageous, and evil.

Incidentally, the word *fascinate* comes from the Latin *fascinatus*, meaning "to bewitch or enchant." The words *bewitch* and *enchant* have roughly the same meaning as *magic*, as do the words *charm* and *glamour*. Magic is everywhere.

POWER

As in ages past, many people interested in real magic today are motivated by a desire to wield power—power to get wealth, fame, love, or sex. All of these applications are possible, and there are plenty of books, videos, websites, and smartphone apps that provide recipes for magical rituals and spells.

Some folks, especially those who subscribe to an orthodox religious faith, may recoil from the idea of spell-casting. Many traditional religions teach that magic and witchcraft are fundamentally demonic and evil. But the way magic is used is completely up to the magician. The power itself, like any fundamental force of the universe, is morally neutral. Atomic fission and fusion are just aspects of the way the physical world works. Questions of morality arise when we use such natural phenomena to create weapons.

Magical power intended to manipulate or exploit others is called *black magic*. It's intensely seductive because, as the existentialist philosopher Jean-Paul Sartre once wrote, "Hell is other people."[10] That is, as social creatures, we must depend on others who may or may not be interested in our desires, and that can easily lead to personal conflicts. Use of magic to resolve these conflicts egregiously violates the Golden Rule, so it's immoral.

By the way, prayers that intend harm to others are also clear instances of black magic. Far right-wing Christians in the United States are constantly railing against the demonic evils of witchcraft, but at the same time they pray intensely to influence others. As an example, one such individual announced during the 2016 U.S. presidential debates that he was praying "that confusion would cloud Hillary Clinton's mind and that fear would come upon her."[11] Then, tit for tat, ceremonial magicians who were displeased with the outcome of the election circulated a "spell to bind Donald Trump and all those who abet him."[12] This type of spell is part of an age-old tradition called *defixiones* magic. It's intended to bind or constrain the object of the spell. Some would argue that a binding spell is not black magic because it doesn't intend to harm an individual; rather, it aims to prevent harm or threats caused by that person to come to others. This reasoning illustrates the slippery slope that justifies the use of magic in a gray area, somewhere between black and white.

When it comes to the consequences of practicing black magic, think of Darth Vader from *Star Wars*, Sméagol from *Lord of the Rings,* or the legend of Faust.[13] Those stories do not end well. Within the magical worldview everything is deeply interconnected, so if you intend to harm others, you are likely to end up harming yourself. This is not just because of a guilty conscience but more like Newton's third law: for every action there's an equal and opposite reaction. Let's just say it would be exceedingly prudent to avoid black magic.

Later we'll look at a few magical practices you can try yourself, to whet your appetite, but this book is not intended to be an instruction manual. Here we're interested in more basic questions, like: Is it possible to study magic using scientific principles and methods? What does that evidence tell us about the reality of magic? And are there any hints within today's science that tell us *how* magic works?

WHERE WE'RE HEADED

In Chapter 2, I'll describe my surprise after it dawned on me that I had been studying magic for about four decades without realizing it. Then we'll survey a potpourri of magical topics, from popular culture to the scholarly study of magic, why magic is both terrific and terrifying, the continuing horrors of witch hunts, and why we can't help but engage in magical thinking (Chapter 3). We'll follow that with an overview of the history of the esoteric traditions, for that's where we'll find clues about how magic works (Chapter 4).

Then we'll look at some elementary magical practices (Chapter 5), and from there we'll examine some of the scientific evidence for magic (Chapter 6). We'll learn that the results of most scientific tests of magical principles are statistically highly significant but generally small in magnitude. So we'll follow up that chapter with case studies of three real-world, Merlin-class magicians. We'll find that the effects typically observed in the laboratory can scale up to jaw-dropping proportions in rare people with high talent (Chapter 7).

That will bring us to a discussion about how magic works (Chapter 8). This involves topics such as the metaphysical foundations of science, the knowledge hierarchies that science uses to carve up reality into separate disciplines, trends in science, and why all of this leads to a new worldview that's consistent with both science and magic. Then we'll wrap up with levitating psychic robots, among other things (Chapter 9).

Chapter 2

SCIENCE AND MAGIC?

To believe that magic will eventually disappear is mere wishful thinking.

—OWEN DAVIES

I'VE BEEN STUDYING MAGIC FROM A SCIENTIFIC PERSPECtive for about forty years. For the first thirty-nine of those years I would have vigorously denied that statement. Magic is associated with fairy tales, Harry Potter, and Las Vegas stage illusionists. Those are all about fantasies, which are fine for entertainment, but scientists aren't interested in frivolous fiction. As Peter Venkman, a character from the 1984 movie *Ghostbusters*, said to prove he's a serious guy, "Back off, man, I'm a scientist."

My formal education included music, physics, electrical engineering, and psychology. In graduate school at the University of Illinois, Urbana-Champaign, I studied cybernetics, computer simulations of cognitive processes, and artificial intelligence. That campus is located in the flatlands of Illinois. During the summer, we'd hear a tornado warning siren almost every day in the late afternoon. Sometimes we would spot an actual tornado headed our way. Watching the sky twist into knots and bear down on you is awesome but also gut-wrenchingly terrifying, so during those episodes I found myself intently wishing that the tornado would go somewhere else. Even in the midst of extreme magical thinking, I knew that my wishes were just a way of coping in the face of peril.

After graduate school, for most of my working career I've focused on the relationships between the brain, the mind (our cognitive and perceptual capacities), and consciousness (awareness). Of those three factors, I've found consciousness to be the most interesting because it raises a baffling problem: how does the three-pound lump of neural tissue inside my head give rise to the awareness that I call me? This "mind-body problem" has been hotly debated by philosophers for thousands of years, and it remains one of the foremost unsolved puzzles in science today.[1] What is consciousness, where does it come from, and what's its purpose?

No one knows.

We don't even know if the way we're posing the question is on the right track. Maybe consciousness is generated by the brain, maybe it isn't. Some neurophilosophers don't even believe awareness exists. They think consciousness is a brain-centric illusion.[2]

What we *do* know is that without consciousness there'd be no "you" to experience the act of reading this sentence. What a lonely universe it would be if ultimately we are just robotic "meat machines," playacting the appearance of reading to a mindless audience that isn't even aware it *is* the audience. Perhaps you can see why trying to understand the nature and purpose of consciousness has kept generations of philosophers enthusiastically screaming at each other.

There are three conventional approaches to studying consciousness. Philosophers analyze the concepts, logic, and assumptions used to describe consciousness. Scientists study consciousness from the outside in, typically by measuring the activity of the brain and body, or by asking people to report their experiences. Meditators study consciousness from the inside out, by introspection.[3] I've used all of those methods, but I've concentrated on a fourth, less conventional approach.

I investigate phenomena that challenge commonly held assumptions about the brain-mind relationship. I do this by investigating psychic phenomena, often abbreviated as *psi*, pronounced "sigh."[4] Psi experiences have been labeled *telepathy* (images or emotions shared between minds separated by distance), *clairvoyance* (perception of distant events or images), *precognition* (perception of distant events or images through time), and *psychokinesis* (influence of distant systems via mental intention). These topics are studied within the discipline known as *parapsychology*.

In the public's mind, parapsychology is associated with exciting tabloid stories about Bigfoot's role in the Illuminati, secret alliances between UFOs and the Transportation Security Administration, telepathic aliens in cahoots with the shadow government, and so on. These stories are fun to read while waiting in the grocery store checkout lane, but from a mainstream perspective only the lunatic fringe takes them seriously. The association between psi and tabloid fare is more than annoying; it's a big problem. The false but *perceived* connection is petrifying to anyone whose career depends on credibility, and in science credibility is essential.

So all fledgling scientists learn to maintain a serious, sober demeanor at all times, even if they're secretly wearing Spider-Man underwear. The saddest people on Earth are junior faculty hoping to get tenure at a university, because they're forbidden to smile in public, crack jokes, or make eye contact, and they absolutely can't be seen as being even mildly interested in tabloid stories. It's the kiss of death to put one's twenty-plus years of education and training in jeopardy by being perceived as too sympathetic about controversial topics.

You may think I'm exaggerating, but I'm not. I once attended a small meeting with the head of an important funding organization, a prominent academic neuroscientist, a junior professor from an Ivy League university, and several others. We were discussing psi research. At one point the eminent neuroscientist suddenly realized that he had no idea what we were talking about, so he asked, "What *is* parapsychology?" Before I could respond, the junior professor brightened up and proclaimed, "Oh, it's like the search for Bigfoot." I knew this fellow had attended lectures on psi research and had even conducted his own psi experiments, so he was well aware that what he had just said was ridiculous. But he said it anyway to let the famous neuroscientist know that he certainly wasn't part of *that* silly crowd.

The upshot of the social taboo is that most academic scientists avoid parapsychology as though it's a virulent strain of a zombie plague. If they're secretly interested in psi—and many are— they first swear everyone to secrecy, and then they approach it slowly while wearing a full hazmat suit, with multiple alibis set up in advance to provide plausible deniability.[5]

This is a pity, because parapsychology involves the application of orthodox scientific and scholarly methods to a class of commonly reported but as yet poorly understood human experiences.[6] That's all it is. The *topics* studied might give some people allergic fits, but the methods used are transparent and completely orthodox.

Because of what parapsychologists *actually* do, as compared to what some imagine that they do, the international organization of academic parapsychologists—called the Parapsychological Association—was elected an affiliate of the largest mainstream scientific organization in the world, the American Association for the Advancement of Science (AAAS). The Parapsychological Association is one of the AAAS's "252 societies and academies of science, serving more than 10 million members, representing the world's largest federation of scientific and engineering societies."[7]

I felt that the aims of the Parapsychological Association— using the tools of science and scholarship to rigorously explore these strange yet commonly reported experiences we call psi—were completely in accord with the highest aspirations of science. So I joined the organization, served on its board for many years, and was elected its president five times.[8] I remain an active member.

What does any of this have to do with magic?

After decades of conducting psi experiments, publishing many journal articles describing the results, and reviewing thousands of other experiments in my popular books (*The Conscious Universe*, *Entangled Minds*, and *Supernormal*), I've come to accept that psi is a real phenomenon. I base my assessment on the fact that telepathy, clairvoyance, precognition, and psychokinetic effects have all been independently repeated in laboratories around the world. Effects we see in the lab tend to be rather small because by design they must be demonstrated on demand and under strictly controlled conditions. But the magnitude of an effect is irrelevant if you're interested in whether the effects *exist*.

For most active psi researchers today, the existential question is no longer interesting, because the data are clear. Those whose knowledge of this field is limited to polemics written by hardened skeptics are, as one might guess, plagued with uncertainties. Sometimes skeptics offer constructive critiques, and those can be very useful for sharpening research methods. But many critiques are bizarrely irrational and positively drip with emotion. Controversy invariably invites disagreements, but there's something peculiar about psi that seems to push otherwise calm, rational scientists beyond civil discourse and into rabid, foaming-at-the-mouth frenzies.

Some portion of those overreactions can be understood as a symptom of an ideological clash. This phrase usually refers to collisions between opposing political or religious beliefs, but science too has its ideologies. If one is taught that psi experiences can only be delusions, because real psi would violate one or more unspecified "laws" of science, then any evidence presented to the contrary can evoke a sense of panic, similar to the body's immune response to a life-threatening allergen. Some people break out in hives when exposed to pollen; others break out in emotional rashes when exposed to psi.

But maybe it's more than that.

After all, a Gallup poll in 2005 showed that nearly 75 percent of Americans believe in at least one "paranormal" phenomenon, like psi, but a mere 0.001 percent of academic scientists are actively engaged in studying the ontological reality of these experiences.[9] What's wrong with this picture? What's the big deal about psi phenomena? The deal is that we all enjoy fictional tales about magic, but real magic is frightening.

And here's the rub: *psi is magic.*

That is, when you boil magic down into its essential forms, it's precisely what psi experiments investigate. Both psi and magic refer to the same underlying consciousness-related phenomena; both are marginalized from the scientific mainstream; both are labeled as demonic by orthodox religions; both saturate popular entertainment; and both are perennially popular in scholarly fields, but not if the phenomena are presented as *real*.

That psi and magic are two sides of the same coin is not a new idea.[10] But discussions from a neutral, scientific perspective are rare. For example, the most comprehensive recent anthology on the state of the art in psi research was published in 2015. Entitled *Parapsychology: A Handbook for the 21st Century*, the book doesn't even list the word *magic* in the index. The psi-magic relationship is occasionally mentioned in the context of anthropology, especially in the study of shamanic or "primitive" practices. But even there, it's only the radicals who propose that shamanic magic is actually *real*.

Books by practicing magicians (the real kind, not stage illusionists) occasionally mention the psi-magic connection. Isaac

Bonewits's 1971 book, *Real Magic*, devoted a chapter to parapsy-chology.[11] But that was published long before modern advance-ments in the field, and much of that one chapter was devoted to a discussion of amusing neologisms Bonewits created for various psi effects.[12] Patrick Dunn's 2005 book, *Postmodern Magic*, is more typical of what modern magicians have to say about psi as the scientific study of magic:

> Looking for a scientific explanation for magic is like trying to find a scientific explanation for poetry. Science simply does not and cannot study magic any more than it can study the phenomenon of "art."[13]

Dunn is overly pessimistic, as we'll see. Another modern magician, Gordon White, favorably mentions the psi-magic re-lationship in his 2016 book, *Pieces of Eight*.[14] But White is an ex-pert on esotericism, and his book appreciates but tends to gloss over the relevant science.

The bottom line is this: (1) practically all conventional aca-demic books and articles that mention psi or magic discuss them as mistaken beliefs, delusions, or aspects of ancient his-tory, (2) the literature on psi research ignores magic, and (3) the literature on magic ignores psi.

That's a strange state of affairs.

I figured that if anthropologists can safely study the magi-cal beliefs of what they used to call "savages," if psychologists are allowed to investigate why modern citizens still believe in magic, and if historians can survey the words used in ancient magical spells, then surely we're mature enough in the twenty-first century to use the lens of science to examine the possibil-ity of real magic without causing the world, or ourselves, to go berserk.[15]

As Rabbi Moses ben Maimon (1135–1204, also known as Maimonides), put it:

Every time you find in our books a tale the reality of which seems impossible, a story which is repugnant both to reason and common sense, then be sure that tale contains a profound allegory veiling a deeply mysterious truth . . . and the greater the absurdity of the letter the deeper the wisdom of the spirit.[16]

Chapter 3

MAGICAL POTPOURRI

The first stage is when you totally believe in witchcraft.

The second is when you realize that it's a complete lot of rubbish.

The third is when you realize that it's a complete lot of rubbish; but somehow it also seems to work.

—Ronald Hutton

When you are studying the history and practice of magic, the first thing you discover is that everyone throughout history has been fascinated by this topic. And it seems that half of them have written at least one book about it. The scope and magnitude of the literature are mind-boggling.

There are hundreds of thousands of scholarly books and articles covering magic from every conceivable angle. Using the search term "magick," Google returns more than 25 million webpages and YouTube returns nearly a half-million videos.[1] The disciplines of anthropology, psychology, sociology, linguistics, semiotics, mathematics, philology, philosophy, religious studies, and history are positively marinated in magic.

Outside of academia, there are hundreds of *grimoires* (books of spells) by ancient, medieval, and modern magicians. There are thousands of articles and books on theatrical magic, sleight-of-hand conjuring, and illusory magic. And there are countless movies, fairy tales, parables, allegories, mythologies, and science fiction and fantasy novels devoted to magical themes.

These books are not merely popular. They rank among the leading bestsellers of any written works in history. They even challenge print runs of religious texts. Such books include *The Alchemist* by Paulo Coelho, *The Little Prince* by Antoine de Saint-Exupéry, *Alice in Wonderland* by Lewis Carroll, the *Harry Potter* series by J. K. Rowling, and *The Lord of the Rings* and *The Hobbit* by J. R. R. Tolkien.[2] Together these books have sold hundreds of millions of copies. If we include the book genre on affirmations and the power of positive thinking, we're talking about a billion books. The same trend is found among the highest-grossing movies of all time, with franchises such as *Star Wars*, *Harry Potter*, *Lord of the Rings*, *The Avengers*, *X-Men*, and *Dr. Strange,* as well as films like *The Sixth Sense,* hovering near the top of the list.[3] Magic is a multibillion-dollar industry and an essential component of popular culture.

SCHOLARLY INTEREST

Christopher Partridge, professor of religious studies at Lancaster University, coined the term *occulture* to refer to the many ways that occult themes are absorbed into and influence popular culture. Many academics are involved in the study of occulture, and within those disciplines magic is a topic of perennial interest.

There are peer-reviewed print and online scholarly journals devoted to the study of magic. For example, the journal *Magic, Ritual and Witchcraft* is published by the University of Pennsylvania Press. The Society for the Academic Study of Magic publishes the journal *Preternature: Critical and Historical Studies on the Preternatural.* There is *Paranthropology: Journal of Anthropological Approaches to the Paranormal.* An online journal, *Esoterica*, is published by Michigan State University.

One of the academic disciplines most entranced by magic is called *esotericism*, the study of hidden, suppressed, secret, or occult knowledge. In the United States there is an Association for the Study of Esotericism. There's a similar society in Europe and a dozen others around the world.

To give a flavor of what scholars of esoterica are interested in, consider the 2010 fall issue of the *Societas Magica Newsletter*, where we find an article on "Jewish love magic."[4] Love magic is one of the most common categories of magical spells, with written evidence traced to Mesopotamia around 2200 BCE.[5] Some two hundred thousand fragments of such spells were found in the Ben Ezra synagogue in Cairo, written from the ninth to the nineteenth centuries. Love spells were intended to encourage ever-popular goals such as attracting a partner, separating lovers, or gaining the favor of someone in authority.

These forms of ancient magic are interesting to scholars because spells written by Jews during that thousand-year period are noticeably different from spells written by non-Jews, and that in turn reflects differences in cultural sensitivities. For example, Greco-Roman love spells were often expressed in flagrantly erotic language with no room for misinterpretation, whereas Jewish love spells were more oblique. That is, a Roman love spell might command, "Now I must schtupp Gloria!"[6] By contrast, a Jewish love spell might go something like this: "If it's not too much to ask, I would humbly request a love match with Bernice in the manner described in the Torah, Genesis 11:29, of the love between Abraham and Sarah. If that's inconvenient, then perhaps in the manner of Isaac and Rebecca. As long as it's not a bother."[7]

TERRIFIC AND TERRIFYING

Real magic is at once terrific and terrifying, awesome and awful. Awesome because from a scientific perspective magic provides valuable clues about who and what we are, and what we may be capable of. From a religious perspective, magic is not just awesome but necessary. It supports the supernatural worldview described in sacred texts.

Theists of most traditional faiths avoid expressing public interest in magic. But many religious people wear a symbol of their faith—a cross, a talisman, a protection amulet given by a guru—and the symbol is not just a public pronouncement of faith but also a form of sympathetic magic (a transcendent symbolic connection to a guru or deity). The promise of magical power is also seductive, especially to those who are told to avoid it. For example, a growing segment of Muslim youth in London are fascinated by a magical healing practice called *ruqya shariya* (lawful incantation). Sorcery is strictly forbidden in Islam, but young people never listen to their elders.[8]

There are some positive role models for magicians, including Glinda, the Good Witch of the South, from *The Wonderful Wizard of Oz*; Samantha, from the 1960s television show *Bewitched*; Jeannie, from the 1960s show *I Dream of Jeannie*; Sabrina, from the 1990s show *Sabrina, the Teenage Witch*; Gandalf, from *Lord of the Rings*; Professor Dumbledore, from the *Harry Potter* series; Merlin, from the tales of King Arthur; and Dr. Strange, from the Marvel Comics series and the 2016 movie.

But these role models are unusual. In fiction, magic is usually portrayed in negative terms, as a struggle between the forces of good and evil, where good only wins occasionally. Horror films based on paranormal themes predictably depict magic in malevolent terms. And the magical arts always seem to attract more than their fair share of angry-looking people dressed in black and decorated with menacing tattoos and alarming facial piercings.

This is where magic becomes terrifying. Magic as something real is fully accepted by the devoutly religious, but to them magic outside the confines of the Church is frighteningly demonic.

Among the secular population, real magic radically challenges basic assumptions about reality. Concepts such as personal and state sovereignty, privacy, and secrecy are regarded as essential features in modern politics and the law. A principal role of the criminal justice system is to expose hidden secrets, and the massive apparatus of the world's intelligence agencies is devoted to that task. Yet magic threatens sovereignty and transcends secrecy. Besides death and taxes, the one other universal truth is that bureaucracies never respond kindly to challenges to their authority. So there's enormous societal pressure to suppress the reality of magic.

Nor would most individuals embrace magic as real the moment they realize that through the application of magic it would be possible, at least in principle, for others to know their private thoughts, manipulate their health, or influence their finances. The mere *idea* that such feats may be possible can evoke severe paranoia. Faced with such perfectly rational fears, we naturally repress the idea of magic. If we deny that there are monsters under the bed, maybe they'll go away.

As we'll see in Chapter 4, many orthodox religions have strictly banned magic, largely as a sociopolitical strategy. It would not do if infidels were allowed to worship anything not under the control of the proper ecclesiastic authorities. Like any struggle for political power, gaining the allegiance of the masses is much easier by inciting fear of the "other" than by encouraging love and compassion.[9]

But religious faith also *requires* an unwavering belief in magic, so certain forms of magic are acceptable. Catholic priests are sanctioned to perform the sacrament of the Eucharist, an explicitly magical transformation of bread and wine into the body and blood of Christ. There are more than 1 billion Roman Catholics in the world, of whom about 400,000 are priests.[10] So quite a few people are approved to perform that particular brand of magic.

But for the rest of us, *no magic for you!*

The early Catholic Church faced the problem of distinguishing between lawful, divine miracles and illicit, selfish, or demonic acts of magic. That problem led to the unequivocal rejection and condemnation of any form of magic (that is, performed outside the Church) by Saint Augustine (254–430 CE). This prohibition was codified within the Catechism of the Catholic Church. So let's turn to your Catechism, Part 3, Section 2, Chapter 1, Article 1.III, the section titled "You Shall Have No Other Gods Before Me." There you will find in paragraphs 2116 and 2117:

2116. All forms of divination are to be rejected: recourse to Satan or demons, conjuring up the dead or other practices falsely supposed to "unveil" the future. . . .

2117. All practices of magic or sorcery, by which one attempts to tame occult powers, so as to place them at one's service and have a supernatural power over others—even if this were for the sake of restoring their health—are gravely contrary to the virtue of religion.[11]

For those who religiously follow the Catechism, these injunctions leave no wiggle room. That's why the *Harry Potter* books are simultaneously the most popular and the most banned books in the world.[12]

IS *HARRY POTTER* HARMFUL?

The *Harry Potter* books are banned because some view them as promoting "unchristian magic." As Carol Rockwood, head of St. Mary's Island Church of England school in Kent, England, explained, "The Bible is very clear and consistent in its teachings that wizards, devils and demons exist and are very real, powerful and dangerous and God's people are told to have nothing to do with them."[13]

So the same book series lauded by parents and teachers for encouraging children to read is disallowed in religious schools and libraries, and in especially zealous cases the books are burned in public. *Harry Potter* is not the only book series banned for its "occult" themes. The popular *Hunger Games* trilogy by Suzanne Collins and *Bridge to Terabithia* by Katherine Paterson are also banned because some see them as promoting satanism.[14]

To fundamentalists, the *Harry Potter* books were always wicked, but in their eyes the presence of evil was highlighted after J. K. Rowling revealed that the character Albus Dumbledore, the revered headmaster of the Hogwarts magic school, was homosexual.[15] That revelation prompted religious conservative Tom Barrett to write,

> In her Harry Potter books [J. K. Rowling] uses material from various pagan religions (including the Druids), witchcraft, Satanism, and dozens of spells and incantations. It should be obvious to anyone who views the books objectively that they are designed to make the evil religion of witchcraft acceptable to young, impressionable children. . . . My daughter will never read one, or see any of the movies, because I love her.[16]

SUPPRESSION

Barrett's profound horror about a popular children's tale is part of a long and important part of the story of magic. It's the reason why magic became an *esoteric* (hidden) tradition instead of an *exoteric* (open) practice. The chilling effect of centuries of religious and scientific polemics against magic cannot be overstated. If I were to seriously suggest that the *Harry Potter* movies are based on a true story, most people would nervously smile and back away. Those with strong religious faith would turn and run. Their stereotyped idea of a witch would cause them to hyperventilate at the thought of hanging out with a coven of friendly witches at the local coffee shop, even if that meeting included a round of delicious chocolate danishes.

The marginalization of magic has been so thorough that until the late twentieth century scholars of religion scrupulously avoided talking about esoteric topics, as though they didn't even exist. Anthropologists too regarded magic as so obviously idiotic that it was erased from the curriculum. Given such prejudices, it's not surprising that academic interest in esoteric studies has evolved at a snail's pace. Wouter J. Hanegraaff, professor of the history of Hermetic philosophy at the University of Amsterdam, is part of a growing group of academics who have specialized in the Western esoteric traditions. Hanegraaff highlighted the academic avoidance of esotericism:

> During the nineteenth and much of the twentieth century, scholars and intellectuals prided themselves on not knowing anything about such matters, so that deliberate ignorance about the traditions in question became deeply ingrained in academic life.[17]

DISENCHANTMENT

What sparked this scrupulously willful ignorance? In 1917, German sociologist and philosopher Max Weber (1864–1920) defined a key feature of modern Western society—its "disenchantment."[18] Weber was referring to a growing conviction among scientists and scholars of the early twentieth century that supernatural concepts were outdated. There was no longer any need for "mysterious incalculable forces," magic, or spirits. There was also no need for institutions that relied on such ideas (hint: religion). Memories of a thousand years of intellectual dominance by religious authorities were painfully fresh, so the rise of the disenchanted world became a welcome gust of freedom.

This cultural sea change inspired scholars to openly and vigorously reject magic, but not just because it was heretical. That was the Church's justification. Now it could be scorned for another reason: magic was a throwback to pre-scientific concepts. It didn't take long for the mere *idea* of magic to be regarded as a dastardly affront to science itself.[19]

Anthropologists were on the front lines in having to deal with the newly disenchanted world, because in their study of "primitive man" they encountered all sorts of curious magical beliefs and practices. Understanding those beliefs and the roles they played in indigenous societies became a major focus of their work. Anthropologists were eager to distinguish themselves from the uneducated (meaning scientifically illiterate) masses, so magic soon became associated with the beliefs of "savages" or the "lower races." It was certainly not the sort of thing that learned men and women should accept.

The first professor of anthropology at Oxford University was Sir Edward Burnett Tylor (1832–1917). Tylor supported the new, scientifically proper way to think about magic, and he wasn't shy about expressing his opinion. He called magic a "monstrous farrago . . . one of the most pernicious delusions that ever vexed mankind."[20] For Tylor, magic was solely a matter of theatrics, superstitions, illusions, and preposterous fantasies. Belief in magic was due to the psychological need to cope with the uncertainties of life by gaining an illusory control over nonexistent supernatural forces.[21]

Tylor's influence over future generations of anthropologists was immense. His insistence that magic was nonsense quickly gathered support among his contemporaries, and it set in stone what nearly all anthropologists believed (or at least what they were comfortable talking about in public) for more than a century. Following Tylor's lead, Sir James G. Frazer's (1854–1941) influential book, *The Golden Bough*, published in 1922, continued the magic-bashing. In referring to "sympathetic magic," Frazer wrote:

> A mistaken association of similar ideas produces homoeopathic or imitative magic; a mistaken association of contiguous ideas produces contagious magic. The principles of association are excellent in themselves, and indeed absolutely essential to the working of the human mind. Legitimately applied they yield science; illegitimately applied they yield magic, the bastard sister of science. It is therefore a truism, almost a tautology, to say that all magic is necessarily false and barren.[22]

The notion that magic was an obviously false practice was widely and uncritically accepted among anthropologists. In 1901, Columbia University granted its first PhD in anthropology, to Alfred L. Kroeber (1876–1960), who incidentally was the father of the well-known fantasy and science fiction author Ursula K. Le Guin. In Kroeber's textbook on anthropology, published a year after Frazer's, we find the following, directly out of Tylor's playbook:

> Beliefs in magic, such as are normal in backward societies, do recur in cultures that by profession have discarded magic, but chiefly among individuals whose social fortune is backward or who are psychotic, mentally deteriorated, or otherwise subnormal.[23]

Half a century later, Hans Dieter Betz, of the Department of New Testament and Early Christian Literature at the University of Chicago Divinity School, edited a large volume on the Greek magical papyri. This is a collection of translated magical spells and formulas, hymns, and rituals from ancient Greco-Roman

Egyptian scrolls. The volume was advertised as an "invaluable resource for scholars in a wide variety of fields, from the history of religions to the classical languages and literatures, and it will fascinate those with a general interest in the occult and the history of magic."[24]

Fascinate, yes, but Betz felt it necessary to add Tylor's damning opinion in his opening remarks to make sure the reader understood that despite spending enormous amounts of time and energy writing a gigantic book on magical spells, of course he didn't *believe* in any of it. Betz's insistence reflected the schizophrenic split that scholars sometimes feel when confronted with magic—they are drawn to it like moths to a flame, but they are also obligated to deny the dangerous attraction. Historian Owen Davies of the University of Hertfordshire describes the academic denial of magic as pronouncements "puffed up with the sense of Western superiority."[25] As an example of that puffery, we find Betz professing,

> Magic is the art that makes people who practice it feel better rather than worse, that provides the illusion of security to the insecure, the feeling of help to the helpless, and the comfort of hope to the hopeless. . . . *Of course, it is all deception.* But who can endure naked reality, especially when there is a way to avoid it? This is why magic has worked and continues to work, *no matter what the evidence may be.*[26]

Not all anthropologists agreed with Tylor. In 1982, Michael Winkelman published an article in *Current Anthropology*, a stolid academic journal published by the University of Chicago Press, on the relevance of psi research to the study of magical beliefs among "primitive peoples."[27] Winkelman's article was followed by nearly twenty commentaries by other anthropologists. This is a common procedure in journals; it's a convenient way to disseminate scholarly debates on controversial topics.

Winkelman began his review by stating the obvious: that most anthropologists had adopted the scientific worldview that magic didn't exist. Most anthropological theories about magic were (and still are) based on psychological or sociological reasons why indigenous peoples can so easily sustain their delusions. To make his case that this common assumption may be mistaken, Winkelman reviewed articles in the anthropological literature from the late 1800s through the 1940s. He showed, based on firsthand anecdotal reports from military officers, physicians, clergymen, and colonial officers, that anthropologists had long noted that *some* aspects of magic practiced by indigenous peoples appeared to be real.

In addition, those magical practices seemed to be consistent with conditions found to enhance psi effects in laboratory studies, including a reliance on altered states of consciousness, concentrated visualization, goal-oriented imagery, positive expectations, strong belief, and intense emotions. Winkelman proposed that the tendency to equate magical beliefs (which are testable) with religious beliefs (which are not) had led anthropologists astray. They regarded magic as a magico-religious *faith*. If instead they had thought of magic as a magico-scientific *practice*, then the idea that magic must be due only to trickery or self-deception could have been put to the test, rather than simply assumed.

Most of the commentaries following Winkelman's article were in the spirit of polite academic debate, some supportive of the article and others more critical. But one commentary was not like the others; it dragged on for seven pages. It was so long that the editor of the journal apologized for its inclusion, noting that it was an extreme departure from their usual policy. The author of the lengthy screed was furious that a dignified academic journal would even consider publishing an article like Winkelman's.

What caused that outburst?

Tylor's ghost.

Some thirty years after Winkelman's article, psychologist David Luke from the University of Greenwich asked if anthropology and parapsychology were "still hostile sisters in science."[28] Luke pointed out that cracks in the resistance had been building since the 1950s. In 1952, an anthropologist elder and past president of the American Anthropological Association (AAA), Dr. John Swanton, wrote an open letter urging anthropologists to take seriously the implications of psi phenomena in the study of magic. Seven years later, the topic was discussed at the AAA annual meeting. The symposium was standing room only and charged with high emotion. Famed anthropologist Margaret Mead (1901–1978) was present, and it took her support for the psi-magic thesis to shatter the impasse.

Around the same time, in his classic text on shamanism, influential University of Chicago philosopher and historian of religion Mircea Eliade (1907–1986) wrote that "a fairly large number of ethnographic documents has already put the authenticity of such (paranormal) phenomena beyond doubt."[29] The formation of the Society for the Anthropology of Consciousness in 1974 was a turning point, especially when that society was formally absorbed into the AAA in 1990.

Anthropologist William S. Lyon, who has studied Native American shamanic beliefs and practices, is representative of modern scholars who are increasingly dissatisfied with making believe that magic doesn't exist. He writes,

> We know academia currently treats magic as the result of "primitive superstition" or "magical thinking." . . . So how did it come to pass that despite throughout all of human history a belief in magic appears in every recorded culture on the planet, in the last 150 years scientists have come to treat it as not real? The simple answer is: magic did not fit our mechanistic view of reality so it needed to be abandoned.[30]

WITCH HUNTS

While some scholars still argue that magic is all based on deception, their pronouncements haven't stopped the tragedy of witch hunts, which are still luridly alive in some areas of the world.[31] In 2014 more than a thousand women in Tanzania, all believed to be witches by frightened neighbors, were lynched, stoned, or hacked to death.[32] And according to a 2014 article in the *New York Times*, the United Nations Office of the High Commissioner for Human Rights reported that "most of the 25,000 to 50,000 children who live on the streets of Kinshasa, the capital of the Democratic Republic of Congo, were abandoned by family members who accused them of witchcraft or demonic possession."[33] The same article mentions how the Catholic Church, which is not known for its historical tolerance of witches, is providing shelter for accused witches in Papua New Guinea.

Besides the fear of being declared a witch in some parts of the world, concerns about being surreptitiously watched by someone or some*thing* at a distance are becoming more common with the flourishing of electronic and drone surveillance. Such concerns are not unreasonable, but paranoia that someone is constantly watching or, worse, *influencing* your thoughts is a classic symptom of schizophrenia. Before you visit a magician or an exorcist, please visit a psychiatrist first to see if there might be an organic reason for you to have such fears. Sometimes these obsessions arise due to misfirings in the brain or to biochemical imbalances. If so, the obsession can be treated.

I mention this because the line between real and illusory can become uncomfortably thin the moment one opens the door to the possibility of genuine magic. In particular, anyone who is casually pursuing magic *as a practice* should be cautious. If you take that path, it's especially important to maintain strong social connections so you can talk about your experiences and remain psychologically well grounded. Magic is a fascinating topic because it raises many interesting questions about the nature of consciousness and its role in reality. But *using* magic in an attempt to manipulate reality or conjure spirits can be psychologically destabilizing. Even the innocent use of the ever-popular Ouija board game can, for a small percentage of people, lead to major psychological problems. Dropping down the rabbit hole into the unknown is exciting, but it's not without risk.

MAGICAL THINKING

While many scientists are quick to dismiss magical thinking as nonsense, the fact is that practically everyone engages in magical thinking, all the time. To account for this, psychologists have proposed four main explanations: (1) believers are wretchedly ignorant or sadly embedded within a religious culture that regards magic to be self-evident,[34] (2) believers are burdened with one or more cognitive or reasoning defects,[35] (3) believers are mentally ill, or are high on a scale of "schizotypy" (that is, they have a tendency toward schizophrenic ideation),[36] or (4) everyone's brains are just hardwired to believe in magic.[37]

In other words, if you believe in magic, either you're stupid, you're nuts, or you can't help it. That last explanation covers everyone, presumably including those who proposed these explanations.

Without being cavalier about it, it's fair to say that *some* aspects of magical thinking can indeed be due to psychiatric problems or cognitive frailties. But it's also recognized that "even smart, educated, emotionally stable adults have superstitions that are not rational."[38] Fortunately, a growing consensus among psychologists suggests that magical thinking may not be so bad after all. It can help us cope with difficult times and decisions. And positive thinking—even if superstitious—can be good for your mental and physical health.[39]

In 2010 in *Scientific American*, psychologist Piercarlo

Valdesolo agreed with the new appreciation for magical thinking in an article entitled "Why Magical Thinking Works for Some People." Valdesolo writes:

> Can belief in [magical] charms actually have an influence over one's ability to, say, perform better on a test or in an athletic competition? . . . The mere suggestion that [a golf] ball was lucky significantly influenced performance, causing participants to make almost two more putts on average. . . . Why? Surely it couldn't be that the same golf ball *becomes* lucky at the experimenter's suggestion—there must be an explanation grounded in the psychological influence that belief in lucky charms has on the superstitious.[40]

Must the explanation *only* be psychological? Are there no other possibilities?

Let's find out.

Chapter 4

ORIGINS OF MAGIC

*I think back in the caveman days, our ancestors would
huddle around the fire at night and wolves would be
howling in the dark, just beyond the light. And one person
would start talking. And he would tell a story so we
wouldn't be so scared in the dark.*

—JOHN LOGAN, from the 2016 movie *Genius*

MAGIC IS TO RELIGION AS TECHNOLOGY IS TO SCIENCE.

That is, one difference between religion and magic is that the
former is essentially a faith-based *theory* about the nature of reality, while the latter involves testable *applications* of that theory.
Theories provide meaningful structures proposed to account for
an otherwise chaotic and bewildering existence, while applications provide the means of controlling some of the chaos.

The religion-magic relationship is actually more complex
than the science-technology connection because there are two
major categories of magic: supernatural and natural. Initially,
everything was considered to be supernatural because our earliest ancestors had no idea about how anything worked. So they
naturally attributed everything to invisible, supernatural causes,
meaning above or beyond the natural world—the divine, or one
or more gods.

Then someone noticed that there were aspects of nature that
were predictable—the movements of the sun and stars, healing

qualities of certain muds and plants—and that realization sparked interest in visible, here-and-now, human-centric natural magic. Supernatural magic was eventually adopted by religion, and natural magic split into two branches, the *exoteric* (outer, physical world) and the *esoteric* (inner, mental world). The exoteric branch evolved into today's science. The esoteric branch is where magic has been hiding.

Natural magic evolved into science as refined methods and technologies were developed that allowed us to control natural forces (like electricity) and to perceive beyond the common senses (as with a microscope). If instruments like the electric battery and the telescope had never been invented, life today in many ways would be as it was in the late Middle Ages. But with such instruments and many others like them, our worldview significantly expanded, theories were developed to account for the new observations, and in the process we've become highly adept at focusing on the outer, physical world. We know that our worldview is accurate because it continues to spawn reliable technologies, many of which would have seemed like pure magic even as recently as the 1950s.

Indeed, in the early twenty-first century it's probably fair to say that most people have no idea how computing or communication technologies work. I don't mean "work" in the sense of knowing how to operate a computer or a smartphone, but rather in the sense of knowing how to build these devices from scratch, or even understanding the main principles underlying these devices. These technologies aren't considered magic because their easy availability gives us faith that someone, somewhere (or, more likely, teams of specialists distributed around the globe) knows how they work. Meanwhile, esoteric magic has also evolved, using its own methods and theories. Not surprisingly, the esoteric worldview is very different from the one that's the basis of today's technologies.

A comprehensive review of the history of esotericism is beyond the scope of any single chapter. This topic is deeply entwined with the histories of science, religion, philosophy, and metaphysics, and it's been explored in fastidious detail by many generations of scholars. But it's important to review it here, even if briefly, to give you a feeling for two central ideas: first, that esoteric ideas have been vigorously suppressed in the Western world for at least a thousand years, and second, that the esoteric worldview provides hints for why magic works.

PREHISTORIC TIMES

Given the mystery of life, its endless uncertainties, and the certainty of death, the first self-aware creatures were strongly motivated to understand how they had ended up in this mess and whether there might be something better to look forward to. Some of those early souls may have gained mystical glimpses of reality through the discovery and use of entheogenic (psychedelic) compounds.[1] A persuasive case for this possibility is made by the esteemed religious scholar Huston Smith in his book *Cleansing the Doors of Perception*.[2] As language developed, the experiences of these early psychonauts, amplified by their creative imaginations, became codified into cosmologies (that is, origin stories).

Individuals who were especially adept at entering these rarefied states of awareness, which afforded visions of reality beyond the here and now, were the first magicians and shamans. Religions developed as the mystical cosmologies were elaborated. Later, those origin stories were supplemented with rules for acceptable behavior and proper forms of homage to authority. Shamans didn't enter these states because all the cool kids were doing it; rather, they did it because their tribe's survival depended on it. They were healers, oracles, and warriors wrapped into one, and they were charged with sustaining their tribe and defending it against rival groups through whatever means necessary, including magical techniques.[3]

ANCIENT TIMES

As tribes' settlements matured into towns, cities, and empires, the cognoscenti of the day gained the luxury of time to turn their thoughts from matters of daily subsistence to grander concepts of spirituality and religion. German-Swiss philosopher Karl Jaspers (1883–1969) labeled the period from about 800 to 200 BCE the "axial age."[4] The term refers to an intellectual swing from matters of basic survival to more abstract and transcendent ideas.

Given today's fast pace, you might have to schlep through a computer or smartphone software update every month or two. But in primordial times thousands of years and untold hundreds of human generations would come and go, and absolutely nothing would change. Considering the almost inconceivably leisurely pace of our ancestors' lives, the six-hundred-year axial age arrived like a historical lightning bolt.

During that period Taoism and Confucianism emerged in China; Buddhism, Hinduism, and Jainism appeared in India; the Hebrew prophets Isaiah, Jeremiah, and others emerged in Palestine; Zoroaster (the Greek name of the Persian prophet Zarathustra) founded one of the first monotheistic religions; and the Greek philosophers, including Pythagoras, Socrates, Plato, and Aristotle, did something new: they questioned the origins of the universe, pondered the meaning, morality, and fate of humanity, and founded the origins of logic, mathematics, and rational analysis.

This shift in perspective is sometimes referred to as the emergence of "second-order" thought, in that humans—at least the ruling classes—began to think about themselves from broader or higher perspectives. The new way of thinking led humanity away from worship of tribal deities and toward contemplation of more universal concepts. Unified kingdoms and "supreme" gods became a new vision. To achieve such goals it was necessary to develop ways other than raw brutality to respond to insults and other aggressions. The new vision was hopeful, an aspiration that has always been difficult to sustain given our hardwired drive to strike first and ask questions later. But the impulse was set, and a case can be made that human violence has steadily declined as civilization has spread throughout the world.[5] Of course, instances of violence tend to saturate the news media, so it might seem like the world is becoming more dangerous. But that's only because breaking-news reports of carnage cause our hearts to beat faster than calm stories about simple human kindness.

One of the sparks that energized the axial age may have emerged from personal experiences within the various mystery schools, which flourished throughout the ancient world. These schools had similar goals: initiation into the mysteries sought "to 'open the immortal eyes of man inwards': exalt his powers of perception until they could receive the messages of a higher degree of reality."[6] In practice, this consisted of experiencing a ritual death of the physical body and subsequent resurrection into a new body, with new capabilities of intuiting secret wisdom, often regarding the functioning of the body itself.[7]

One of the longest-lasting schools was the Greek Eleusinian Mysteries, active from about 1500 BCE to 392 CE.[8] Most of the Greek philosophers regarded the Mysteries with awe. Even the Roman skeptic Cicero (106–43 BCE) wrote, "Nothing is higher than these mysteries . . . they have not only shown us how to live joyfully but they have taught us how to die with a better hope."[9] Hundreds of years later, the Greek philosopher and statesman Themistios (317–385 CE) mentioned the Eleusinian Mysteries in an essay he wrote on the soul:

The soul [at death] has the same experience as those who are being initiated into great Mysteries. . . . [A]t first one wanders and wearily hurries to and fro, and journeys with suspicion through the dark as one uninitiated: then come all the terrors before the final initiation, shuddering, trembling, sweating, amazement: then one is struck with a marvelous light, one is received into pure regions and meadows, with voices and dances and the majesty of holy sounds and shapes: among these he who has fulfilled initiation wanders free, and released and bearing his crown joins in the divine communion, and consorts with pure and holy men.[10]

The Lesser Rites of the Eleusinian Mysteries involved a theatrical allegory of what (supposedly) happened after death. It was unusually democratic for its time, being available to both citizens and slaves. But the Greater Rites were available only to selected patrons. These were said to provide a personal *experience* of the afterlife. The ritual included drinking a potion known as *kykeon*, a mixture consisting of barley, mint, and water.[11] Kykeon might have been similar to *soma*, the potion mentioned in the Hindu Vedas that some scholars now believe was an entheogenic compound. While the actual composition of these concoctions is unknown, we do know that they were made from grains, and ergot—a poisonous fungus that commonly grows on grains—contains lysergic acid, the core component of the most powerful psychedelic drug, lysergic acid diethylamide, or LSD.

The Eleusinian Mystery School was forced to close in 392 CE when Christian emperor Theodosius I, head of the Holy Roman Empire, officially declared the rites pagan and therefore heretical (that is, they were so popular that they interfered with the Church's authority).[12]

One of the more famous mystery school initiates was Plato (427–347 BCE), student of Socrates and teacher of Aristotle. Plato proposed the existence of a "higher domain" of pure Ideas.

To help explain his concept, Plato used an allegory of prisoners in a cave. As the story goes, these prisoners spent their entire lives chained up in a cave in such a way that all they could see was the cave wall in front of them. They couldn't see a fire that was glowing behind them, nor that a group of actors was holding up puppets and casting shadows on the wall of the cave. For these prisoners, their entire world consisted of those shadows.

One day a prisoner was released from the cave and taken outside. At first blinded by the light, after a while his eyes adjusted to the brilliance, and for the first time he saw the vibrant colors and depth of "real" reality. His former ideas about the world were shattered, and when he was allowed to return to the cave he excitedly explained to the other prisoners that their shadow existence was an illusion. There was a richer, intensely luminous world just a few steps outside the cave. But regardless of what he said, or the arguments he used to try to convince them that their reality was a pale cartoon of reality, the other prisoners thought he had gone mad.

Plato used this allegory to argue that there was a difference between the everyday *appearance* of the world, shaped by everyday language and concepts, and the world *itself*. Common sense provides a poor facsimile of what is really "out there," so to grasp the true nature of reality—Plato imagined that this consisted of what he called eternal Forms or Ideas—requires a special form of knowing, called *gnosis*. Knowledge gained through gnosis is different from intellectual or rational knowing. American psychologist and philosopher William James (1842–1910) provided a definition for a similar word, *noetic*, in his famous book *The Varieties of Religious Experience* (1902). Noetic experiences were, as he described in the flowery language of the early twentieth century,

states of insight into depths of truth unplumbed by the discursive intellect. They are illuminations, revelations, full of

significance and importance, all inarticulate though they remain; and as a rule they carry with them a curious sense of
authority.[13]

Gnosis is thus a type of deep intuition, a means of knowing
that transcends the ordinary senses and rational thought, like
knowing "from the heart." A mother knows she loves her child;
it's not something she has to rationally, logically, or analytically
figure out. Note that gnosis being *non-rational* does not mean
it's *irrational*, for that would imply faulty knowledge.

From the perspective of magical practice, gnosis may be
thought of as an "intense consciousness of something."[14] The
term *grok*, from Robert Heinlein's 1961 science fiction novel
Stranger in a Strange Land, also gets at this idea. At one point in
that novel the character Mahmoud describes *grok* as

> to understand so thoroughly that the observer becomes a part
> of the observed—to merge, blend, intermarry, lose identity
> in group experience. It means almost everything that we
> mean by religion, philosophy, and science—and it means as
> little to us [ordinary humans] as color does to a blind man.[15]

During the Hellenistic period in Greece (from the death of
Alexander the Great in 323 BCE to the emergence of the Roman
Empire in 31 BCE), Plato's ideas evolved into an esoteric worldview. A key figure associated with development of what is now
called Neoplatonism was Plotinus (204–270 CE), a philosopher
born in Egypt half a millennium after Plato.

Neoplatonism proposed the existence of deep interconnec-
tions among all things, including what is normally viewed as
the distinction between mental and physical phenomena. From
the everyday, ego-based state of awareness (I'll call this personal
form of consciousness [c]), mind and matter *appear* to be fundamentally different. But from the rarefied state of gnosis, which

provides direct access to higher states of existence (I'll call this state of Universal Consciousness [C]), the apparent distinctions between mind and matter, or space and time, are revealed as illusions. That is, from [c] we see objects separated in space and time, and we see obvious differences between mental and physical phenomena. But from [C], all such differences dissolve and naked reality is experienced as entangled relationships in a holistic reality, completely free of the constraints of space or time.

From [C], you directly perceive what [c] experiences as the future or the past. From [C], you also transcend the distinctions that separate you from other objects, and by so doing, you can directly influence the physical world. That is, in a domain without separation you may "become one with," say, a dark cloud, whereupon you could introduce an intention to rain. Or by becoming one with a friend, you could know your friend's thoughts and emotions. By proposing the notion of a "higher" reality beyond the shadow existence of ordinary experience, Plato and later Neoplatonism provided a worldview that opened the door to the possibility of real magic.

Treatises on Neoplatonism and many other esoteric ideas were collected in one of the supreme accomplishments of ancient times: the library of Alexander of Macedonia (356 BCE–323 BCE), better known as Alexander the Great. Alexander charged this library with collecting all of the world's knowledge. He began it in 334 BCE, and in its prime the Alexandrian library was the largest single repository of knowledge in the world—the Internet of the ancient world. The library contained over a half a million documents collected from Assyria, Greece, Persia, Egypt, India, and many other places. More than a hundred scholars from all civilized countries traveled to the library to live, study, and translate the documents into all known languages.

After being the hub of the world's knowledge for two hundred years, the library was partially destroyed by an accident in 48 BCE, when Julius Caesar ordered ships in the harbor to be burned during a military campaign. The fire spread to the docks and eventually destroyed part of the library. Over the next five hundred years the library was slowly whittled away as the city came under the control of different factions and religious authorities. Stories have been told about how one or another individual was responsible for burning or gutting the library, but scholars today agree that most of those stories were apocryphal.[16] There are undoubtedly many reasons the library slowly dissolved, but the full story is lost in the mists of time.[17]

Fortunately, over the centuries of its existence many of its documents were copied by scholars from other countries, so portions of the ancient world's knowledge were retained. Much of that knowledge was about magic. This is not to say that real magic was uniformly accepted by ancient scholars. Some regarded claims about magic with disdain.

An example is the Greek historian Pliny the Elder (23–79 CE), author of one of the earliest known encyclopedias. Entitled *Naturalis Historia* (Natural History), Pliny's work was consulted by scholars for a thousand years. Regarding magic, he wrote: "Without doubt magic arose in Persia with Zoroaster. On this our authorities are agreed, but whether he was the only one of that name, or whether there was also another afterwards, is not clear."[18] He also wrote:

> I have often indeed refuted the fraudulent lies of the Magi, whenever the subject and the occasion required it, and I shall continue to expose them. In a few respects, however, the theme deserves to be enlarged upon, were it only because the most fraudulent of arts has held complete sway throughout the world for many ages.[19]

And yet, after that opening dismissive salvo, Pliny goes on to describe more than sixty recipes that the magi of the day used to treat various ailments. Some of those methods were based on sympathetic magic, the idea that objects with certain appearances or properties would sympathize, or resonate, with similar objects. Thus, to reduce a fever the magi might create an amulet that looked like a snake, or contained bits of a snake, because a snakebite can produce the sensation of a fever. But not all folk medicine was based on magical concepts. Many treatments were developed by pure trial and error. Here's Pliny's description of how to treat a cold and sore throat:

I find that a heavy cold clears up if the sufferer kisses a mule's muzzle. Pain in the uvula and in the throat is relieved by the dung, dried in shade, of lambs that have not yet eaten grass, uvula pain by applying the juice of a snail transfixed by a needle, so that the snail itself may be hung up in the smoke, and by the ash of swallows with honey.[20]

Kissing a mule on the snout and gargling with dried, grassless lamb dung sounds a lot worse than suffering through a cold and sore throat. Maybe patients just *said* that the treatment was soothing so they didn't have to do *that* again. But there's also an alternative explanation. Some of these ingredients, as odd as they sound, may have had chemical properties that were medically useful.

For example, an article in the *European Journal of Pharmaceutical and Medical Research* describes how cow urine, a traditional Ayurveda elixir, has antioxidant, anti-diabetic, wound-healing, and immunomodulatory properties.[21] We are so used to synthetic drugs today that it's easy to forget that modern pharmaceuticals are a recent invention. For millennia, the pharmacopeia consisted exclusively of natural ingredients, because that's all that was available. Sometimes those forms of natural magic worked wonders, and for reasons that we're only now beginning to understand in modern terms.

EARLY MIDDLE AGES

Also known as the Dark Ages, the Middle Ages refers to a period of about a thousand years in Europe, from the fall of the Roman Empire to the beginning of the Renaissance, roughly from the fifth to fourteenth centuries. After Rome fell to the "barbarians," other than a few pockets of civilization most of Europe turned into one of those post-apocalyptic zombie movies. All forms of scholarship in Europe significantly subsided.

To further tarnish the image of the early Middle Ages as a desirable travel destination for future time-travelers, during that period the Catholic Church's tolerance of magic rapidly dissipated as Church leaders clamped down on the widespread popularity of pagan beliefs. In the early thirteenth century, Pope Gregory IX created the holy police force known as the Inquisition, to combat heresy.[22] In 1252 Pope Innocent IV formalized the Inquisition and authorized it to use torture to force confessions and to burn people alive for their heretical beliefs.

About two hundred years later, Pope Innocent VIII authorized two inquisitors, Jakob Sprenger and Heinrich Kramer, to accelerate the holy work of the Inquisition. Sprenger and Kramer wrote a book entitled *Malleus Maleficarum* (The Witches' Hammer), which essentially turned witch-hunting into a religiously sanctioned sport. Hundreds of thousands of people, perhaps as many as a million, were arrested, tortured, and killed at the hands of the Inquisition. These horrific acts forced esoteric interests deep underground, and the cultural memory of the terror associated with being declared "deviant" because of one's ideas or beliefs continues to affect us today.

Now—for reasons you'll presently discover—we'll briefly jump five hundred years into the future, to 1945 in Nag Hammadi, a city on the Nile in Upper Egypt. At that time a set of thirteen ancient papyrus manuscripts was discovered. These texts, which were not fully translated until the 1970s, altered our understanding of the Christian Bible.[23] Known as the Nag Hammadi codices, they describe "gnostic gospels" that were left out of early efforts to establish the orthodox interpretation of Christianity, perhaps because the information provided by these gospels differed from the stories included in the New Testament.

The gnostic gospels include the Gospel of Thomas, which begins with a startling opening sentence: "These are the secret words which the living Jesus spoke, and which the twin, Judas Thomas, wrote down."[24] Elaine Pagels's book *The Gnostic Gospels* provides an excellent description of the discovery and mysteries of the Nag Hammadi manuscripts and their influence on understanding the origins of Christianity as we know it today.[25]

Returning to the early Middle Ages: The esoteric tradition of Gnosticism, like Neoplatonism, viewed the central importance of gnosis as a way of directly perceiving higher states of being. But it also added a distinct sense of purpose to Neoplatonism's cosmology. The Gnostics taught that we are like the prisoners chained up in Plato's cave. That is, we have a spark of the divine within us, but we're unaware of it. Fortunately, even though we fell from grace, we can work our way back up the spiritual hierarchy by attaining gnosis of our true being. In this way the gnostic allegory provided a way to escape from the chains of ignorance and the suffering of the material world. We can be like Plato's prisoner who escaped from the cave.

The Gnostics regarded the Catholic Church with disdain, seeing it as having lost its way through corruption and politics and having neglected the teachings of Christ. As one might imagine, Church authorities were not amused by this criticism, as dramatically exemplified by the plight of the Cathars. The Cathars were a group of Gnostic Christians in the town of Béziers, in southern France. The thirteenth-century pope Innocent III was increasingly annoyed by the Gnostics because their criticism was becoming a major challenge to his authority. The Cathars even went so far as to accuse the Pope of being the puppet of Satan. So the Pope sent his army of Crusaders to Béziers, accompanied by his representative, a French monk named Arnaud Amalric. The military leader of the Crusaders was Simon de Montfort, a French nobleman who was offered a cruel incentive by the Pope—de Montfort could keep the land of any Cathar heretic that he dispatched.

On July 22, 1209, de Montfort arrived at Béziers and demanded that the town turn over the Cathar heretics. The town refused and the Crusaders attacked. During the siege a soldier asked Amalric how were they supposed to tell who was a heretic and who was a proper Catholic. Amalric famously replied, "Kill them all. Let God sort them out." All twenty thousand people in the town were massacred and the city was burned to the ground.[26] On July 22, 2009, the town of Béziers observed the eight-hundredth anniversary of this massacre.[27]

History lesson: it is advisable to think twice about annoying those in power.

THE RENAISSANCE

During the Renaissance, from the fourteenth through the seventeenth century, translations of manuscripts long held in Arabic, Greek, and Asian states were slowly being reintroduced to Western scholars. The invention of the printing press in the fourteenth century and distribution of the translated texts resulted in an explosion of renewed ideas and relief from the stagnation of the previous thousand years. This in turn stimulated an upheaval in religion, politics, economics, and scholarship, and it established the basic structures and Western cultural beliefs that would come to define the modern world.

Religious reformers such as Martin Luther challenged the

rigid authority of the Catholic Church, its increasingly corrupt practices, and its monopoly in defining what Christian practice meant. That challenge provoked decades of wars and persecutions, but it also dramatically changed European politics and national boundaries. As old structures began to crumble, the dust generated a heavy price in the form of nearly continuous conflicts. Fortunately, it also fostered a new intellectual openness that eventually allowed for the rediscovery of Hermeticism.

Hermeticism is named after Hermes, the son of the Greek gods Zeus and Maia. Hermes is known as Mercury in the Roman pantheon and Thoth in the Egyptian pantheon. Hermes/Mercury/Thoth was considered an emissary between the gods and humans, the god of writing, wisdom, and magic, and a trickster. Thoth was held in such high regard by the Egyptians that referring to him as Thoth the Great was simply not good enough. Even Double-Great Thoth wasn't adequate. But, like in the Goldilocks tale, Great-Great-Great Thoth was just about right. That honorific title led to Thoth's better-known Greek name, Hermes Trismegistus (Hermes three-times-great).

Hermetic cosmology contends that reality consists of a single Universal Consciousness, known by many names: the One Mind, the Divine, the Tao, Brahman, Allah, God, Source, and so on. To avoid religious connotations of these terms, I've referred to this concept as consciousness with a big *C*, or [C]. In Hermeticism, [C] appears in two complementary aspects, like the two sides of the same coin. One form is a manifested, primordial, "plastic" energy, sometimes referred to within the alchemical tradition as the One Thing.[28] The other form is a non-manifested, transcendent element known as the One Mind. The One Thing reacts to and is shaped by the One Mind.

The One Thing is similar to the Hindu idea of *akasha*. In Swami Vivekananda's book *Raja Yoga*, akasha is described as follows:

It is the omnipresent, all-penetrating existence. Everything that has form, everything that is the result of combination, it is evolved out of this Akasha. It is the Akasha that becomes the air, that becomes the liquids, that becomes the solids. . . . It cannot be perceived; it is so subtle that it is beyond all ordinary perception. . . . At the beginning of creation there is only this Akasha.[29]

Because the One Thing is viewed as a consciousness-shaping "substance," its appearance depends on who's looking and what they're expecting to see. Moses was stunned to encounter a burning bush that spoke to him. On October 13, 1917, three children near Fatima, Portugal, saw the Virgin Mary, while tens of thousands of others who were present witnessed anomalous lights and atmospheric effects that seem very much like what we'd today describe as a UFO.[30]

Hermeticism may sound like a dualistic concept, with the One Mind and the One Thing being starkly different from each other. But that's only because [C] is beyond human comprehension, so it's just described in two forms that are easier to grok.[31] That is, the One Mind only has the *appearance* of being different from the One Thing. Similarly, personal consciousness, [c], is not separate from the physical world. In other words, from the Hermetic perspective reality is not just physical, it's *psychophysical*. This interaction is commonly studied in the form of mind-body connections within the mainstream scientific disciplines of psychoneuroimmunology, psychophysiology, and the neurosciences. It's also the basis of psychosomatic medicine and the placebo effect. But when [c] influences the physical world *outside* of the body, which it can do because [c] has properties similar to [C], then that's called magic.

Hermeticism was considered heretical by the Church because it asserts that all humans have an inherent spark of divine power within us. That is, we have God-like abilities because [c] is a part of [C]. As a result, from the Hermeticist's perspective there were no special benefits conferred by following someone else's dogma, because each of us could achieve enlightenment on our own. As you may imagine, such insolence was unacceptable, so the Church applied its well-honed strategy for maintaining control, and like Neoplatonism and Gnosticism, Hermeticism was forced to go underground.

Hermeticism was rediscovered in the fifteenth century largely due to the efforts of Prince Cosimo de Medici of Florence, Italy, and that was allowed to happen only after the Church's millennium-old stranglehold on scholarship began to loosen. At this point an important figure enters the picture: Marsilio Ficino, head of the Florentine Academy. Ficino was commissioned by de Medici to translate a set of seventeen ancient manuscripts that had been found in the Middle East.

Ficino's translation, subsequently called the *Corpus Hermeticum* and published in 1471, thrilled scholars who were in the process of rediscovering the ancient Greek, Egyptian, and Jewish traditions, all of which were thought to predate the Church. The *Corpus Hermeticum* manuscripts were originally imagined to be ancient, harking back to the time of Plato or even before the Greek philosophers, but modern scholars now consider them most likely to be a combination of ideas from Egypt and Greece from the first and second centuries.

In Ficino's day, the excitement over these manuscripts was due to the belief that Hermes Trismegistus might have been a contemporary of Moses, or maybe he *was* Moses.[32] In either case, scholars hoped that the translations might reveal an ancient wisdom that preceded the Bible, because if that knowledge were brought to light it could demonstrate the long-fabled dream of a *prisca theologia,* or first true religion, and that in turn might break the Church's domination of acceptable scholarship and allow fresh ideas to flourish.

Another promise was that the *Corpus Hermeticum* might be

able to liberate long-suppressed prohibitions against the study of magic. Scholars reasoned that if the Church's doctrine was found to be compatible with much older ideas, then the magical concepts within Hermeticism should also be allowed to be studied. Unfortunately, their hopes did not pan out because by then the Protestant Reformation had all but eliminated the magical rituals popular in Catholicism, such as the Eucharist. And that in turn forced Hermeticism to retreat even further into the background.

But Ficino's translation was not forgotten.

Ficino was one of the first to popularize the idea that there was an ancient secret wisdom at the core of all the world's religions. This *philosophia perennis* would be the fundamental, first-principles truth around which the whole universe revolved. This idea was so appealing that it never faded away. The search for this particular holy grail can be found in today's physics in the form of the many proposed Theories of Everything. Trying to develop a fundamental theory that explains everything remains the obsession of thousands of scientists who, like the esoteric scholars of the Middle Ages, hold the conviction that there *must* be one "secret truth," or key principle, underlying all of reality.

One of Ficino's students, Count Giovanni Pico della Mirandola (1463–1494), later added portions of the Jewish Kabbalah to Hermeticism. The Kabbalah was an ancient cosmology even in Pico della Mirandola's time, based on *sephiroth* or spheres of "cosmic vibration" that connect the transcendent divine with the everyday world. The Hebrew word *kabbalah* means "to receive," as in "received wisdom." It refers to the Jewish mystical tradition discussed in texts such as the *Zohar*, a commentary on the Hebrew Bible.

Pico della Mirandola's analysis of the Kabbalah proposed not only that Christianity was contained within pagan beliefs but also that it was part of the secret tradition of Kabbalah that (tradition tells us) Moses received on his second expedition up

Mount Sinai.[33] Like Ficino before him, Pico della Mirandola was motivated by a search for the *prisca theologia*. He claimed that his Hermetic-Kabbalistic synthesis, consisting of twenty-six "magical conclusions," did the trick.

Incidentally, the Kabbalistic text known as the Sepher Yezirah (Book of the Creation) describes a cosmology that some scholars claim is identical to the Emerald Tablet, another key source of the Hermetic tradition.[34] The *Corpus Hermeticum* is said by some to expand on principles written (in extremely compact form) on the Emerald Tablet.[35]

Like other esotericists in the Middle Ages, Pico della Mirandola was nervous about attracting unwanted attention from the Church, so he described his magical synthesis as "the practical part of natural science."[36] This strategy was an attempt to separate magic from religious concepts and place it firmly within the bounds of the natural world. Pico della Mirandola's synthesis was part of a long line of *syncretic* efforts, meaning a fusion of different religious ideas. Examples of popular syncretic rituals include Valentine's Day, Halloween, Easter, and Christmas. All of these holidays are hybrids based on a blending of pagan and Christian rituals.

Ficino and Pico della Mirandola's work sparked a flood of new combinations and syntheses of the esoteric traditions, many of which were instrumental in the development of the early sciences. A few of the key magician-scientists during this period were German scholar Heinrich Cornelius Agrippa, English mathematician John Dee, Italian friar Giordano Bruno, and Swiss physician Paracelsus.[37] These and many other individuals made the study of magic part of the scientific mainstream during the late fifteenth and sixteenth centuries.

Briefly, Heinrich Cornelius Agrippa (1486–1535) wrote his first and most famous work on magic in 1510. Entitled *De occulta philosophia* (Occult Philosophy), the book was based on a Christian Kabbalistic framework. John Dee (1527–1609), adviser to Queen Elizabeth I, combined the study of the natural sciences with magical evocations aimed at establishing contact with spirits from (what he called) the angelic realm. Italian philosopher, mathematician, and Dominican friar Giordano Bruno (1548–1600) was attracted to Neoplatonic and Hermetic ideas. In his 1584 work, *De l'infinito, universo e mondi* (On the Infinite Universe and Worlds), he proposed that the universe contained an infinite number of worlds and that these were all inhabited by intelligent beings.[38] This idea flatly contradicted Church dogma, and Bruno paid the ultimate price for his heresy.

Philippus Aureolus Theophrastus Bombastus von Hohenheim (1493–1541), who called himself Paracelsus because it took too long to say his whole name, was one of the first modern medical theorists, the founder of homeopathy, and a pioneer in wound surgery. Paracelsus stressed that exercise of the imagination was the beginning of all magical operations. For the youth of the early twenty-first century, Paracelsus is perhaps better known as a character on one of the collectible Chocolate Frog Cards in the *Harry Potter* novels.

THE ENLIGHTENMENT

The Enlightenment was a period of accelerating advancements in science, technologies, philosophy, society, and politics. The medieval worldview was slowly being transformed by the new rationalism and its accompanying disenchantment of ancient religious ideas. Intellectuals felt a new sense of freedom to explore the world without the constant fear of the Inquisition.[39]

By the end of the sixteenth century, the Freemasons—a medieval guild of stonemasons—were able to freely move among European countries to practice their craft. They were also collecting esoteric traditions along the way, following the lead of the twelfth-century Knights Templar. The Freemasons were especially fond of adopting Hermetic symbolism and lore. Over time the Freemasons slowly evolved into an esoteric organization open to all men (and much later to women) across all social classes. The Masons, as they are now more commonly known, would become an important forerunner of future esoteric organizations.

During the first two decades of the seventeenth century, a legend arose about a certain Christian Rosenkreutz and his mysterious Brotherhood of the Rosy Cross. Manuscripts attributed to Rosenkreutz described a new syncretic philosophy combining ideas about magic, alchemy, Kabbalah, medicine, healing, and mathematics. It also described a secret brotherhood working behind the scenes for the benefit of humankind, an enticing idea that would hold endless fascination for generations to come. The new idea offered by the Rosicrucians was that this knowledge was held by an *organization* that one could join and learn from, rather than by the occasional rare and wise individual.[40]

Legendary origins and secret fraternities have always stimulated the imagination because they suggest that the never-ending chaos in human affairs is not random but is under control by someone or some group, somewhere. We'd all like to know who's at the steering wheel, but even if we don't know the identity of the driver, there's still some comfort in the belief that at least *someone* is driving the bus. Even Einstein didn't like it when he was confronted with the idea (from quantum theory) that uncertainty rules the universe. He refused to believe it, responding with his famous retort, "God does not play dice with the universe."

As often happens with fun stories passed down through history, there is no clear evidence that the secret invisible masters of the Rosicrucian Brotherhood ever existed, or even that Christian Rosenkreutz was an actual person. Some scholars now regard the original Rosicrucian Manifestos as an invention of a

Lutheran theologian, Johann Valentin Andreae (1586–1654), and his friends in Tübingen, Germany.[41] The secrecy and anonymity were undoubtedly due to the ever-present danger of invoking the declining but still powerful wrath of the Church.

Because Rosicrucianism was said to be founded on an exotic combination of ancient Egyptian lore, the Greek Eleusinian Mysteries, and concepts borrowed from Gnosticism, Hermeticism, Renaissance alchemy, and the Kabbalah, its influence on future esoteric societies was immense, as was that of the Masons.

POST-ENLIGHTENMENT

A major personality in the history of science was Sir Isaac Newton (1642–1727). It is less well known that Newton also played a key role in the history of esotericism, where he is referred to not as the "first of the Age of Reason" but as the "last of the magicians." Because he was the single most famous scientist of the day, for many years Newton's official biographies did not even mention that he spent more time studying alchemy and other esoteric subjects than he did physics or mathematics. Then, in 1936, economist John Maynard Keynes bought an obscure collection of Newton's personal papers and discovered to his and everyone else's amazement that the earlier biographies of Newton as the idealized scientist left out the majority of what Newton was really interested in.

Some contemporary biographers, like Michael White, have had difficulty understanding why Newton spent any time at all with alchemy. White's bewilderment was based on his certainty "that the alchemical tradition is so illogical, [and] the obvious fact that no single alchemist has succeeded through history [is] so clear."[42] To explain this odd juxtaposition, White speculated that Newton's "ego could simply never allow" someone else to find the fabled alchemical philosopher's stone, which was supposedly able to turn base metals into gold.

White correctly noted that the alchemical tradition included the consciousness of the alchemist as a key part of the process. But it was precisely because of that esoteric element that White wrote, "It was this which pushes the subject into the realms of magic and left it forever beyond the boundaries of 'Science'."[43] He's correct about the first part of that statement, but wrong about the second. The fact is that one of the most famous scientists in history, presumably a fairly bright guy, owned one of the most extensive collections on alchemy in his day.[44] I think it's safe to assume that Newton was well aware of what he was up to.

Emanuel Swedenborg (1688–1772) was another prominent force in both scientific and esoteric history. While still in his twenties, Swedenborg had already worked with Newton, Edmund Halley, and other leading scientists of the day. He traveled widely throughout Europe and published original research in practically all of the sciences, including astronomy, physics, engineering, chemistry, geology, anatomy, physiology, and psychology. He was prominent in Swedish public finance and politics, he had no interest in religion, and he had gained a reputation as a renowned member of the Swedish Academy of Sciences. From all appearances, Swedenborg was the very model of a modern major scientist.

Then, in the spring of 1744, when Swedenborg was about fifty years old, he had a mystical experience, one of many that would dramatically change the course of his life. Those experiences sparked an interest in esoteric concepts, and they eventually led him to write many books on mysticism, magical correspondences, and conversations with what he perceived to be angels. Swedenborg's influence on esoteric and religious movements continues to the present day.

Another major figure of the eighteenth century was German physician Franz Anton Mesmer (1734–1815). Mesmer created a healing practice that was translated into English as the term "animal magnetism." The word *animal* in this context refers to life or living systems, and not to the usual English connotation of a four-legged beast. Mesmer's ideas were explored in his 1766 doctoral dissertation, "The Influence of the Planets on the Human Body," in which, inspired by the idea of universal gravitation, he proposed the existence of an invisible, universal "fluid." This fluid was said to flow continuously everywhere; it also served as a means by which the planets, the Earth, and all living creatures interacted.

Mesmer's idea was similar to Paracelsus's "cosmic fluid" or *archaeus*, the yogic concept of *prana*, the Chinese *chi* or *qi*, the Lakota tribe's *wakan*, Greek philosopher Pythagoras's *pneuma*, Austrian psychotherapist Wilhelm Reich's *orgone*, and so on. The concept of a living or "vital force" permeates the esoteric traditions.

Like most scholars of the Enlightenment, Mesmer was determined to advance beyond the quasi-religious concepts of earlier times, so he attempted to put a scientific spin on the nature of his proposed fluid. His healing technique produced some astonishing cures, which made his practice wildly popular. This impressed some but also raised significant jealousy and suspicion in others who subsequently attacked Mesmer, claiming that their instruments could not detect his claimed magnetic fluid.

The explosion of popular interest in Mesmer's method eventually triggered an investigation by the French Academy of Sciences in 1784, chaired by renowned American polymath Benjamin Franklin. Franklin was in France attempting to gain France's support for the American Revolution. The French Academy was charged with evaluating the scientific status of Mesmerism, and a commission within the French Royal Society of Medicine was asked to determine whether Mesmerism was useful in treating illness.

After numerous tests, both commissions reported that there wasn't any evidence for Mesmer's magnetic fluid, and that the medical effects were explainable as the result of the patients' expectations (today we'd call this a placebo effect). However, the Royal Society's medical conclusion wasn't completely unanimous; their minority report found that some of the healing outcomes could not be explained by simple expectation.[45]

Fifty years later, Mesmerism was still raging throughout Europe, so the French Royal Society of Medicine launched another investigation. This time the report was uniformly *favorable*, not only to the medical usefulness of Mesmerism but also to psychic effects that were induced in some deep-trance patients. Their report ended by recommending that the Royal Society continue to study the psychic effects. Over the next five years investigators described many examples of phenomena that they had witnessed firsthand. This caught the attention of Jean-Eugène Robert-Houdin, the most famous stage magician of his day.[46] Robert-Houdin investigated an individual named Alexis who was said to be able to demonstrate highly accurate clairvoyance while in a mesmeric deep-trance state. Robert-Houdin later "confessed that he was completely baffled" at what Alexis could do.[47]

INDUSTRIAL AGE

While the rest of the world was busy building the modern industrial age, the practice of magic was on a parallel track. The demonstrable success of scientific rationalism influenced the magicians of the day, leading to new ways of interpreting magic. No longer would magic have to rely solely on religious concepts that permeated esoteric lore. Magic was always about pragmatics, so as language and scientific concepts became more sophisticated, so did theories of magic.

In Paris, in the second half of the nineteenth century, Alphonse-Louis Constant, better known by his magical moniker, Eliphas Lévi (1810–1875), played an important role in the modern revival of magic. Lévi's synthesis of the Western magical tradition echoed the Perennial Philosophy, which we'll explore in more detail in Chapter 8.[48] Lévi proposed that humans are a microcosm of the universe, and that there are sympathies or correspondences between the "lower" physical worlds and the "higher" metaphysical or spiritual worlds. This correspondence allowed the magician to exercise her powers through rituals like Kabbalistic incantations, by use of talismans, or by focusing on magical symbols.

Lévi further proposed that rituals transformed forces *within* the magician, which—because of the lower-to-higher correspondences—would then manifest in the external world. Lévi explained the underlying "substance" of magic in terms of what he called the Astral Light, conceived as a subtle fluid that pervades the universe but is not constrained by the usual boundaries of space-time. This fluid, which we've already encountered in Mesmer's ideas and the alchemical notion of the One Thing, was said by Lévi to be sensitive to human intention, and likewise, mental impressions could be influenced by it. The former would allow for psychokinetic (mind-matter) influences and manifestations, and the latter for psychic perceptions such as precognition and clairvoyance.[49]

Meanwhile, in 1848 in Rochester, New York, sisters Kate (1837–1892) and Maggie Fox (1833–1893) claimed that they were receiving messages from spirits in the form of rapping noises at their family home. This inauspicious-sounding event fired the imagination of Americans, and what became known as Spiritualism quickly spread throughout Europe as an entertainment for some, and as a serious pursuit for others.

Spiritualism was immensely popular because it promised personal proof of the existence of a spirit world, which in turn counteracted the disenchantment of the rising materialistic worldview. Spiritualism, as practiced in the form of séances, was a modern form of the ancient magical practice of theurgy.

Because smartphones and video-streamed movies had not

been invented yet, the public's demand for séances as a form of quasi-spiritual entertainment sparked an industry only too glad to provide those services. Many of these individuals, called *mediums* because they were the intermediaries through which the spirits could communicate with the living, were frauds. Unlike prestidigitators and stage illusionists, most of whom did not hide the fact that they were performing tricks, fraudulent mediums swore that what they were doing was for real. And each time a medium was unmasked as a fraud, it led to growing skepticism—which persists to the present day—and to the notion that *all* mediums were necessarily frauds and fakes. This wasn't true then, nor is it true today.

The rising popularity of Spiritualism in the late nineteenth century also gave rise to the first organized scientific studies of psychic phenomena. Many prominent scientists and philosophers of the day, including William James, Sir William Crookes, Sir Oliver Lodge, and Lord Rayleigh, became members of the Society for Psychical Research (SPR), founded in London in 1882. The SPR remains a vital organization in the twenty-first century. Its peer-reviewed academic journals report an unbroken line of scientific studies about psychic phenomena, and its online encyclopedia, launched in 2016, is a valuable resource for those interested in learning more about psi research.[50]

The SPR's use of scientific controls offered a way to avoid the biases and frailties associated with earlier investigators' case studies, which relied mostly on eyewitness testimony. But the new methods also introduced a disadvantage. Carefully controlled scientific experiments are artificial constructs that require psychic effects to occur on demand. Such experiments rarely capture the motivational or emotional context that seems to spark spontaneous psychic effects. Fortunately, they do work often enough, even with solid controls in place, as we'll see later.

While America exported Spiritualism to Europe, an esoteric import arrived from Europe in the form of Frenchman Charles de Poyen. His demonstrations of Mesmerism were eagerly embraced by American spiritualist groups. An American physician with the delightful name of Phineas Parkhurst Quimby (1802–1866) witnessed Poyen's presentations and was so impressed that he combined Mesmerism with faith healing and developed a new healing technique that involved guiding the patient's imagination.

One of Phineas Quimby's successful patients was a woman named Mary Patterson. Based on Quimby's treatments, she fully recovered from a long, debilitating illness. In 1879, Patterson founded a religious teaching that included a mental-healing practice; she called it the First Church of Christ, Scientist, better known today as Christian Science. By then she was using her married name, Mary Baker Eddy.[51]

Other movements, also inspired by Quimby, adopted names such as Mental Science and New Thought. These new approaches to health and healing were thoroughly pragmatic efforts formed out of a mixture of Spiritualism and esoteric concepts. They presaged elements of the human potential movement that would unfold with increasing vigor over the next century.

In a development more closely associated with magic, in 1866 a small group of master Masons in Anglia (Britain) formed a Masonic-Rosicrucian study group called the Societas Rosicruciana. In 1887, this led to the formation of the Hermetic Order of the Golden Dawn, a syncretic resurrection of classical ceremonial magic practices. Israel Regardie (1907–1985) published the magical order's history and rituals.[52] The Golden Dawn would become an influential model for modern magical organizations.

This brings us to the Theosophical Society, co-founded in New York in 1875 by Russian-born Helena Petrovna Blavatsky (1831–1891) and retired American military officer Henry Steel Olcott (1832–1907).[53] Blavatsky had become disillusioned with the superficiality of Spiritualism and its reliance on séances, so she set out to review all of the major Western esoteric traditions.

She also added some new, exotic elements—materials from the Far East, mainly Hinduism and Buddhism. Like esoteric authors before her, Blavatsky claimed that her synthesis revealed a perennial set of ideas found throughout history and across all cultures.[54]

Blavatsky continued the trend that began in the Enlightenment, as religious and spiritual ideas were transitioning from supernatural to natural magic, and then from natural magic to scientific concepts. As this transition proceeded, it became clear that the developing scientific worldview was enormously powerful, but it also painted a picture of reality, and life, that was intensely nihilistic and purposeless. The promise of Spiritualism was that it posited some sort of survival after death, which addressed one of the major concerns about nihilism.

In this context, one of Blavatsky's aims was to restore human dignity and destiny by combining the concepts of reincarnation, karma, and secret masters with a syncretic pastiche of Hermetic magic, Neoplatonism, Gnosticism, Renaissance alchemy, Kabbalah, Egyptian and Greco-Roman mythology, Buddhism, and the Hindu philosophy of Advaita Vedanta.[55] In other words, she threw into the bouillabaisse pot every esoteric idea she could find. Her masterwork, *The Secret Doctrine*, was published in 1888.

Similar to the legendary origins of the Rosicrucians, Blavatsky claimed that she was taught by secret Tibetan masters. These were, she said, advanced adepts hidden deep in the Himalayan mountains, working for the benefit of all humanity. Stories about secret masters can still be found in much contemporary New Age spirituality.[56]

Blavatsky's efforts succeeded remarkably well, with Theosophy becoming a major blueprint for the modern esoteric revival and for much of New Age thought. Blavatsky's successors, Annie Besant (1847–1933) and Charles Leadbeater (1854–1934), added to Theosophy the practice of psychic abilities, explorations of the

astral plane, and past-lives research. This was a major break from
Blavatsky's approach because she had steered Theosophy away
from occult practices. Under Leadbeater's influence, magic became a central topic of interest.[57]

THE INFORMATION AGE

There were many important developments in the history of esotericism during the twentieth century. I will briefly mention just
six notables whose work has been especially relevant to the development of magical theory.

The first is British magician Aleister Crowley (1875–1947).
While at the University of Cambridge in 1898, Crowley became
a member of the Hermetic Order of the Golden Dawn. He eventually left it to join and then lead another magical group called
the Ordo Templi Orientis, which emphasized sexual magic. A
few years later, while traveling in Egypt, Crowley reported that a
discarnate intelligence (one of those ever-popular secret masters)
named Aiwass dictated to him "The Book of the Law," a work
about a new magical system he called Thelema. Crowley's intentionally provocative approach to magic, perhaps developed in
reaction to the proper British rules of conduct in the Victorian
era, was expressed through his motto "Do what thou wilt shall
be the whole of the Law." In other words, toss aside restraints of
tradition and laws and do whatever you want, including brazen
hedonism. This was the Victorian version of an unabashed call
for sex, drugs, and rock and roll (the last hadn't been invented
yet, but if it had been, Crowley would surely have promoted
that too).

Crowley's approach to magic was an idiosyncratic mix of
ceremonial magic, yoga, astrology, Kabbalah, a Western form
of Tantrism, and his own inventions. Crowley reveled in being
a nonconformist, but he also made important contributions to
practical magic. He recognized that ancient ceremonies and

rituals were needlessly obscure, and like most intellectuals of the day, Crowley was determined to bring magic up to date and to "naturalize" it based on the fast-rising influence of science.[58]

Crowley's definition of magic reflected this goal, as it stripped away any religious or esoteric connotations: "Magick is the science and art of causing change to occur in conformity with will." In alignment with his scientific approach, Crowley insisted that fledgling magicians record their magical efforts in detail, noting the physical and mental conditions, time and place, and any other circumstances that might have any result on their "experiments." They were also expected to share their records with others.[59] Magic, in Crowley's view, was basically a branch of science. It was all about consensus interpretation of data and independent replication.

One of Crowley's contemporaries was a leading popularizer of early twentieth-century magic, Violet Mary Firth (1890–1946). She too was a member of the Hermetic Order of the Golden Dawn, where like others she eventually became disenchanted with its ponderous ceremonial rituals. She left and cofounded a magical order called the Fraternity of the Inner Light, which she—like Blavatsky and Crowley—claimed was inspired by invisible "ascended" masters. Her family's motto, "Deo non fortuna" (from the Latin meaning "From God, not chance"), provided the pen name by which she is better known: Dion Fortune.[60] Fortune authored many popular books on magic in the 1920s and 1930s, including titles such as *Esoteric Orders and Their Work* in 1928, *Psychic Self-Defense* in 1930, and *The Mystical Qabalah* in 1935.[61]

The third major promoter of early twentieth-century esotericism was the Austrian philosopher and mystic Rudolf Steiner (1861–1925). Steiner was the general secretary of the Theosophical Society in Germany in 1902. In 1912, Steiner founded a new society devoted to his Christian-oriented interpretation of Theosophy, which he called anthroposophy. Steiner was a prolific author whose influence continues today through his founding of the Waldorf schools, biodynamic farming, and anthroposophical medicine. Steiner promoted the idea that esoteric knowledge was not just limited to the few. For example, in his 1904 book, *Knowledge of the Higher Worlds and Its Attainment,* Steiner wrote:

> There slumber in every human being faculties by means of which individuals can acquire for themselves a knowledge of higher worlds. Mystics, Gnostics, Theosophists, all speak of a world of soul and spirit which for them is just as real as the world we see with our physical eyes and touch with our physical hands. . . . As long as the human race has existed there has always been a method of training, in the course of which individuals possessing these higher faculties gave instruction to others who are in search of them. Such training, and the instruction received therefrom, is called occult (esoteric) teaching or spiritual science.[62]

A fourth influential figure was Greek-Armenian spiritual teacher George Ivanovitch Gurdjieff (1866–1949), whose work was popularized by his Russian student Piotr Demianovich Ouspensky (1878–1947). Gurdjieff developed an original esoteric school that included a neo-gnostic cosmology and spiritual self-development training program, which Ouspensky helped to promote through his popular books, including *In Search of the Miraculous* and *A New Model of the Universe.* Like Steiner, one of Gurdjieff's main contributions was the idea that esoteric ideas were not beyond the reach of the ordinary person. Through disciplined effort, transformation could be achieved by nearly anyone. In his book *Meetings with Remarkable Men,* Gurdjieff "meant to bring to the West . . . not only a new statement of what has been called 'the primordial tradition,' but the knowledge of *how* modern man might conduct his own search with the conditions of twentieth-century life."[63]

The fifth important contributor to modern esoteric thought was Swiss psychiatrist Carl Gustav Jung (1875–1961). Jung's symbolic analysis of alchemy, his concept of synchronicity, his dialogs about the relationships between mind and matter with quantum physicist Wolfgang Pauli, and his long fascination with mythological and archetypal influences all countered the scientific trend toward disenchanting the world.[64] Scholars have noted that Jung's process of depth psychology could be compared to the processes of transformation and initiation of the ancient mystery schools, and that Jung was well aware of and exploited that relationship.[65]

The sixth person who advanced magical theory in the twentieth century was British magician Peter Carroll. His development of "chaos magic," named after the new field (at the time) of chaos mathematics, was introduced in a 1987 two-part book entitled *Liber Null & Psychonaut.*[66] Carroll's work continued the "naturalization of magic" approach begun by Crowley and others. Carroll proposed:

> After some centuries of neglect, advanced minds are turning their attention to magic once more. It used to be said that magic was what we had before science was properly organized. It now seems that magic is where science is actually heading. Enlightened anthropology has grudgingly admitted that beneath all the ritual and mumbo-jumbo of so-called primitive cultures there exists a very real and awesome power that cannot be explained away. . . . In this new aeon the thrust of magical endeavor is toward making the actual experimental techniques work regardless of their religious or symbolic associations. The techniques of magic will be the hypersciences of the future. . . . Science has brought us power and ideas but not the wisdom or responsibility to handle them. The next great advance that humanity will make will be into the psychic domain.[67]

No overview of the modern esoteric tradition would be complete without mentioning individuals said to "channel" esoteric information.[68] Channelers speak of ascended masters that they hear in their mind or that speak through them while in a trance state. Examples of channeling can be found in virtually all religious texts; they're usually described as the sayings of the prophets.

Transpersonal psychologist Arthur Hastings, in his book *With the Tongues of Men and Angels*, surveyed the history of channeling. Six centuries before Christ, the oracle at Delphi was said to channel the Olympian god Apollo.[69] A thousand years later the prophet Muhammad channeled the Angel Gabriel. Another thousand years later and a photographer in Kentucky named Edgar Cayce (1877–1945) became known as the "sleeping prophet." Alice Bailey (1880–1949) channeled more than a dozen books dictated to her between 1919 and 1949 by "the Tibetan," whom she called Djwhal Khul. The British poet William Blake wrote his epic poem *Jerusalem* by listening to the dictation of an inner voice. Indian mathematician Srinivasa Ramanujan (1887–1920), who grew up in a small Indian village and learned everything he knew about mathematics from a book, developed thousands of original mathematical theorems, many of which have been proven to be correct and are still discussed today in scholarly journals. Ramanujan claimed that he received his ideas from the Hindu goddess Namagiri. On one occasion, as he described it,

> while asleep, I had an unusual experience. There was a red screen formed by flowing blood, as it were. I was observing it. Suddenly a hand began to write on the screen. I became all attention. That hand wrote a number of elliptic integrals. They stuck to my mind. As soon as I woke up, I committed them to writing.[70]

There are hundreds of contemporary channelers; some of the better-known include Ruth Montgomery, Elizabeth Clare Prophet, Kevin Ryerson, J. Z. Knight, and Jack Pursel. Two of the more influential channelers of the twentieth century were academic psychologist Helen Schucman (1909–1981) and author Jane Roberts (1929–1984). Their channeled books, *A Course in Miracles* and *Seth*, respectively, have sold millions of copies. The Seth material in particular closely reflects the esoteric and magical traditions:

> Your thoughts, studied, will let you see where you are going. They point clearly to the nature of physical events. What exists physically exists first in thought and feeling. There is no other rule. . . .[71] Matter is formed by those inner qualities that give it vitality, that structure follows expectation, that matter at any time can be completely changed by the activation of the creative faculties inherent in all consciousness.[72]

Finally, a key development in practical magic in the twentieth century was the repackaging of esoteric ideas into forms designed to appeal to the American impulse toward pragmatism, prosperity, and personal success. These books exalt the power of affirmations and positive thinking. This genre has become one of the most successful categories in the history of publishing. One of the first examples was *As a Man Thinketh* by James Allen, published in 1903. The book opens with this:

> The aphorism, "As a man thinketh in his heart so is he," not only embraces the whole of a man's being, but is so comprehensive as to reach out to every condition and circumstance of his life. A man is literally what he thinks, his character being the complete sum of all his thoughts. . . . Let a man radically alter his thoughts, and he will be astonished at the

rapid transformation it will effect in the material conditions of his life.[73]

Other successful works along these lines include *It Works!* by Roy Herbert Jarrett, published in 1926. This little booklet sold well over 1.5 million copies and has remained continuously in print since it first appeared. *How to Win Friends and Influence People*, published by Dale Carnegie in 1936, is ranked as one of the top twenty bestselling nonfiction books of all time.[74] *Think and Grow Rich*, published by Napoleon Hill in 1937, has sold over 100 million copies worldwide.

Then we have *How to Manifest Your Desires* by Neville Goddard in 1948. *The Power of Positive Thinking* by Norman Vincent Peale in 1952. *The Strangest Secret* by Earl Nightingale in 1956, a spoken record that sold over a million copies, making it the first audio recording to achieve gold album status. *Hidden Power for Human Problems* by Frederick Bailes in 1957. And *The Power of Your Subconscious Mind* by Joseph Murphy in 1963.

All of these books, and dozens more, assert the same basic idea: if you have very clear goals, concentrate on them, and unquestionably believe that the goals will manifest, then they will. This concept, simplified into the New Age shibboleth "You create your own reality," comes directly out of the esoteric traditions and is at the very core of magical practice.

Today the power of positive thinking tends to be interpreted in conventional psychological terms, but it is a fast-growing movement in academia. There are university-based courses devoted to positive thinking, and there's even a Positive Psychology Center at the University of Pennsylvania, where you can earn a master's degree in applied positive psychology.[75] Academic courses on the power of positive thinking may not include *As a Man Thinketh* or the esoteric origins of this concept, but as we'll see, there's more to affirmations than *just* psychological effects.

THE INTERNET AGE

The affirmations genre has continued unabated in the twenty-first century. Examples include *Ask and It Is Given: Learning to Manifest Your Desires* by Esther Hicks in 2004, the worldwide bestseller *The Secret* by Rhonda Byrne in 2007, *The Secrets to Quick and Lasting Life Change with Neuro-Linguistic Programming*, published in 2008 by Richard Bandler, and a rash of other popular books by authors such as Louise Hay, Jack Canfield, Anthony Robbins, Wayne Dyer, Jean Houston, Marianne Williamson, and Paul McKenna.

There are also many health-oriented books with similar themes, usually cast in terms of the power of intention, including bestsellers like *The Extraordinary Healing Power of Ordinary Things* by Larry Dossey in 2007, and *Mind over Medicine: Scientific Proof That You Can Heal Yourself* by Lissa Rankin in 2013. Among modern magicians we find the trend toward the scientific normalization of magic proceeding apace. As Patrick Dunn proposes, "If reality at an even more fundamental level than the quantum level is symbolic in nature, then manipulating symbol systems manipulates the semiotic web, and therefore manipulates reality."[76]

The urge to develop a "scientific magic" is accompanied by an increasing willingness to let go of the baggage of archaic ceremonial practices. A consequence of esotericism having lived underground for so long is that it has become moldy. Much of that literature today feels positively medieval. But there are signs of refreshing progress. Esoteric scholar Gordon White writes:

> Chaos magic first emerged in 1980s Britain as a reaction against the moribund state of occultism in general, having staggered out of the seventies with malodorous coatings of Castaneda and Ascended Masters layered atop a long-

stagnant core of Victorian magical order nonsense and taw-
dry in-fighting. . . . Chaos magic lacks any certificates of
participation. You achieve what you set out to do or you have
failed. Success could be lasting apotheosis or it could be bed-
ding your secretary. This only looks like elitism to failures.
To scientists, it looks like science.[77]

This brings us up-to-date. Now we are prepared to look at the
practice of magic.

Chapter 5

PRACTICE OF MAGIC

Don't only practice your art, but force your way into its
secrets, for it and knowledge can raise men to the divine.

—Ludwig van Beethoven

The essence of magic boils down to the application of two ordinary mental skills: attention and intention. The strength of the magical outcome is modulated by four factors: belief, imagination, emotion, and clarity.[1] That's basically it. The ceremonial robes, somber settings, black candles, secret hand-shakes, chanting in ancient languages, sex, and drugs—all are good theater, which may help in withdrawing the mind from the distractions of the mundane world. But ultimately, they're unnecessary.

GNOSIS

The single most important aide to developing magical skills is to learn how to enter the state of consciousness known as gnosis. The time-honored and safest way to do this is through medita-tion.

As recently as the 1960s, meditation in the Western world was regarded as so exotically alien that it was difficult to find a meditation teacher or training materials. Now any moderate-sized town will have at least one meditation class offered at a school, library, or community center. Meditation instruction can certainly benefit from a wise teacher, but there are hundreds of books, audio programs, and smartphone apps that provide excellent introductions to meditation. Some apps now work along with relatively inexpensive neurofeedback hardware that is supposed to accelerate the learning process.

The effectiveness of these programs varies a great deal, so the only way to tell if a particular method works for you is to try it. If you manage to read only one book about meditation, I recommend *The Science of Enlightenment: How Meditation Works*, by Shinzen Young, published in 2016. It's also available as an audiobook. It's an exceptionally clear exposition written for the Western mindset, covering what meditation is, how to do it, and how it works.

The basic practice of meditation is straightforward. Sit in a comfortable position. Relax your body. Close your eyes. Then quiet your mind and stop thinking. That's all there is to it. Simple.

Well, not so simple. If you're a novice, three seconds after beginning this practice your mind will start to wander and you'll enjoy one enticing fantasy after another. After dreaming about tasty cheeseburgers for ten minutes, you'll suddenly realize that your mind was wandering. So you start again. Relax your body. Drop your jaw a bit and relax the muscles around your eyes. Let it go. Empty your mind. No thoughts.

This time, after a whole six seconds of calm silence, your mind will wander again. Progress! So you do it again, and again. It may take months or years of practice to achieve extended periods when the mind remains still. While engaged in this practice, you're essentially reprogramming your nervous system, even if you don't notice it. You'll start to feel better physically and mentally. You'll see the world more clearly. As Shinzen Young puts it, as a result of this practice "clarity and equanimity are slowly but surely trickling down into the subconscious. They rewire us at the most fundamental levels."[2]

Some meditation techniques involve mentally repeating sounds, words, or phrases to help keep your mind focused. Others train you to visualize complex patterns. Still others just involve watching your breath. There are scores of variations. One of the more popular methods today is called mindfulness. This is a secular version of the Buddhist practice called Vipassana, which literally translated means "to see in various ways." The goal is to see things as they actually *are*, not as they may appear to be.

It wasn't always so easy to find information about meditation. The cover story of an issue of *Time* magazine in 1975, "The TM Craze," reported on the rising popularity of the Transcendental Meditation movement. A dozen years later, the cover featured actress Shirley MacLaine holding a quartz crystal. The photo caption read, "A strange mix of spirituality and superstition is sweeping across the country." In 1996, a cover story asked, "Can prayer, faith and spirituality really improve your physical health? A growing and surprising body of scientific evidence says they can." In 2001, the "power of yoga" was on the cover. In 2003, we learned about "the science of meditation." By 2014, the cover story was on "the mindful revolution: The science of finding focus in a stressed-out, multitasking culture."

Over a mere four decades, the cultural pulse in the United States evolved from a worried befuddlement at what those crazy hippies were doing to an appreciation of a widespread beneficial practice with obvious value that's covered by medical insurance. Given this shift in opinion, what else may we expect to become self-evident about meditation? One likelihood is that science will rediscover what has been known for millennia but, like magic, was denigrated as a superstitious belief. This involves the original purpose of meditation and some of the less well-known but exceptional consequences of engaging in a disciplined practice. As I discussed in my book *Supernormal*, the goal of meditation across many traditions is to achieve a state of awareness where one gains the realization that the personal self and the Universal Self are one (in my shorthand, [c] = [C]).

Within the [C] state, abilities naturally arise that allow the meditator to manipulate or to transcend the world. Within the path of yoga, the goal of meditation is transcendence, or personal liberation. In that tradition the *siddhis*, or powers, that are gained are strongly deemphasized. In the magical tradition, gaining those powers is the goal.

It's worth mentioning that the *Yoga Sutras*, the classical book of yoga written by the Indian sage Patanjali about two thousand years ago, assures us that these powers have nothing to do with faith, religious doctrine, divine intervention, spirituality, or the supernatural. These powers are just another aspect of the natural world. As Buddhist scholar Alan Wallace put it:

> In Buddhism, these [abilities] are not miracles in the sense of being supernatural events, any more than the discovery and amazing uses of lasers are miraculous. . . . What may appear supernatural to a scientist or a layperson may seem perfectly natural to an advanced contemplative, much as certain technological advances may appear miraculous to a contemplative.[3]

Many variations of the superpowers are described in the yogic tradition. They range from vanilla psi to supermagic such as levitation. Levitation may be regarded as a high-level magical skill that involves hanging in the air in much the same way that bricks don't.[4] For most people, most of the time, psi experiences are spontaneous and tend to occur mainly during periods of crisis or extreme motivation. By contrast, the siddhis are regarded as reliable and under full conscious control. Some magicians are said to have developed that level of ability as well, but as with the siddhis, achieving conscious, robust control of superabilities is rare.

One way to investigate if meditation really does amplify natural psi and magical skills is to ask meditators about their experiences. At the Institute of Noetic Sciences, my colleagues conducted a survey of more than a thousand meditators to ask about their experiences. They found that three out of four reported increases in meaningful synchronicities as a result of their practice. Nearly half reported sensing "nonphysical entities," and a third reported experiences such as clairvoyance or telepathy. This suggests that meditation works as the yogic and other traditions claim it does, at least when it comes to subjective reports. The next step is to see if those experiences are supported by objective evidence. We'll address that question in Chapter 6.

The bottom line: If you want to perform magic effectively, maintain a disciplined meditation practice. Learn to quiet your mind. See the world as it is, not as it appears to be when viewed through multiple layers of cultural conditioning.

FORCE OF WILL

It's unrealistic to expect that you'll become the legendary Merlin after lighting a candle and practicing meditation for five minutes. Throwing "battle magic" lightning bolts from your fingertips looks great in the movies, but for the majority of us magic is expressed in subtle ways. Performing potent magic, like any refined skill, requires talent and disciplined practice.

Perhaps you are the one in a million who's gifted with strong natural talent. If so, you'll be able to achieve dramatic effects fairly quickly. But the rest of us have to work at it. Fortunately, nearly anyone who's able to follow instructions and is serious about practicing can perform some degree of magic because— according to the esoteric worldview—whether you know it or not, within you there's a spark of the same source that manifests the entire universe.

With that as a brief introduction, here then are two variations for exercising your force of will: affirmations and sigils.

Affirmations

Force-of-will magic involves the application of focused attention, intention, imagination, and belief. It's preposterously simple, but many claim that it works. We'll use a slightly elaborated example from the appropriately entitled book *It Works!*[5] This book provides a prime example of "writing magic," one of the earliest forms of magical practice. The four steps are as follows:

1. *Know what you want.* The clearer the intended goal, the more likely it will manifest. *Believe* that the goal will be achieved. *Imagine* that it has already been achieved in the future and it is inexorably headed your way. Write the goal on a piece of paper to focus your attention. Use a pen and paper exclusively reserved for this purpose. While writing, imagine that the surface of the paper represents Universal Consciousness and the ink represents your unconscious.[6] As you write your goal, imagine that you are casting your unconscious intentions onto the medium that creates and sustains reality itself.

2. *Review what you want.* Review your goal daily. Between reviews do not dwell on it. You want to strengthen your intention and keep it clear, but you also want to allow the goal to seep into your unconscious, because that's where magic is catalyzed. You may want to secure the writing paper with a special ribbon or place it in a box set aside specifically for this purpose.

3. *Maintain secrecy.* Don't share your goal with others; they may inject doubt, and you need to maintain strong belief.

4. When it works, accept the outcome with gratitude and use it to *strengthen your belief.*

This method, like any form of magical manifestation, is neutral with respect to morals or ethics. However, virtue is its own reward, and it's useful to keep in mind Spider-Man's motto: "With great power comes great responsibility." This means it would be morally questionable to use this technique to influence someone else, even in a way that you would consider to be positive, without that person's permission.

In addition, from a pragmatic perspective it is useful to begin with simple, easily measurable outcomes, like finding a small amount of money or achieving a modest goal. Avoid jumping straight away into grandiose schemes like world peace, not because it wouldn't work (at least in principle) but because gaining crystal clarity on what an accomplishment of that type of goal would *mean*, and how one would know if it happened, isn't as simple as it may seem.

Sigils

Before considering how to create a *sigil* (pronounced "SIDG-ul"), a bit of background is in order. First, a sigil is simply a symbol for a desired goal.[7] It has an advantage over writing because crafting a sigil requires more focused attention than just writing it, and because use of a symbolic goal reduces the grasp of the analytical mind. In addition, after the sigil is created, the magician traditionally "charges" and then "releases" it. The charging is meant to forcefully concentrate emotion, intention, and belief on the goal; the releasing is intended to push the goal from the conscious mind into the unconscious.

There's another reason a sigil is useful as a magical tool. Consider the word *spell*. As a verb, *spell* means an action where symbols are combined to form larger symbols, which in turn refer to objects, actions, or concepts. That is, letters → words → sentences. The magical meaning of the noun *spell* is similar to the meaning of the verb, except it assumes a worldview where everything is interconnected beyond space-time; this is the meaning of the magical Law of Correspondences. Now consider the word *draw*. One meaning of the verb *draw* is to devise a picture or a symbol; the other is to pull together.

From the magical perspective, a symbol is more than something that points to a relationship. It's also an integral part of the structure of reality itself. By drawing a symbol, you pull the meaning of that symbol into existence. If the word-symbol *Fido* corresponds to a real dog named Fido, then operations on the symbol will also influence the actual Fido. This is the concept underlying homeopathy, the wearing of good-luck charms, and voodoo. Comb the hair of a doll made in the likeness of your distant friend, and your friend may thank you later about the wonderful new hairdo that she spontaneously decided to adopt. (Note: This example is on the razor's edge of black magic, so don't try this at home.)

The idea that signs and symbols reflect, or literally *are*, the relational structure that holds the universe together was famously explored in Robert Heinlein's *Stranger in a Strange Land*. The main character in that story, Valentine Michael Smith, was raised on Mars. In learning the Martian language, Smith gained powers that looked like magic. He taught others Martian words, and they too were able to gain these exceptional powers. A similar idea, of an alien language evoking special powers, was the leitmotif of the 2016 science fiction movie *Arrival*. In that story the scientist who figures out how to interpret an alien language based on circular time begins to literally experience time differently.

This notion jibes with informational interpretations of quantum theory, which we'll explore in more detail in Chapter 8. Perhaps the most famous of those interpretations was proposed by Princeton University physicist John Wheeler. He described it as the physics of "it from bit," which means that an object in the physical world (an "it") is derived from pure information (a "bit," a digital representation of information). As Wheeler put it:

> Every it—every particle, every field of force, even the space-time continuum itself—derives its function, its meaning, its very existence entirely—even if in some contexts indirectly— from the . . . answers to yes-or-no questions, binary choices, bits.[8]

MIT physicist Max Tegmark generalized Wheeler's "it from bit" by proposing that physical reality literally *is* a mathematical structure, an abstract set of relationships. From that viewpoint, if one manipulates those abstract relationships, then one manipulates the physical world.[9] That's the idea of a sigil (and of force-of-will magic in general).

Making and Using a Sigil

1. Write your desire. Example: "I find a ten-dollar bill."
2. List the first letters of words in the sentence, ignoring words that begin with a vowel. You'll end up with FTDB.
3. Fit the letters together into an abstract symbol, as in Figure 1.

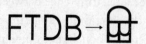

Figure 1. Letters arranged into a sigil.

4. Focus on the symbol, projecting either intense calm or intense emotion through the symbol to "charge" it and amplify your desire. Magicians provoke this charge within the state of gnosis through deep meditation, by firing up a fierce concentration, by engaging in strong physical activity, by evoking

anger, or by using the moment of sexual orgasm to provide an explosive point of focus.

5. After the sigil is charged, release your attention by putting the sigil away. Some magicians will go as far as to burn it; others will momentarily glance at the sigil every so often or place the symbol in a location where they'll see it now and then. The idea is to deflect the intention of the sigil from the conscious mind to the deep unconscious, where it will simmer and draw the desired outcome into being.

6. As with writing magic, maintaining strong belief is an important factor, as is secrecy. So keep the meaning of the sigil private, and heed the age-old wisdom about using magic for benign purposes only.

Does This Really Work?

In my experience in both life and the lab, yes, it does. Not every time, and not always with great fanfare. But it works often enough to raise an eyebrow. In life, the desired outcome usually manifests in the form of a meaningful synchronicity. In a laboratory study, it manifests as a statistically significant test of a hypothesis. The key elements in both cases are focused intention, an openness to the idea that the desired outcome has already been achieved, and very clear goals.

Of course, there's a big difference between magic in everyday life and magic in the lab. With the latter, we know by design what is a chance versus a nonchance outcome. But with the former, there's no way to know for sure *why* a desired outcome occurred. Coincidences do occur. But occasionally a synchronicity seems so unlikely that chance is no longer a viable explanation. I'll give an example of a four-part synchronicity.

Synchronicity #1

Early in the year 2000 I was searching for office space for a research institute that a colleague, Richard Shoup, and I were establishing. We called it the Boundary Institute because its mission was to scientifically explore the boundaries between mind and matter using the disciplines of physics, mathematics, and computer science. This organization would continue a program of psi research that I had been in charge of at a Silicon Valley technology company called Interval Research Corporation, funded by Paul Allen, the co-founder of Microsoft.

The dot-com craze was at its peak at the time, with new Internet start-ups popping up all over Silicon Valley. As a result, office rental rates, already at astronomical levels, were continuing to rise. We looked at four potential locations and ended up rejecting the first three because they were too expensive. That left only one clear choice, in the town of Los Altos, a suburb of Silicon Valley. It was a nice space with four offices, a common area, and a conference room, and it was located in a complex that housed accountants, therapists, real estate agents, dentists, and so on. The plan was that I would move in first and get things set up.

After moving furniture into a room that would become my office, I became curious about our neighbors. I found a directory sign listing the office suites. Most were ordinary businesses, but one was named PsiQuest, Inc. I took this as a delightful coincidence, because our new institute was also a sort of psi quest, namely, psi research of the parapsychological kind. There are only a handful of psi research facilities in the world, and we are all well aware of each other. So I was certain that the "psi" in PsiQuest must have meant "Personnel Service Investigations," or something like that. The "psi" similarity was surely just an amusing coincidence.

Synchronicity #2

About a month later, I took a new route to walk to our office and noticed that the sign on the suite next door to ours, which I hadn't noticed before, was "PsiQuest Research Labs." Now this was suddenly more interesting, because what in the world was Personnel Service Investigations, as I imagined PsiQuest to be, doing with a research lab? The miniblinds on the PsiQuest Research Labs window were closed, and what little I could see through the blinds revealed only a well-appointed reception space. No one was visible.

I checked every day for the next two weeks. Finally someone was in the PsiQuest Labs office. I knocked and tried the door. It was unlocked, so I entered and prepared to say hello to a man behind a desk. He looked up and his eyes widened as though he saw a ghost. I thought maybe he was startled, so I extended my hand and said, "Hello, I wanted to introduce myself. I'm your neighbor next door. My name is. . . ." But before I could finish he managed to croak: "Dean Radin?"

I hesitated. "Yes," I replied cautiously, wondering how he knew who I was, and if he was feeling okay. He said nothing. He just continued to stare at me. After an uncomfortable pause, I said, "I'm your neighbor next door. I just wanted to introduce myself and see what kind of work you do here."

After a moment the man replied, "I'm doing what you're doing."

Confused, I asked, "What do you think I'm doing?"

He replied, "Psi research . . . parapsychology."

Now it was my turn to stare, dumbfounded. Unbeknownst to me or to any of my colleagues around the world, here was another group engaged in the same kind of research that we were, and they were located *next door* to our new offices.

Synchronicity #3

It turned out that the president of PsiQuest, Jon K., not only was thoroughly familiar with psi research but was specifically engaging in a magical practice to *manifest me*! Jon was using a Tibetan dream yoga technique, which involves alternating three-hour periods of sleeping and waking over the course of twenty-four hours. During the waking periods, he was intensely wishing for a sign that his business was on the right track, and one of those signs would be for me to show up, somehow, so I could join his board of directors. But he had no idea where I was or how to contact me. Hardly anyone at the time knew that I was living in Silicon Valley, and even fewer knew where our new institute was located.

That's why when I opened the door to Jon's lab that day he was speechless. He couldn't tell if he was awake or dreaming. From his perspective, my appearance on his doorstep was literally an act of magic based on his clear, repeated affirmations. When he was finally able to tell me what was going on, I too felt seriously disoriented. We both had to sit down.

Synchronicity #4

The month before all this unfolded, I was focused on visualizing what our new offices and laboratory space would look like. I was drawing sketches of my ideal lab configuration on the whiteboard in my office and imagining a certain kind of reclining leather chair, a shielded room, and other types of equipment that would be useful to have in the lab. I knew all this would be expensive, and our budget was limited, so I figured we wouldn't be able to afford it in the short term. But that didn't stop me from visualizing what I wanted.

Returning to the story, after recovering from the shock of

our meeting, Jon invited me to tour the rest of his facility. As we moved from one room to the next, I could hardly believe my eyes. Jon had the reclining leather chair, the shielded chamber, and all the other pieces of laboratory equipment I had been actively imagining. And all of it was located *on the other side of the wall* from my desk, no more than six feet from where I had been sketching what our lab would look like. I literally drew what I wanted into being.

A Half-Baked Speculation

After discussing that series of synchronicities with the other members of our institute, we agreed that this couldn't be a case of dumb luck. It's as though sustained intention on the part of Jon and myself had acted as a sort of force that drew PsiQuest and the Boundary Institute together, analogous to gravity drawing a moon and a planet together. In Einstein's general relativistic concept of gravity, the planet doesn't reach out with "gravity beams" to pull on the moon. Rather, the fabric of space-time is distorted by the planet's mass, and the warped geometry naturally guides the moon and the planet to drift toward each other.[10] (Later I'll describe an experiment we did that more formally explored this idea.) With this analogy in mind, we thought that perhaps intense intention also warps or distorts aspects of reality. Events that might otherwise be completely separate and never meet are naturally drawn (incorporating both meanings of the verb *to draw*) together by the resulting warp in space-time.

Like magic.

DIVINATION

Divination involves perceiving beyond the ordinary boundaries of space and time. In the early nineteenth century this ability was called clairvoyance (French for "clear-seeing"). Later it was called extra-sensory perception, or ESP. Today the euphemism *remote viewing* is more commonly used.

Training techniques to help develop remote viewing abilities were designed by artist Ingo Swann as part of a classified program of psi research funded by the U.S. government from 1972 to 1995. Swann based his picture-drawing technique on methods used in the 1880s by British researchers Frederic W. H. Myers and Edmund Gurney, in the 1920s by the American social activist Upton Sinclair, and in the 1940s by British psychologist Whately Carington and French researcher René Warcollier.

The method involves making fast, abstract sketches of impressions gained when asked to mentally perceive a distant target image or location. This is intended to capture not only fleeting visual images but impressions from the other senses as well. The reason Swann's technique focused on fast sketching, at least in the initial stages of remote viewing, is that the single greatest inhibitor of remote viewing ability is the analytic mind, which gets in the way. In the jargon used in this type of training, this problem is called an "analytical overlay."

To explain, let's say our task is to use remote viewing to describe a hidden or distant target. A taskmaster assigns the target a randomly assigned label, say "X2395," which is associated with the real target. This association can be accomplished by simply placing the label on an envelope containing a photo of the target. Now let's say the target is a person wearing a yellow raincoat. When a remote viewer directs her attention toward that target she might instantly perceive a vague flash of something yellow. But then, within a fraction of a second, the analytical portion of her mind will jump in and associate that bit of information with typically yellow things. Before she's even consciously aware of it, she'll start thinking that the target is a banana. And once that thought enters her mind, it's extremely difficult to let it go.

Other than using meditation to achieve a state where these flashes of information are not overwhelmed by the buzz of everyday thoughts, learning to *not name* the target is the primary challenge one faces in remote viewing training. For reasons that make sense in evolutionary terms, over millions of years our brains have been hardwired to take a pinch of information and instantly fill in the blanks with the most likely description. The reason is simple: If you see a glimmer of black and orange stripes out of the corner of your eye, your brain will instantly assume it's a tiger and your legs will start running before you realize it. If your assumption is wrong, you'll get a momentary scare and it won't matter much. But if you're right, it could save your life. In the wild you survive by acting first and thinking later.

But for more subtle types of perception like remote viewing, that same tendency has to be unlearned. This is what Swann's method taught. One of his earliest techniques, designed to baffle the analytical mind, was called "coordinate remote viewing," because the only information provided about the target was map coordinates. Without thinking about it or looking at a map, what's your impression of what's located at 37.819732° latitude and -122.478762° longitude?[11] Later techniques by Swann used more abstract targeting methods, like the randomly constructed label "X2395." And that worked just as well.

After the secret government program was declassified, variations of the original training methods were developed and taught by former members of the U.S. Army's remote viewing unit. As time went by, variations of the original method were developed by second- and third-generation students who capitalized on the burgeoning popular interest in remote viewing training. Each new method seems to carry increasingly bolder claims about its amazing new and improved, super-duper, double-secret enhanced learning technique. But the essence of all of these various methods is the same.

Remote Viewing Training

Swann's original technique was based on a series of stages that I've simplified into eight steps.[12] We'll assume that you have no idea what the target is or where it's located. It might be a photograph inside a sealed envelope, a person who will travel tomorrow to a location only she knows, or an object that a friend lost a week ago. To make the exercise useful as an experiment you'll eventually need to know what the right answer is; otherwise you won't be able to tell if the remote viewing attempt was accurate.

This method may be easier if the remote viewing session includes a partner who can guide you through the various stages.[13] In that way you won't need to engage the portion of your mind that's required to keep track of the process. Most classroom remote viewing training, as well as most of the operational remote viewing employed in the U.S. government program, used a human interviewer for this reason. Obviously in a valid experiment the interviewer can't know anything about the target either. For a novice this process may take a half hour or more. For an expert it can take five minutes. The eight steps are as follows:

1. Start with a blank piece of paper and a pencil. Holding the target in mind, quickly draw lines, curves, or squiggles. Don't think about it, just sketch the first thing that comes into your mind. Remote viewing information initially appears as a very brief impression; a flash, a mere glimmer. It's not like watching a full-color 3-D Imax movie. Also, your sketch might reflect how you *feel* about the target and have nothing to do with what the target looks like. So don't analyze what you've drawn. Just quickly sketch while keeping your goal in mind: describe the target.

2. List your initial sensory impressions of the target, focusing on movement, odor, taste, touch, and sound. After listing those, add any visual impressions that come to mind, including

shape and color. The moment you realize that you've *named* an impression, note it but add that it's "AOL," for "analytical overlay."

3. Mentally examine the target from other perspectives: from far away, close up, low, and high. Capture the impressions you gain from each new perspective. Avoid naming the impressions.

4. Note any emotional feelings you may have about the target.

5. Combine all of the impressions you've gained so far and use them to make a sketch or series of sketches that describe the target. Now, based on your accumulated perceptions, write down what you think the target is. This is the first step where analysis should be used.

6. Mentally reexamine the target and look for anything you may have missed. Watch for new insights, novel feelings, surprising elements, or any other aspect that might feel out of place. Sketch and write down these impressions.

7. Compare your sketch of the target with any new information you've gained. Revise if necessary.

8. Now compare the actual target with your final description.

Factors involved in enhancing remote viewing performance, or improving divination skills of any sort, were studied by parapsychologist Rhea White in the 1960s.[14] She focused on reports by individuals who had consistently demonstrated high-level psi performance to see if there were any similarities. She found a number of them:

1. *Relax.* Achieve a state of deep physical relaxation.

2. *Stabilize the mind.* Meditation may be helpful in encouraging what some adepts refer to as a "blank mental screen," or what a magician might call the initial stages of achieving gnosis. The goal is to avoid mind-wandering.

3. *Direct the mind.* After achieving a period of mental stability,

ask yourself, "What is the target?" The idea is to direct the mind, which at this point should be in a calm, blank, or idling mode, so it can focus without distraction on the task at hand.

4. *Wait with expectation.* To explain this, Rhea White recounted a metaphor of the winding of a toy top as a preliminary to its spinning. That is, don't just wait passively; create a sense of tension, belief, and excitement that the information will arrive. Be patient and don't force it.

5. *Look for a feeling of conviction.* To help discriminate between mind-generated fantasies and acquisition of genuine information, you may notice that when the impression is correct it is accompanied by a strong feeling of conviction, or by a burst of joy, vividness, or certainty.

In today's fast-paced world, we want instant results. Five steps times thirty seconds is two and a half minutes. Who has that kind of time to spare? The talented people that Rhea White studied would sometimes spend an *hour* or more on a single trial: fifteen minutes to relax, a half hour to create a mental blank screen, then another half hour before perceiving target information and "knowing" that it was correct. Sometimes no suitable impression would arrive, so there goes an hour, wasted. You could have been watching the latest cat videos on YouTube and enjoying a refreshing beverage and a biscotti. Magic is real, but no one said it's going to be fast or easy.

THEURGY: CALLING ALL SPIRITS

Why is it when we talk to God it's called praying, but if God talks back it's called schizophrenia?

—JANE WAGNER

People have different reactions to the concept that there are dis-embodied spirits around us all the time. For those who believe in guardian angels, or that their departed loved ones are still present in some form, the idea can be comforting. For those who've been frightened by tales of demons, the same idea is horrific.

There are endless stories about such entities.[15] And a case can be made that all of it, from legends of the wee people, fairies, and forest sprites to tales of angels, demons, and even extraterrestrial aliens and UFO encounters, arises from a common source.[16] But so far scientific evidence that such experiences involve intelligent, independent, nonphysical *entities,* as opposed to a mixture of human-centric psi and psychological *effects,* has not been established in such a way that people who are intimately familiar with the evidence, and even sympathetic to the idea of entities, will reach the same conclusion. In my opinion, the scientific jury is still out regarding the reality of such spirits or entities.

Of course, my hesitation doesn't mean that such entities don't exist. It just means that we don't have methods yet that can strictly discriminate between psi effects in the living and independent, disembodied intelligences. Some claim that we can communicate with spirits using electronic devices and computers. And some of the evidence for what is known as electronic voice phenomena or instrumental transcommunication (ITC) is intriguing. But there too the methods do not *strictly* exclude explanations based on psi. One source of information about electronic methods used in this line of research is the *ITC Journal,* run by Dr. Anabela Cardoso.[17]

As far as the practice of theurgy goes—the act of evoking spirits—it should not be taken lightly that ghosts and demons are indispensable plot points in horror films. Or that skeptics laugh at the notion of disembodied spirits, even if that laugh is nervous and one eye twitches uncontrollably.

The esoteric literature on theurgy suggests that if you don't know what you're doing, don't do it. There are plenty of books on theurgic spells and ceremonial rituals that appear to be relatively benign.[18] But given that scientific guidance for these practices is so thin as compared to the other two classes of magic, and because of the potential psychological consequences of shattering your belief system by encountering something that scares your pants off, I will pass on providing practical exercises. This is a topic that requires expertise and wisdom, and because of that, it's inadvisable to learn from a book. Don't say I didn't warn you.

Chapter 6

SCIENTIFIC EVIDENCE

The only way of discovering the limits of the possible is to venture a little way past them into the impossible.

—Arthur C. Clarke

The scientific literature relevant to understanding magic has been published in peer-reviewed journals over the past century and a half. It consists of roughly three thousand laboratory experiments, each of which involved one or more researchers testing anywhere from a handful to hundreds of participants over years or even decades. With very few exceptions, these experiments were not designed to test magical concepts. They were conducted in the context of applying scientific methods to investigate psi experiences. But when these same studies are viewed through the lens of the esoteric traditions, testing magic is exactly what these experiments were all about. Force of will has been studied in the context of investigating mind-matter interactions, also called psychokinesis. Divination has been studied as variations of clairvoyance or precognition. Theurgy has been investigated in the laboratory typically in the form of mediumship studies.

From a mainstream scientific perspective, the existence of psi phenomena remains controversial. Some claim that the persistent debate indicates that despite a century of smoke there's still no fire, and so psi probably doesn't exist. For stronger skeptics, all of the supporting scientific evidence—100 percent of it—can be due only to flukes, flaws, or fraud.

I am confident that the dismissive skeptical opinion is wrong. In my opinion, the primary reason for the continuing uncertainty is due to assumptions about the nature of reality that are formalized within the scientific worldview. If one completely accepts today's worldview as inviolate or absolute, then the strength and quality of the evidence for psi simply don't matter. The phenomena are considered impossible, and that's that.

This may be surprising to those who've been taught that science is dispassionately rational and evidence-based. Science certainly aspires to be driven by evidence, but as in any domain of human affairs, a few leading figures in each discipline establish fads and fashions that others are expected to follow. Those same figures enforce the status quo by deciding who gets promoted and who gets grants to fund their research. This helps to define the boundaries of each discipline, but of course it also constrains genuine innovation.[1] The realpolitik of science is a fascinating subject, and it's central in understanding why psi and magic are taboo within the academic world. But it also threatens to deflect us from our main interest, so I'll set it aside for now and instead address the evidence from a different perspective.

AN EXPERT ANALYSIS

The mathematical discipline that specializes in the evaluation of experimental data is statistics. Professor Jessica Utts is chair of the statistics department at the University of California at Irvine. In 2016, she was also president of the American Statistical Association (ASA), the world's largest community of professional statisticians.[2] In her presidential address to the ASA, speaking at a meeting attended by six thousand statisticians from sixty-two countries around the world, Utts said something that undoubtedly surprised many of the attendees.[3] I quote a segment of her talk at length because it's directly relevant to understanding the evidence for psi. She said the following:

> For many years I have worked with researchers doing very careful work in [parapsychology], including a year that I spent full-time working on a classified project for the United States government, to see if we could use these abilities for intelligence gathering during the Cold War. . . .[4]
>
> At the end of that project I wrote a report for Congress, stating what I *still* think is true. The data in support of precognition and possibly other related phenomena are quite strong statistically, and would be widely accepted if it pertained to something more mundane. Yet, most scientists reject the possible reality of these abilities without ever looking at data! And on the other extreme, there are true believers who base their beliefs solely on anecdotes and personal experience. I have asked the debunkers if there is *any* amount of data that would convince them, and they generally have responded by saying, "probably not." I ask them what original research they have read, and they mostly admit that they haven't read any. Now *there* is a definition of pseudo-science—basing conclusions on belief, rather than data!
>
> When I have given talks on this topic to audiences of statisticians, I show lots of data. Then I ask the audience, which would be more convincing to you—lots more data, or one strong personal experience? Almost without fail, the response is one strong personal experience. . . . I think people are justifiably skeptical, because most people think that these abilities contradict what we know about science. They don't, but that's the subject for a different talk![5]

SIX SIGMA

Another take on the overall evidence for psi is provided by classes of experiments that have exceeded the six-sigma threshold. This refers to studies where the overall odds against chance, after careful consideration of all known experiments investigating the same topic, are assessed to be over a billion to one.[6] Each of these experiments used protocols that avoided all known design flaws. An extensive due diligence list of possible design faults has developed after years of intense scrutiny and criticism of these studies, leading to bulletproof designs.

Each class of experiments has been repeated from a dozen to more than a hundred times by independent investigators at different labs around the world, with each class cumulatively involving hundreds to thousands of participants. The vast majority of these studies involved ordinary people, most of whom were not claiming any special psi abilities. This recruitment strategy was employed in most cases for pragmatic reasons (it is expensive to find and work with highly talented specialists), but it also provides an important benefit because the results are not based on extraordinary claims. That is, tests involving celebrity psychics inevitably invite attacks because it's easier for critics to believe that those individuals were just clever tricksters rather than genuinely talented. The other advantage of working with ordinary people is that the resulting evidence then applies to the general population. In other words, we're talking not about X-Men but about what is true among the general population.

CLASSES OF EXPERIMENTS

The six classes of scientific experiments with overall strong positive evidence are:[7]

- *Telepathy,* specifically an experimental protocol called the *ganzfeld,* for testing the existence of conscious telepathic impressions between pairs of isolated people.[8] This experiment has been repeated by dozens of investigators around the world for four decades, including by avowed skeptics who, to their consternation and surprise, successfully replicated the effect.

- *Remote viewing,* otherwise known as clairvoyance and precognition, a method for testing perception that transcends space or time.[9]

- *Presentiment,* a technique for measuring unconscious physiological reactions to future events.[10]

- *Implicit precognition,* a test that measures future influences on present-time behavior.[11] This type of study was popularized by Cornell University psychologist Daryl Bem.

- *Random number generators* (*RNGs*), a laboratory protocol used to test if mental intention affects the outputs of random physical systems. This is a more refined version of older tests involving tossed dice. An RNG is an electronic device designed to produce truly random sequences of 0s and 1s, each with probability 1/2, like an automated coin flipper.[12] The source of randomness in these devices is not a software algorithm but true random events such as electron tunneling in electronic circuit components. Tunneling is a quantum mechanical phenomenon considered in physics to be fundamentally random.

- *Global Consciousness Project,* a worldwide version of an RNG experiment, where the outputs of RNGs located around the world are compared against long-term baselines during events of major global interest (e.g., terrorist attacks).[13] This experiment differs from the previous five classes because it doesn't involve individuals studied in the laboratory but rather is a global experiment including everyone. It also tests not the effects of intention but rather the simultaneous focused attention of millions of people. All of the data from this project have been publicly available through its website from 1998, when the project began. After collecting five hundred worldwide events (which took eighteen years, because—fortunately—major worldwide events don't happen very often), the experiment had achieved an overall result above seven sigma. That's associated with odds against chance greater than a trillion to one.[14]

Other classes of studies that haven't reached the six-sigma level yet but may do so after enough data are collected include experiments investigating the effects of distant mental influence on human physiology and behavior.[15] In one variation of this type of experiment, a total of fifty-one experiments were conducted between 1977 and 2000 by multiple investigators at different labs around the world. The experiments involved more than a thousand pairs of participants, with one member of each pair attempting to mentally influence the other's physiological state. The combined results were odds against chance of 15,600 to 1. The second type of experiment involved a laboratory test of Obi-Wan Kenobi's Jedi mind trick, as memorialized in his famous line in the first *Star Wars* movie, "These aren't the droids you're looking for." These experiments explored if one person's intention could "cloud" or distract another person's mind. In a combined 576 test sessions, the associated odds against chance in these studies were a modest but statistically meaningful 100 to 1.[16]

In sum, when considering Utts's statements to the world's statisticians, the six classes of experimental protocols that exceed combined odds against chance of 1 billion to 1, and two other protocols headed in that direction, there is no need for further proof-oriented scientific evidence. Debates will persist over ways to best explain and interpret these data, but the *existential* question—that some forms of psi exist—is for all practical purposes settled. And that means what we've called "magic," because we don't know what else to call it yet, also exists.

In the rest of this chapter we'll explore how certain aspects of magical lore have been studied in the laboratory. We'll look at experiments that have investigated how the force of will works, the role of belief in modulating performance, studies on divining the future, the power of collective consciousness, the Law of Correspondences, and evidence of communication with non-physical entities.

Most of the following studies were not endlessly repeated like the six-sigma experiments. I've reviewed those proof-oriented studies in other books, so there's no need to repeat them here. Instead, we're interested in experiments that were designed to probe beyond the edge of the known and into the frontiers of magic.

FORCE OF WILL

Quantum Consciousness

A February 2017 "Big Questions" article in the BBC's online magazine *BBC Earth* was on the topic of "the strange link between the human mind and quantum physics." It reviewed the observer effect in quantum mechanics, whereby observing an elementary quantum object (such as a photon or an electron) affects its behavior. This "shyness" effect, which is well accepted in physics but still quite mysterious, is thought by some to have something to do with consciousness. The BBC article describes that possibility, but then disparages what it calls the New Age cottage industry for using quantum concepts to support ideas like psychic phenomena. The popular association between what skeptics have labeled "quantum flapdoodle" and actual quantum physics makes it difficult for legitimate physicists interested in the observer effect to propound on its implications.

But not everyone is so reticent. Adrian Kent is a respected professor of quantum physics at the University of Cambridge. In an interview with the BBC, Kent proposed that it might be possible that consciousness affects the behavior of quantum systems, and that someday it might even be possible to detect such effects in laboratory experiments. He then went out on a limb and cautiously predicted that there might be a 15 percent chance that his proposal was correct and a 3 percent chance that this would be confirmed within the next half century.[17]

That's very exciting. It's too bad we have to wait fifty years to learn if consciousness is related to physics.

Then again, maybe we don't have to wait that long. We've already seen that one of the six-sigma classes of psi experiments involves testing the effect of intention on RNGs where the randomness is based on quantum properties. Hundreds of such experiments have been published since the 1960s. In 2003, the effect was even successfully replicated by a staunch skeptic.[18]

Starting in 2008, my colleagues and I began a series of experiments to look more closely at the quantum observer effect.[19] In journals including *Physics Essays* and *Quantum Biosystems*, we described seventeen experiments using various types of optical systems to test, as Adrian Kent proposed, whether consciousness would affect the behavior of quantum systems in a detectable way. Most of our experiments used double-slit optical systems. These are elegantly simple devices used extensively in physics to explore the quantum nature of photons ("particles" of light). They consist of a source of light, two tiny parallel slits that light can pass through, and a camera that records the resulting pattern of light. The source of light might be an incandescent bulb or a laser, both of which can produce umpteen trillions of photons per second. Or it might be a fancier arrangement that's designed to generate one photon at a time. The two slits in our optical setups were about 200 microns (millionths of a meter) apart, and each slit was about 10 microns wide. The camera can be a high-resolution digital camera, or it might be a device called a line camera, which has a line of sensors all in a row, each of which is extremely sensitive to variations in light intensity.

The reason this simple setup is so popular is because it's easy to mathematically describe the behavior of light in the apparatus, and also because it's a convenient way to demonstrate the quantum observer effect. This effect refers to the fact that the light pattern produced by this apparatus differs depending on whether one knows (or can know, in principle) if the photons pass through the left slit or the right slit. If you know, then the pattern that the camera sees is what one would expect if the photons were acting like little particles. But if you don't know, then the pattern looks like the photons were behaving like waves.[20] This wave-like versus particle-like difference suggests that there's something peculiar about the role of observation, and that strangeness opens the door to the possibility that consciousness and the physical world might interact in fundamental ways.[21]

Overall, our experiments suggest that what Adrian Kent was pondering is in fact true. The overall odds against chance in our series of studies ranged from a conservative 27,000 to 1 to a liberal 17,000 trillion to 1, depending on the assumptions used when combining the experimental results.

Four of our double-slit systems used continuous beam lasers as the source of photons; one used a light source that produced one photon at a time. We even ran a series of experiments over the Internet to study the role of distance between the participants and the optical system. More than fifteen hundred people participated in that study over the course of three years; some were as far as eighteen thousand kilometers away from our laboratory. We found that the distance between the participants and the optical systems didn't matter; the average effects were the same, regardless of distance. Two independent physicists reviewed our raw data from these experiments and both confirmed that our reported results were correct.[22] Of greater significance, a series of independent replications of our work, by a physicist at the University of São Paulo in Brazil, were highly successful.[23] A talk I gave at a conference in April 2016 that summarized our seventeen studies was posted on YouTube, and as of July 2017 it had been viewed over a half-million times.[24]

The Role of Resonance

A series of experiments at the University of Edinburgh in the 1970s and 1980s used RNGs to explore mind-matter interactions. Participants were asked what kinds of mental strategies they used and which ones produced the best outcomes. The most successful participants reported that a subjective sense of *resonance* or "feeling at one" with the RNG was the key factor. Another was the paradoxical concept of "effortless striving." This means you must absolutely want the desired outcome more than anything you've ever desired—a passionate, obsessive, overwhelming desire—but at exactly the same time you must also maintain zero anxiety about it. This contradictory state is by no means easy to achieve, but it does bear similarity to states that *can* be achieved in meditation, visualization exercises, and focused concentration.

Of the different intentional strategies participants used in the RNG studies, the most successful in terms of their actual performance were, in decreasing order, resonance, then asking entities (spirits or angels) for assistance, using emotion to help "power" the will, one-pointed concentration, physical relaxation, visual imagery, and finally, talking to the RNG as though it was a sentient creature, much as children might talk to their teddy bears or as a car mechanic might talk to a misbehaving engine.[25]

Princeton University's PEAR Laboratory, active from 1979 to 2007, conducted a long series of RNG studies, and they too asked the participants what strategies they were using when they got the best response from the RNG.[26] Their comments were similar to those found at Edinburgh:

> A state of immersion in the process which leads to a loss of awareness of myself and the immediate surroundings. Similar to the experience of being absorbed in a game, book, theatrical performance, or some creative occupation. . . . I don't feel any direct control over the device, more like a marginal influence when I'm in resonance with the machine. It's like being in a canoe; when it goes where I want, I flow with it. When it doesn't, I try to break the flow and give it a chance to get back in resonance with me.[27]

A third series of experiments using RNGs explored the role of *absorption* in more detail. This refers to a state of mind where the distinction between oneself and the RNG dissolves. Psychologist Lonnie Nelson, then at the University of Arizona, explored how the subjective depth of absorption affected psi performance. He consistently found a positive relationship between his influence of the RNG and the depth of absorption. He concluded:

> The results are consistent with the hypothesis that states of absorption associated with changes in perception of time and experience of trance-like awareness are associated with replicable alterations in an electromagnetically shielded REG device.[28]

In sum, laboratory observations and experiments indicate that experiences described as resonance, absorption, and effortless striving are all associated with improved performance in intentional tasks. These experiences are in alignment with a key goal in magical practice, especially for spell-casting and other intentional acts, of working from a state of consciousness that sees through the illusion of separateness.

Blessed Chocolate

In the ritual of the Eucharist, a Catholic priest is said to be the instrument through which the power of the Holy Spirit transforms bread and wine into the body and blood of Christ.[29] For the devout, this act, called transubstantiation, is not just a symbolic act. It's a genuine miracle, an act of pure magic. The act of blessing water, wine, and bread plays a dominant role in many religious rituals, and the practice of offering a toast with food or drink is universal. On occasion, consuming blessed food or water is said to result in remarkable healings. The conventional explanation for such reports is that *belief becomes biology*, that is, that any such healings are due to the placebo effect.

There is another possibility.

Blessing food may be regarded as a magical expression of the force of will. That is, one common type of food blessing is an expression of gratitude for the plants or animals sacrificed on your behalf. But another type includes the *intention* that the food about to be consumed is safe and nourishing. If you haven't thought much about the second type of blessing, you may want to spend a few hours learning about foodborne diseases, and then read the health inspection reports of your favorite restaurants. Then again, perhaps you shouldn't, because according to the U.S. Centers for Disease Control and Prevention, more than 200 known diseases are transmitted through food, and bad food causes an estimated 76 million illnesses, 325,000 hospitalizations, and 5,000 deaths every year in the United States alone.[30]

In other words, it goes beyond mere academic interest to wonder if intentionally blessing your food may prevent your delicious restaurant meal from accidentally killing you.

To find out, we conducted a double-blind experiment to see if beneficial intentions—a blessing—directed toward chocolate would elevate the mood of people who ate it, more than the exact same chocolate that wasn't blessed. This is not like testing if "blessed salmonella" can be magically cured of its toxic effects, but you've got to start somewhere without putting people at risk. A double-blind design is used to offset ordinary expectation effects, so if we see an interesting result, we'll know it's not due to the placebo effect.

We used dark chocolate for the test substance partially because it's one of the most craved foods in the world, and also because chocolate is a mild stimulant. Dark chocolate's bittersweet taste, creamy texture, and sensuous aroma, combined with its unique biochemistry, are known to produce short-term elevations in mood. We wanted to know if a blessing would further increase those mood-enhancing properties.

The study was designed for sixty participants, fifteen assigned to each of four groups. Most of our recruits lived in the San Francisco Bay Area. Each was told that he or she would be randomly assigned to receive a small amount of blessed or unblessed dark chocolate, all from the same source.

The intention applied to the treated chocolate was encapsulated into a specific statement: "An individual who consumes this chocolate will manifest optimal health and functioning at physical, emotional and mental levels, and in particular will enjoy an increased sense of energy, vigor and well-being." We didn't tell the participants exactly how those intentions would be applied to the chocolate.

Unlike many experiments we've conducted, as soon as people learned that we were recruiting volunteers to eat a gourmet brand of dark chocolate as part of an experiment, they told their friends, and it didn't take long before we were overwhelmed with enthusiastic volunteers. They're not called chocoholics for nothing.

After we selected the participants, we randomly assigned them to the four groups, balanced by age, gender, and the average amount of chocolate that each participant consumed per week.[31] Then we asked each person to fill out a personality questionnaire, and gave them seven blank copies of a standardized mood questionnaire along with six half-ounce packages of dark chocolate. They filled out the personality questionnaire on day one of the test, and then during each evening over the next seven days they filled out the mood questionnaires based on their self-assessment.

On days three, four and five of the week-long test, they were asked to eat a half-ounce package of chocolate at 10:00 AM and another at 3:00 PM. They were requested to mindfully savor each piece and pay attention to their experience. At the end of the week they sent the completed questionnaires back to us.

Mood is known to be influenced by the personality factor of neuroticism, a hardwired tendency toward anxiety or depression. People rated high on neuroticism experience stronger mood swings than people with lower neuroticism. We measured this factor in each person and balanced the average level of neuroticism among the four groups to create the statistical equivalent of a level playing field.[32]

Three different methods were used to bless the chocolate: a pair of senior Buddhist monks, an electronic device "imprinted" by six experienced meditators, and a ritual performed by an experienced Mongolian shaman.[33] A fourth group—the control group—was given the same chocolate from the same source, but it wasn't blessed. The experiment took place during one week in October 2006 with nearly all of the participants recruited from the San Francisco Bay Area; the timing and location of the experiment were constrained to reduce local environmental effects on mood. A total of sixty-two people completed all phases of the study.

What we found was that by the third day of eating chocolate, the average mood measure had improved more in the groups eating the blessed chocolate than in the control group, with odds against chance of 24 to 1. While this outcome is only modestly significant from a statistical perspective, it suggested that based on the gold-standard design for conducting clinical tests—a double-blind, placebo-controlled randomized trial—the blessed chocolate altered subjective mood in a positive way.

Then we analyzed a subset of individuals who consumed less than the overall average of 3.2 ounces of chocolate per week (this is why we asked each person how much chocolate they ate during an average week). We examined the results of this low-chocolate group because we posited that people who habitually ate a lot of chocolate might not show much of an effect by eating a little more, whereas people who didn't eat much chocolate might be more sensitive to the blessing. This subset of non-chocoholics did indeed show a much stronger improvement in mood, with odds against chance of 10,000 to 1.

From a skeptical perspective, the results of this experiment are explainable only as a flaw or a fluke. The use of the gold-standard protocol argues against its being a flaw, and the very strong results observed with the subset of people who didn't eat much chocolate argues against a fluke. Still, many scientists might find it difficult to believe that eating intentionally blessed chocolate would do *anything* other than make you gain weight. But when we shift our perspective to a magical worldview, where consciousness affects the physical world, this study outcome isn't surprising at all. A magician might only wonder why the effect we obtained wasn't even stronger.

Cryptochrome

The chocolate experiment provided intriguing results, but it would have been more impressive if we had found an *objective* outcome associated with the blessing. To explore this idea, Professor Yung-Jong Shiah from the National Kaohsiung Normal University in Taiwan ran an experiment to see if blessed water would influence the growth of seeds. Dr. Shiah asked if I would like to collaborate on the project, and I was glad to assist.[34]

For the seeds, Shiah chose a small flowering weed in the mustard family called *Arabidopsis thaliana*; its common name is mouse-ear cress. The full genome of this plant was completely sequenced in the year 2000, and shortly afterward the human genome was also sequenced. It was then discovered that a majority of genes suspected to play a role in human disease had close analogs in *Arabidopsis*. That made this little plant, which grows quickly and easily in the laboratory, a key resource in the study of the genetics of both plant and human health.

Arabidopsis also contains a photosensitive protein called cryptochrome. This protein plays an important role in many aspects of plant growth, including circadian rhythm, flowering time, and seed germination. Of interest to us was the fact that cryptochrome is found in both plants and humans, and that there is evidence that cryptochrome has quantum properties.[35] Among other things, the quantum nature of this protein is thought to account for cryptochrome's exquisite sensitivity to weak magnetic fields. Cryptochrome is found in the retina of certain birds, which apparently allows the birds to literally *see* the Earth's magnetic lines of force.[36] Shiah speculated that because *Arabidopsis* contains cryptochrome, it is a potential "living quantum system," that is, it might act as a super-sensitive target for use in an intention experiment.[37]

The water used to hydrate the *Arabidopsis* seeds was purchased from a commercial water bottling plant in Taiwan. Twenty-four bottles were used in the study; they were randomly assigned by a third party into blessed and untreated conditions, and then labeled A or B. The intentional treatment itself was provided by Master Lu Cheng, a respected monk and director of the Bliss and Wisdom Buddhist Foundation in Taiwan, along with two senior monks from the same Foundation. The intention they provided was similar to the chocolate experiment: "The *Arabidopsis* that absorbs this water will manifest optimal growth; in particular, it will have increased nutrition, energy, vigor and well-being." The monks mentally directed this blessing toward half of the bottles of water in a room at the foundation for twenty minutes. Then, to avoid accidentally influencing the control bottles of water, which were located in the same room as the treated bottles, they added: "This enhancement," referring to the blessed bottles, "is only for this batch of water."

During this procedure only a research assistant and the three monks were present, and none of them was involved in any other aspect of the experiment. Also, none of the other participants or investigators in the study knew which bottles were blessed or in the control group, maintaining the strict double-blind design.

After the intentional treatment process, a third party who was blinded to the meaning of the labels A and B on the bottles was in charge of all of the watering, seed germination, and measurement procedures. After all of the measurements were completed and analyzed, only then was the blinding code broken.

We used three types of *Arabidopsis* seeds. One was called the "wild type," which means the seed found in the wild; it's known as Columbia-4. A second seed was a "loss-of-function" mutation, meaning its genetic makeup made it less sensitive to blue light than the wild type. The third seed was a gain-of-function mutation, which has enhanced sensitivity to blue light. All of the seeds were prepared in the usual way for laboratory growth and then placed in a temperature-controlled incubator. Some seeds were hydrated with the blessed water, others with the untreated water. The dishes of seeds were distributed randomly within the incubators.

In each experiment, three measurements were taken on the germinated seedlings: the amount of chlorophyll (a green pigment), the amount of anthocyanin (a red-orange to blue-violet pigment), and hypocotyl length (the stem of a seedling). Increased levels of chlorophyll and anthocyanin are known to be beneficial for human health, and a shorter stem length is associated with improved seed growth. Based on these properties, we predicted that seeds grown with blessed water would show increased levels of chlorophyll and anthocyanin and a shorter hypocotyl length as compared to seeds grown with the control water.

And that's what we observed. The average hypocotyl length in seedlings hydrated with the blessed water was much shorter than in seedlings hydrated with control water. This enhancement occurred mainly in seeds with the gain-of-function mutation (see Figure 2). The experiment was repeated four times, each using different intensities and combinations of blue and red

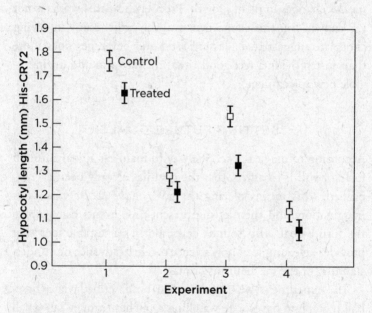

Figure 2. Results of four experiments conducted under double-blind conditions, with different intensities and combinations of blue and red light, using treated (blessed) vs. control (untreated) water to hydrate *Arabidopsis thaliana* seeds. The measurement of interest here is hypocotyl (seedling stem length). The error bars are 95 percent confidence intervals. The combined result is associated with odds against chance of 38 trillion to 1. This suggests that blessed water caused the seeds to grow more robustly than seeds hydrated with untreated control water from the same source.

light (to see how the plants would respond to different energies), and overall the effect was a robust demonstration of the force of will.

Over the four experiments the difference in seedling stem length was associated with odds against chance of 38 trillion to 1. Significant increases in anthocyanin and chlorophyll were also observed in the gain-of-function mutations, the former with odds against chance of 33,000 to 1 and the latter at a more modest 20 to 1.

This study showed that force of will produced *objectively measurable* changes in plant growth. Precisely how this works is not yet known. But this experiment and the earlier study involving chocolate suggest that blessing food and beverages does more than just provide a feel-good ritual. It may also add an intangible new spice: magic.

SETTING FUTURE GOALS

According to magical lore, one way to manifest a goal through force of will is to affirm that the goal has already been accomplished. This means placing the goal *in the future* with your imagination, and then letting present-time events catch up to the future goal. This sounds crazy, but it's a testable idea that provides an example of how science can help advance our understanding of the mechanisms of magic.

The experiment we'll look at can be described via a baseball metaphor. Say you're watching a pitcher throw a curveball toward the plate. Over the 60-foot-6-inch distance from the pitcher's mound to the plate, a curveball can deviate from the centerline by as much as seventeen inches.[38]

Now imagine that you've been watching the pitcher throw a couple dozen curveballs, and the deviations are all roughly in the same range, about a foot and a half. Then the pitcher winds up for another throw and fires toward the plate, but this time the ball curves *eight feet* from the plate. You blink in astonishment, and the hot dog you've been chewing falls out of your open mouth. The umpire faints, and the catcher stares at the ball careening sideways off into the distance. Then you turn to your friends to see if they just saw what you did, and they too are standing with mouths agape. This is impossible. There was no blast of wind or other mundane reasons that might have caused the ball to behave that way. And no human can spin the ball fast enough to make it curve from the centerline by eight feet.

And yet it did.

This metaphor is roughly what happens in successful experiments involving mind-matter interaction. The outcomes appear to be impossible. The only force in physics that's clearly associated with mental activity is electromagnetism, generated by neuronal activity in the brain. But that force is so weak that at the surface of the scalp it's measured in microvolts—millionths of a volt. That miniscule force is exceptionally difficult to detect just a few feet away from the scalp. So electromagnetism is a very unlikely explanation for the effect of intention on the physical world. Then how else might it work?

What if the pitcher intensely *imagined* that the ball was curving, and the act of intention itself caused the metaphorical equivalent of a gravitational attraction? As mentioned earlier, Einstein's theory of general relativity describes gravity as a distortion in the fabric of space-time caused by the presence of mass. If such a distortion—introduced in this case by focused intention—was able to bend the space between the pitcher and the plate, then the ball would naturally follow that bend. To a casual observer the ball's movement might *look* like a force had shoved it, but no explicit force need be involved.

From a conventional physics perspective, linking intention with gravitational space-time warps is of course outrageous. But when considering "impossible" outcomes, we're obliged to consider all sorts of radical possibilities. The point of the metaphor is to play with the idea that maybe intention warps *something* about space-time, because if that were indeed the case, then intention could make all sorts of surprising things happen.

The beautiful thing about science is that we don't need to engage in endless debates about the merits or demerits of such wild speculations. Even the strangest ideas can be put to the test. So that's what we did.[39]

In our experiment, a tossed curveball was modeled by a mathematical structure known as a Markov chain. This technique, named after the early twentieth-century Russian mathematician Andrei Andreyevich Markov, is used to model systems that evolve over time, such as the incremental positions of a ball thrown from the pitcher's mound to the plate. Each successive event in this sequence of events depends on the previous event according to a set of probabilistic rules. In our case, these probabilities determine if the tossed ball continues on a straight line (defined as 80 percent of the time in our experiment) or gets nudged to one side or the other (20 percent of the time). By design, when the ball reaches the plate it will end up either a little to the left or a little to the right of the center line; we won't let it land *exactly* in the center. The probabilities in our experiment were generated by a truly random RNG, and the goal was to see if force of will could cause a simulated ball to curve in the intended direction.

The Experiment

If you were a participant in this study, you wouldn't know anything about the baseball metaphor. I'd just ask you to press a button while maintaining the intention to hear an engaging audio clip selected randomly from a pool of five hundred possible clips. Each of these clips is just a few seconds long; they're famous spoken lines or other snippets extracted from soundtracks of popular television shows, movies, and news reports. An example is the spoken phrase "I have a dream," from the famous speech by Martin Luther King Jr.

Once the button is pressed, you would immediately hear either a randomly selected audio clip or a short click sound. Your goal is to get the interesting audio clip each time you press the button. You repeat this task one hundred times, and then you're finished. Each trial takes about five seconds, so the experiment is fast and easy.

This experimental design guarantees that if intention has no influence on the virtual ball, then it would curve according to chance expectation, about fifty times to the left and fifty times to the right. But if intention *does* influence the ball, then it would curve more in one direction than one would expect by chance.

Recall that we're not talking about baseballs. The experiment used a computer program and an RNG to *model* a pitched ball. What's actually going on is straightforward but more abstract than baseball. When you press the button to initiate each trial, an RNG generates a random bit, like a coin flip, either a 1 or a 0. If the bit is a 1, that's assigned the direction *left*, and if a 0 it's assigned *right*. That decision takes place in the P bubble (P for "pitcher") at the bottom of Figure 3. This decision indicates the way the simulated ball is spinning as it leaves the simulated pitcher's hand.

Because the RNG outcome is completely random, each time we press the button to begin a trial we'll end up in the Stage 1 *left* bubble about half the time and in the Stage 1 *right* bubble about half the time. Once we're at Stage 1, the RNG generates a random number from 1 to 100. If the resulting number is between 1 and 80 and we were in the left bubble, then we'll continue straight ahead and move to the left bubble at Stage 2. If the number is greater than 80, then we'll switch to the right bubble. We repeat this same process at Stage 2 to advance to

Stage 3. Each *trial* in this experiment consists of three jumps, each associated with whether the virtual ball curves left or right as it moves from the initial P decision to Stage 3.

If at Stage 3 the ball ends up in the *left* bubble, then the interesting audio clip is played. If it ends up in the *right* bubble, then the uninteresting click sound is played. In the actual experiment this three-step process is completed in a fraction of a second, so you get an audio clip or a click almost instantly after pressing the button.

Before we conducted this experiment we tested the setup to see if it was biased in some way that might have inadvertently caused the virtual ball to drift to the left or right. To do this we automatically ran it through thousands of trials while no one was paying attention. For each trial we had the computer count how many times the virtual ball ended up in the left and right bubbles at each of the three stages. The hit rate at each stage was the count divided by the number of trials. Not surprisingly,

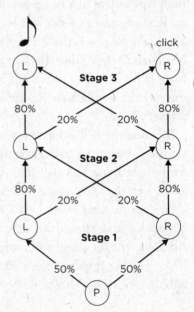

Figure 3. Markov chain as a two-state, three-stage random target system for a force-of-will experiment. The circles represent states, and the lines represent transitional probabilities. See the text for an explanation.

because all of the random decisions were made with a truly random RNG, and no one was applying intention, we found that the hit rates at stages 1, 2 and 3 were all about the same, very close to 50 percent. So the system was working as expected.

What happened when participants intentionally tried to influence the RNG?

Results

Figure 4 shows three lines (see page 118). The one labeled "Stage 1" shows the proportion of time that the virtual ball landed in the left versus right bubble at Stage 1 after each of one hundred repeated trials (remember, each *trial* consisted of one full pass through the Markov chain). The Stage 1 line indicates that after the first couple of trials the ball tended to drift toward the right bubble (in the graph this is shown as below the 50 percent line). By the twenty-fifth trial it was drifting toward the left bubble (above the 50 percent line), and then after about the fortieth trial it stayed right around 50 percent, meaning about half the time drifting left and half the time drifting right, with no clear preference. So far, so good. Nothing unusual happening.

For the Stage 2 line in Figure 4, after about fifteen trials the cumulative hit rate clearly drifted left (above the 50 percent line) and stayed there over the course of the remaining eighty-five trials. For the Stage 3 line, the curve strongly moved toward the left. Recall that Stage 1 was associated with the direction in which the ball deviated from the centerline immediately after it left the pitcher's hand. Stage 2 was when the ball was about halfway to the plate. And Stage 3 was when it arrived at the plate. The goal was to cause the ball to curve as far to the left as possible at the plate, so if the experiment was successful, we'd see a large deviation to the left at Stage 3. In Figure 4, this would manifest by getting a hit rate above the 50 percent centerline.

And that's what we got. The hit rate of 56 percent at trial 100

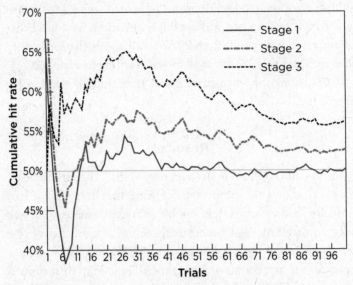

Figure 4. Results of the Markov chain experiment in terms of cumulative hit rates at Stages 1, 2, and 3. The goal was that by trial 100 the hit rate at Stage 3 would be significantly above chance expectation. And it was, at 56 percent.

in Stage 3 was associated with odds against chance of about 1,000 to 1.[40] Somehow mental intention caused a virtual curveball to swerve in the intended direction to such an extent that it would have occurred only once in a thousand times by chance. But we ran the experiment only once. So how did this happen?

Could these results have been caused by a malfunctioning RNG that was generating too many 1s and not enough 0s? No. We can exclude this possibility because in Figure 4 the Stage 1 line hugs the 50 percent chance expectation line after about forty trials. So we know right off the bat (so to speak) that the RNG was working properly.

Maybe there was a small but constant bias that caused the RNG to slightly favor generating 1s at the initial P bubble, and then that same bias trickled over into the random decisions at Stage 2 and Stage 3? In our baseball metaphor, this could be imagined as a small force that was somehow pushing the ball to spin faster to the left. To see if that might have explained our outcome, we calculated what amount of constant bias in the RNG would have been required to cause the hit rate at Stage 3 to reach 56 percent at trial 100. That figure turns out to be 3 percent. So we took the original data from Stage 1, applied a continuous 3 percent bias, and then calculated what the curves would look like at Stages 2 and 3. Figure 5 shows the results, which don't look anything like our actual experimental results. A constant-bias explanation doesn't work.

Now, what if—as magical lore suggests—intention bypasses the ordinary flow of time, manifesting the goal *in the future* and thereby causing events unfolding in the present to be "pulled" toward that goal? To test this wild idea, we ran the known results at Stage 3 *backward* through the Markov chain. Through this

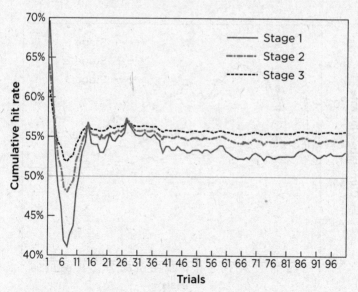

Figure 5. Results of a constant 3 percent forward-time bias. This produces the observed terminal hit rate at Stage 3 (56 percent), but the shape of these curves do not resemble our actual results, as shown in Figure 4.

method we could see what the hit rates would have looked like at Stages 2 and 1, assuming no external influences were applied. We can easily do this because a Markov chain is a mathematical abstraction that doesn't care in which direction we step through it. It operates in a completely "time-symmetric" fashion. The result is shown in Figure 6.

The line labeled "Stage 3" in Figure 6 is exactly the same as in Figure 4; it's our original data. The line labeled "Stage 2" shows the result after running the Stage 3 data backward through the Markov chain. Likewise, the line labeled "Stage 1" is what we get after running backward from Stage 2. These curves are now much closer in appearance to our original results as shown in Figure 4. This suggests that some intentional effects may involve processes that—from a conventional perspective—*run backward in time.*[41]

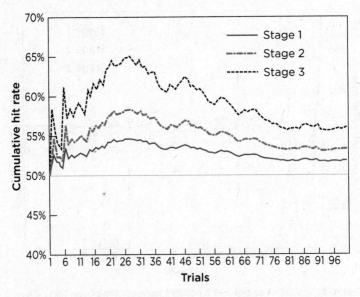

Figure 6. Results of running the Stage 3 curve backward through the Markov chain.

I conducted this type of experiment a number of times using Markov chains of different lengths. The conclusion was that intention influences RNG outputs not by "pushing" the RNG by force but rather through a goal-oriented or *teleological* effect. I did not reach this conclusion lightly. The cause → effect sequence is so deeply ingrained into our ways of thinking about how events unfold in time that a retrocausal influence seems like a gross violation of common sense. But after testing numerous possible explanations, I felt obligated to let go of commonsense prejudices and entertain stranger possibilities.

Some like to argue that retrocausation is a *logical* impossibility, so it can't be true, regardless of any evidence to the contrary. But those objections haven't prevented mainstream physics journals from publishing many articles speculating about time-reversed and time-symmetric concepts. The mathematics of classical and quantum mechanics allow for such strange things.[42] Of course, those articles usually assume that weird things happen to the flow of time only in exotic domains, like in extremes of gravity or in the quantum domain.

A feature story on retrocausation in *Discover* magazine noted: "A series of quantum experiments shows that measurements performed in the future can influence the present. Does that mean the universe has a destiny—and the laws of physics pull us inexorably toward our prewritten fate?"[43] Perhaps. And experiments like the present one, as well as dozens of other studies investigating precognition and retrocausation, also suggest that time behaves in enigmatic ways at the everyday, human scale, and in particular that goals pulling from the future might be associated with our *intentions*.[44] Sounds like magic.

THE ROLE OF BELIEF

We only see what we want to see; we only hear what we want to hear. Our belief system is just like a mirror that only shows us what we believe.

—DON MIGUEL RUIZ

A central tenet of magical lore is that belief modulates magical efficacy. What do experiments say?

Sheep and Goats

In the early 1940s, psychologist Gertrude Schmeidler, of the City College of New York, proposed that people who don't believe in psi subconsciously avoid psi experiences because they don't want to experience them.[45] On the flip side, people who do believe in psi want to see them, so they do. She turned this idea into what she called a "sheep-goat" hypothesis, where the skeptics are the stubborn goats and believers are the acquiescent sheep.

In a typical sheep-goat experiment, participants fill out a questionnaire asking about their beliefs in psi, and about any psi experiences they may have had. Based on their responses, they would be classified as sheep or as goats. All of the participants then take the same type of psi test, and the average sheep and goat performance is compared. Schmeidler found that her hypothesis was supported: sheep tended to score *above* chance, and goats tended to score at or *below* chance.

Many clever variations have been tried in examining this effect. To give just one example, in 2007 Kevin Walsh and Garret Moddel, of the University of Colorado at Boulder, ran an experiment where individuals were categorized as sheep or goats based on their prior beliefs, and then they were randomly assigned to read either a commentary strongly supportive of psi or one harshly against psi, and each then conducted the same psi test. The participants fell into four groups: believers who received a pro-psi fact sheet, believers who received an anti-psi sheet, skeptics who received a pro-psi sheet, and skeptics who received an anti-psi sheet.

The result was what you'd expect if belief modulates performance. The sheep who read the pro-psi fact sheet obtained a significantly positive hit rate; the sheep who read the anti-psi fact sheet performed positively, but not to a statistically significant degree; the goats who read the pro-psi fact sheet performed as well as sheep who read the anti-psi sheet; and the goats who read the anti-psi fact sheet performed at chance. The authors concluded that "innate psi ability alone cannot explain why some subjects perform better. Belief in psi is required."[46]

In 1993, psychologist Tony Lawrence of the University of Edinburgh, Scotland, reported a meta-analysis of all sheep-goat psi experiments that had used "forced choice" designs (the participant is forced to select one out of a set of possible targets, like in a classic ESP card test). Lawrence included all studies from Schmeidler's original experiment through the year of his publication. He found seventy-three reports by thirty-seven different investigators, involving more than 685,000 guesses contributed by 4,500 participants. The overall result was strongly in support of the sheep-goat effect, with believers outperforming disbelievers with odds against chance of over a trillion to one. Lawrence concluded that "the results of this meta-analysis are quite clear—if you believe in the paranormal you will score higher on average in forced choice ESP tests than someone who does not [believe]."[47]

In 2015, psychologists Lance Storm of the University of Adelaide, Australia, and Patrizio Tressoldi of the University of Padua, Italy, brought the sheep-goat meta-analysis up-to-date. They searched for all published sheep-goat forced-choice experiments conducted after Lawrence's 1993 meta-analysis, and they found forty-nine additional studies reported by forty-three investigators. The overall result was again supportive of the sheep-goat effect, and associated with odds against chance of 12 million to 1. They concluded that "a belief-moderated communications anomaly in the forced-choice ESP domain . . . has been effectively uninterrupted and consistent for almost 70 years."[48] In sum, just as the magical traditions have maintained, belief modulates psi performance. In other words, if you don't believe in magic, then *no magic for you*.

Blessed Tea

Given the evidence in favor of the sheep-goat effect, Yung-Jong Shiah (whom we've already met) and I set out to test this idea using a design similar to the blessed chocolate experiment. We asked if blessed *tea* would affect people's mood differently than the same tea that wasn't blessed. We also explored the effect of the participants' *beliefs* about what they were drinking to see if their beliefs modulated the blessing effect.[49]

We used tea in this study because the experiment was conducted in Taiwan, and the tea ceremony in Asia is an honored tradition. It's not just an aesthetically pleasing performance; it's also about achieving a meditative, intentional state of awareness whereby the drinker becomes "one with the tea." A refreshing gnostic beverage, if you will.

We were interested in two ways that belief might modulate mood in this study. In the first case, we looked at all of the participants who *believed* that they were drinking the intentionally blessed tea, but in fact some of them actually did while others drank unblessed "control" tea. This was a classic placebo-controlled comparison, because everyone's expectations were controlled to be the same.

The second case involved a group of participants where everyone was given the same blessed tea to drink, but some believed that they got it and others believed that they didn't. In a double-blind experiment the participants can't be told what condition they are in, but of course they can guess which condition they think they're in. This is called a "placebo-enhanced" comparison because everyone drank the same blessed tea, but they were separated into two categories of belief, pro and con. This comparison would tell us if the participants' beliefs modulated the "blessing effect."

Dr. Shiah and his team in Taiwan recruited 221 people. Each was asked to fill out a form collecting basic demographic information and an estimate of the amount of tea consumed on an average day. They also took a personality questionnaire to assess their degree of neuroticism, for the same reason that we took this measure in the chocolate experiment: mood fluctuates more in neurotic people, so to balance each group we needed to know each person's baseline level of neuroticism.[50]

Each participant was then given a mood questionnaire and six bottles of tea. They were asked to not drink any other tea during the week-long experiment. Every evening for a week each person filled out a mood questionnaire. On the three middle days of the week they drank one bottle of tea at 10:00 AM and a second at 3:00 PM. On the last day of the week, they were also asked to indicate if they *believed* that they were drinking the intentionally blessed or the unblessed tea, or if they had no opinion.

The tea we used was a variety of oolong, a pleasant aromatic tea that's especially popular in Southeast Asia. The name *oolong* comes from the Chinese name for this tea, which means "black dragon tea." It was prepared in a big batch in a large container and then poured into separate bottles. As in the *Arabidopsis thaliana* seed experiment, Master Lu Cheng and two senior monks from the Bliss and Wisdom Buddhist Foundation were invited to provide the intentional blessing. The monks mentally directed their blessings toward the tea for twenty-two minutes.

Then, to avoid including the untreated tea in the intentional process, the untreated bottles were placed in a distant room and an additional intention was added: "This enhancement is only to this batch of tea," referring to the blessed bottles.

After the bottles of tea had been prepared, a research assistant who had no other connection to the monks or to the participants in the study packaged up bottles of tea and questionnaires appropriate for the blessed tea and control tea groups. The packages were labeled only as A or B, and given to Professor Shiah, who did not know the meaning of the labels. He then distributed the packages to the participants. After the week-long study was completed, another assistant, also blind to the meaning of A and B, recorded the data from the participants' daily questionnaires. Those entries were double-checked by a third, blinded assistant. At this point, I analyzed the results without knowing the conditions, and finally Dr. Shiah contacted the research assistant to break the blinding code. All of this obsessive blinding and double-checking is standard fare for placebo-controlled experiments. It's necessary to avoid personal biases from influencing the results.

As expected in all clinical trials, some people dropped out. This left us with a total of 189 participants. Of them, 95 had been assigned to the blessed tea group and 94 to the control group. Each participant's mood score on the first two days of the week was averaged and then their change in mood was calculated for the rest of the days of the week. The results are shown in Figure 7.

The placebo-controlled test (left-hand panel in Figure 7) showed that even though everyone in the two groups *believed* that they were drinking the blessed tea, people who *actually* drank the blessed tea reported better moods than those who drank the control tea. The mood difference between the two groups was associated with modest odds against chance of about 50 to 1. The "nocebo"-controlled group (right-hand panel in

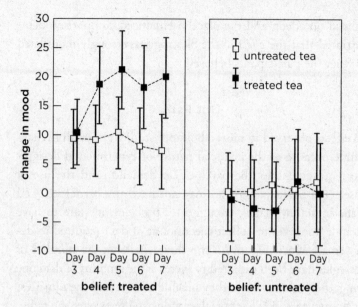

Figure 7. Average change in mood in blessed tea experiment, with 95 percent confidence intervals. Left panel is the placebo-controlled group; the right panel is the nocebo-controlled group.

Figure 7) compared groups where everyone did *not believe* (nocebo is the opposite of placebo) they were drinking the blessed tea, but some of them actually did. This comparison found no mood differences between the groups.

What we'll call the placebo-enhanced comparison was more interesting. This is the comparison between the curve with black squares in the left panel of Figure 7 and the same type of curve in the right panel. Everyone in these two conditions in fact drank the same blessed tea, but some believed that they did and others believed that they didn't. The odds against chance for this comparison were a healthy 50,000 to 1.

What this showed is consistent with the idea that belief modulates magical efficacy. The placebo-controlled comparison indicated that the blessing modestly improved people's mood who drank the treated tea, the nocebo-controlled comparison showed no effect, and the placebo-enhanced comparison demonstrated that the *effect* of the blessing was strongly modulated by what the participants believed.

Got Psi?

Psi effects observed in most laboratory studies are small in magnitude because of the artificial nature of experimental designs, the requirement to "be psychic" on demand, and the use of unselected participants who may not have any psi talent. And if those factors weren't enough of a problem, it's rare to have enough resources to collect the amount of data required to detect small effects. To overcome these challenges, a number of strategies have been explored to increase the amount of data one can gather at lower cost. They include conducting the same test for many years in the same lab, conducting tests over the radio, via TV, or in magazines, or performing meta-analyses where the results of many similar experiments are statistically combined.

All of these methods have enjoyed some success. Long-term experiments, such as RNG tests reported by Princeton University's PEAR Laboratory from 1979 to 2007, or the ESP card tests reported by J. B. Rhine's laboratory from the 1930s to the 1960s, have each provided sound evidence for psi. But persuasion in science rests on independent replications, so critics have been suspicious of the evidence produced by those individual long-term efforts. They imagine that those labs just kept making the same mistakes over and over again, or maybe that they were cheating, or maybe . . . You get the picture.

With the rise of the Internet, a new approach has been used to inexpensively collect lots of psi data: online tests. In 1977, I conducted what may have been the first computer-networked psi experiment.[51] I used a large-scale computer network at the University of Illinois to provide a public-access precognition test.[52] The study outcome was interesting and suggestive of pre-cognition, but I was a graduate student at the time and heavily involved in my doctoral work, so I didn't get around to publishing the results.

In 2000, I launched a suite of psi tests on the Internet that are still accessible at the website www.GotPsi.org. From then through mid-2017 the site had collected more than 225 million trials from some 350,000 people around the world. Over the years, the programming infrastructure was revised a number of times, but from the user's point of view the tests have remained the same. This has provided many years of continuous data collection on several kinds of simple psi tests.

When a person signs up for the GotPsi.org tests, they select a nickname and fill out a few short questionnaires. What we'll focus on here is the user's response to a question on "the degree to which you believe in psychic phenomena," which ranges in five levels from none to certain. From that answer we can see if belief modulated the average user's performance.

Location Test

One of the GotPsi.org tests is called "Location." The user sees an empty square on the screen and is asked to imagine where the computer will place a target spot inside that square. The user makes her choice; then the Web server immediately and randomly selects a location, displays it, and compares the distance between the user's and the computer-selected locations versus all possible distances if the Web server had selected other locations. That comparison is then used to determine the odds against chance for each trial. The user is asked to repeat this task in sessions typically composed of twenty-five repeated trials, and then the results are shown in terms of overall odds against chance for the session.

Remote Viewing Test

The other test we'll consider is a simple remote viewing task. The user sees a blank rectangle in the browser window and is asked to imagine a photograph that the computer would randomly select and later display in that same rectangle. After using remote viewing to imagine the photo, the user fills out two short questionnaires asking about various shapes and elements in the image, like arcs, squares, water, people, or plants. Performance on the task is evaluated by comparing how the user responded to those questions versus how judges responded to the same questions while actually looking at the target photographs. Then the user's responses are compared to the judges' scores for all of the other photos that the computer might have selected. The performance on each trial is presented as a score ranging from 1 (a poor description of the target) to 100 (the best possible match).

Results

Let's first consider the results of the location test. Since the website went online, we collected data in 589,920 sessions, each of which was contributed by one person per day, and where each session consisted of a full complement of 25 trials.[53] Overall, those sessions comprised a total of 48.5 million trials. Figure 8 shows the average score on the location test for each level of belief in psi, from lowest to highest.[54] The differences in the size of the error bars tell us that there were many more users of this test who had higher levels of belief than lower levels. This isn't surprising because skeptics generally aren't interested in trying psi tests. We also see from the graph that the performance levels were in accordance with the sheep-goat effect, with negative scores for lower belief and positive scores for higher belief. The average size of these effects was very small, but with the statisti-

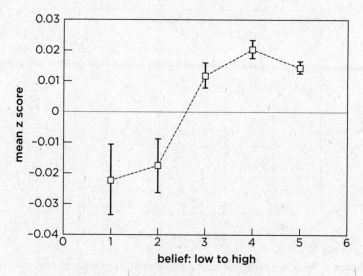

Figure 8. Location test results by belief, in terms of mean *z* scores (standard normal deviates), with one-standard-error bars.

cal power afforded by nearly 50 million trials, the outcome is clear.

The same sort of analysis for the remote viewing test is shown in Figure 9. In this test we collected a total of 1.2 million individual trials, where the data considered were only the first trial contributed by each unique user per day. The results are similar to the location test. Poorer remote viewing performance was associated with lower levels of belief, and better performance with higher levels of belief.

The bottom line: sheep get magic, goats do not.

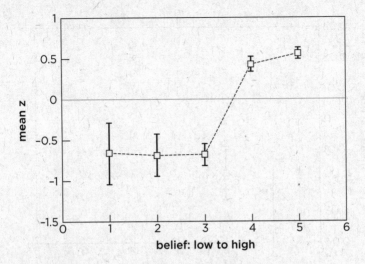

Figure 9. Remote viewing results by belief, with one-standard-error bars.

DIVINATION

The people who demand that the oracle predict for them really want to know next year's price on whalefur or something equally mundane. None of them wants an instant-by-instant prediction of his personal life.

—Frank Herbert, *Heretics of Dune*

Study After the Test

If divination is a real phenomenon, then when you're taking a multiple-choice test today you ought to be able to peek at your future self, tomorrow, when you'll be looking at the answer sheet. You can then use that future knowledge to improve your performance today. That would be nice. It's also a testable idea and known as an experiment involving "implicit precognition."

I discussed the initial results of these tests in my 2013 book,

Supernormal. Briefly, Cornell University psychologist Daryl Bem designed several experiments to see if present-time behavior can be influenced by future events. He published the results of his experiments in 2011 in the well-regarded *Journal of Personality and Social Psychology.*[55] Because those experiments showed strong evidence for precognition, and because that journal is held in such esteem, it created a firestorm of controversy. A science writer at the *New York Times* warned scientists, without a hint of irony, to prepare to be outraged before the article was even published.[56]

A typical response to Bem's work by a journalist appeared in November 2010, in *Wired* magazine. An article entitled "Feeling the Future: Is Precognition Possible?" was appropriately descriptive until we encounter this paragraph:

> [Here] is the dirty secret of anomalous phenomena like telepathy and clairvoyance: They've been demonstrated dozens of times, often by reputable scientists. (Bem is an extremely well-respected psychologist, best known for his work on self-perception.) Why, then, do serious scientists dismiss the possibility of psi? Why do rational people assume that parapsychology is bullshit? Because these exciting results have consistently failed the test of replication.

For anyone who knows the relevant literature, this is a great example of "It's what you know for sure that just ain't so." Journalists can't spend the time to become experts on everything, so they'll spend a few minutes surfing Wikipedia, they'll chat with a couple of critics they found online, and then they'll dash out a summary of what they think they've learned. That approach might work for conventional topics, but it fails miserably when it comes to understanding scientific controversies. The *Wired* article continues:

And this is why Bem's paper is so important: It provides the first testable framework for the investigation of anomalous psychological properties. Unlike most tests of psi or ESP, Bem's research builds upon well-known experimental paradigms, and minimizes the contact between the experimenter and the subject. The data collection was automated and accurate; the paper passed peer-review. . . . Only time will tell if the data holds up.[57]

This paragraph is so far out in left field, it's not even in a ballpark. It was by no means the "first testable framework" in psi research; there are dozens of other well-designed classes of experiments. But the author did get one thing undeniably right. Beyond all the gnashing of teeth and lamenting, controversies in science ultimately rest on a single question: can independent researchers successfully replicate the effect?

In the early days of the hullabaloo a few investigators tried to replicate Bem's experiment, they failed, and then they rushed to publish their results. Those reports caused a second splash in the news: it was now safe to dismiss Bem's claims as mistaken because his experiment wasn't repeatable after all. Whew. The story quickly disappeared from the popular press. Nothing to see here, move along. In *Supernormal*, I concluded my discussion of this controversy with this line: "Bem's innovative approach is relatively new, and as such the jury is not yet in on whether the effect will be easily repeatable by others."[58]

Well, here we are a few years later. And the jury is definitely in.

In 2015, and later updated in 2016, Bem and his colleagues published a meta-analysis of all known replications conducted up to that point: ninety studies reported by thirty-three labs in fourteen countries. The overall result was associated with odds against chance of *8 billion to 1*.[59] Bem's experiments are in fact independently repeatable. This should have been front-page news.

Not a peep.

The article reporting this result was published in a new and relatively unknown online journal, rather than where one might expect—a prominent, top-tier journal reporting an earth-shattering discovery. Why? Because *no mainstream journal would publish it.*[60]

Bem later told me that this was the first time in his fifty-year career as a well-respected academic psychologist that he could not get an article published in the same journals he had been regularly publishing in throughout his career. Why not? Because most psychologists don't appreciate how slippery the concept of time is, so they don't believe that precognition can be real.

A March 1, 2017, feature story in *New Scientist* addressed this issue with the question "Does time go both ways?" In the article we learn that

> in quantum mechanics, where a system's evolution is proba-
> bilistic, you can specify conditions for the initial state and
> final states of the system, and both of these conditions will
> influence the evolution. Apply this idea to the universe as a
> whole and "information could be coming from plus infinity
> and propagating back through time," says [physicist Sandu
> Popescu of the University of Bristol]. . . . There's no evidence
> of any of this so far, Popescu cheerfully admits. "No one yet
> has investigated it seriously," he says.[61]

No one, that is, except for the ninety replications of Bem's experiment and literally hundreds of other experiments on precognition with positive results published since 1935.[62] When it comes to controversial topics such as precognition, zombie myths (ideas that die hard) take on a life of their own. In the March 17, 2017, issue of the *Chronicle of Higher Education*, we find an article mentioning Bem as a "quirky psychologist," because if his claims about precognition are true, then all hell will break loose:

Bem's finding would upend what we understand about the nature of time and causation. It would be a big deal. [Bem's] paper, "Feeling the Future," was widely ridiculed and failed to replicate, though Bem himself has stood by his results.[63]

Similarly, in a May 17, 2017, article in *Slate* magazine, we find academic psychologists panicking because Bem had gone to "crazyland" and broke science.[64]

Sigh. Perhaps someday when our supersmart robot overlords are in charge, they'll do a better job at reporting science news because they won't have hair on their shiny metal heads, and thus they won't have to tear their hair out every time an experiment challenges their naive beliefs about the nature of time and causation. If we just calmly stick with the experimental facts, then there is no question that Bem's experiment is in fact repeatable. And that means we're influenced not only by our past, but also by our future, as seers throughout history have tried to tell us.[65]

What Does Precognition See?

Divination is often imagined to reveal the absolute future, as though the future were fixed or fated to unfold in a predetermined way. But the nature of the future isn't all that clear, nor is it obvious what precognition "sees." We usually behave as though we have free will, but maybe we really have unalterable destinies and free will is just an illusion. This raises the question: does precognition perceive the actual future, the one that *must occur*, or does it perceive a probable future, a future that *might occur*? And how can we tell which is a better explanation?

By now you've learned that with a little thought it's possible to devise experiments that can explore even the most mind-boggling puzzles, including this one. We included such an experiment as a secret feature in one of the online tests at GotPsi.org.

This test is modeled after the famous twenty-five-card, five-symbol ESP test popularized by J. B. Rhine at Duke University in the 1930s. In the Web browser, the user sees the backs of five cards, as in the top image of Figure 10. The task is to click on a card that the user thinks the computer will randomly select. After her selection, the computer shows which card it selected, as in the bottom image of Figure 10, along with feedback for the number of trials completed so far.

HIT! Good job! 2 hits in 4 trials = 50%

Next Trial

Figure 10. From the www.GotPsi.org card test. (Top) The user sees the backs of five "cards" and selects one. (Bottom) The computer randomly selects one card and displays it. In this example the user selected the correct future target.

It is implied in this test that the computer randomly selects the future target uniformly among the five possible cards. But that's actually not the case. There's a hidden feature. Before the Web server displays the backs of the five cards, it selects one of those cards at random (call this card T1, for target 1), and then it randomly assigns a *bias* (B) to that card. The bias determines how likely T1 will end up being the actual target. The value of B ranges from 5 percent, meaning the card is very *unlikely* to end up as the target, to 100 percent, which guarantees that it *will definitely* be selected as the target.

After the Web server selects both T1 and B, the backs of the cards are displayed and the trial begins (Figure 10, top image). All of this takes a fraction of a second, so the user doesn't know about the hidden feature. (But now *you* know.)

At this point the user selects which card she thinks the computer is going to select. Call her chosen target R (for "response"). Now the Web server decides whether the first card it selected, T1, should end up as the final target, based on the value of bias B. For example, say the computer initially assigns for T1 the bias level B = 90 percent. In that case, T1 will become T2 90 percent of the time, but there's also a 10 percent chance that the computer will select a new target, call it T2, at random from one of the remaining four cards. The bottom line is that if the user ends up selecting T2 (i.e., R = T2), then that trial is declared a *hit* (Figure 10, bottom image). If R ≠ T2, then the trial is declared a *miss*.

After collecting some 80 million trials with this hidden feature, we tested to see whether precognition tends to see the *actual* or the *probable* future. If precognition sees the actual future, which we've defined as T2, then the bias B—which as you recall is randomly assigned to a different card on each successful trial—shouldn't influence the user's performance. But if precognition sees the probable future, then when T1 is very likely to become T2 (because its associated bias was a high probability), the more likely it ought to be perceived and thus selected.

The result is shown in Figure 11, which plots the hit rate for each level of bias B (in twenty steps, from 5 percent to 100 percent). The relationship between B and the resulting hit rate is a statistically significant correlation of $r = 0.45$, which is associated with odds against chance of 40 to 1. This suggests that precognition accuracy is influenced by the present *probability* of the future target.

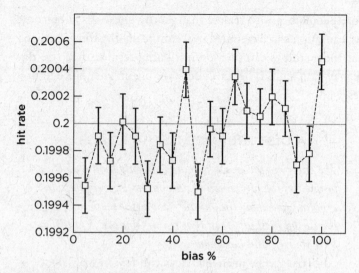

Figure 11. Hit rates for each level of a priori bias in the GotPsi.org card test, with one-standard-error bars.

The outcome of this experiment cannot be attributed to the participant's conscious choices, because nothing reveals that there's a hidden factor. So this probabilistic influence is a completely unconscious tendency. This suggests that if we look at a subset of trials where the cards were selected by rote rather than by conscious deliberation, then we might find that the hidden biases would have an even stronger effect. To do this, we looked at trials where the user selected the middle of the five targets, which was the most common, unthinking response. For those trials the bias–hit rate correlation increased to $r = 0.603$, associated with odds against chance of 400 to 1. And if we remove one outlier, the correlation increases to $r = 0.762$, now with more impressive odds against chance of 10,000 to 1.[66]

What all this suggests is that precognitive perceptions are influenced by the *probable* future. It still doesn't tell us unequivocally if future events are flexible or fated, or if we have free will. But it does hint that the future is probable, and not fixed. As more people begin to realize that thorny questions about time and causation can be studied in scientifically rigorous ways, and that these studies can provide intriguing results, then one day we may gain a much better understanding of what precognition sees.

A DISTURBANCE IN THE FORCE

The energy of the crowd is insane. Twenty thousand people. It's the biggest jolt of adrenaline. It's very hard to explain. You know the old story about the woman lifting the car off her kid? It's in that realm. You can actually hurt yourself and not know it.

—TOM PETTY in an interview with *Esquire* magazine

Schools of fish and flocks of birds are common ways of observing collective behavior in animals. Humans too are influenced by group behavior. Crowd psychology, a branch of social psychology, studies behavior in vigilante mobs, consumer fads, stock market booms and busts, and political movements. These collective, often highly contagious phenomena demonstrate that otherwise rational behavior by individuals can, depending on context, quickly devolve into destructive mob violence or remarkable acts of altruism. Theories of crowd behavior note that because we are social animals, we are exquisitely sensitive to the herd instinct and are hardwired to imitate.

Here we consider another possibility related to collective consciousness. An artistic portrayal of this phenomenon was a scene in the movie *Star Wars*. At one point the Jedi knight Obi-Wan Kenobi suddenly staggers as if in pain, then says, "I felt a great disturbance in the Force, as if millions of voices suddenly cried out in terror and were suddenly silenced." This happened just as the evil Galactic Empire was using the Death Star weapon to blow up an inhabited planet. The Force was described by Obi-

Wan as "an energy field created by all living things. It surrounds us and penetrates us; it binds the galaxy together."

The question posed by such a story is whether the esoteric concept of an *anima mundi* or "world soul" is a measurably real phenomenon. Within psi research this idea was first encountered by noticing that during participation in engaging rituals, whether sports, meditation, or music, people sometimes reported a strange, expansive feeling as though they had merged with the group's collective mind. Such moments are described as an "energetic shift," a feeling of "electricity in the air" or "being in the zone." The term *energetic* in this context is not what a physicist means when discussing the four known forces of physics, but rather what people describe as a palpable subjective sense of vibrancy or excitement, or as an unusual feeling of liveliness.

This phenomenon may be similar to the concept of resonance in physical systems. Resonance can be demonstrated by placing a group of metronomes running at similar—but not exactly the same—frequencies on a flexible surface. That allows the metronomes to shift from a state of maximum entropy (randomness), where each metronome acts independently and creates a noisy cacophony of random ticking sounds, to a state of maximum negentropy (order), where the separate movements become tightly synchronized and generate a single, uniform, loud tick.

From the perspective of each separate metronome, the transition from acting independently to becoming part of the collective might be felt (in an anthropometric sense) as a release of personal effort, accompanied by a huge rise in collective "energy." That's because it's easier in nearly any context to swim with the current than against it. As the resonance increases, a metronome might feel that it's becoming "one with" with the collective.

Previous studies investigating these collective effects, like the Global Consciousness Project mentioned earlier in this chapter, have used RNGs designed to produce truly random bits (0s and

1s). Those studies suggest that when collective mental coherence intensifies it causes something like a "disturbance in the Force."

An example of such an episode was the unusually contentious 2016 presidential election in the United States. Analysis of data from the Global Consciousness Project, using that project's standard method of analysis, showed that the combined results of the first three presidential debates showed a modest but statistically significant deviation from chance, with odds of 330 to 1.[67]

But the big event was November 8, 2016, the day of the election itself. Perhaps 100 million people around the world were rapt with attention throughout the day, with nearly all opinion polls predicting that the Democratic candidate would win. But as the day lengthened and election results started to come in, the results were tipping in favor of the Republican candidate. As the election drew to a close just after midnight (Pacific time) on November 9 and collective emotions had reached a feverish pitch, the Republican candidate was finally declared the winner.

This stunned everyone, not only because most of the pollsters were dead wrong but also because the popular vote was strongly in favor of the Democrat by nearly 3 million votes, the third-highest vote count received by any presidential candidate in U.S. history.[68] It was also only the fourth time in U.S. history that the winning candidate failed to receive the majority of popular votes; the mismatch between winning the popular vote and losing the election was due to the archaic peculiarities of the U.S. Electoral College system.

To study shocking mass events like these, we developed a new kind of RNG. Instead of turning random electronic noise into bits (1s and 0s), as most commercial RNGs do, we recorded the noise itself. We did this because while RNG studies have produced interesting results, because of the way they're constructed it's not possible to "reverse-engineer" what happened inside the RNG during the attention-riveting events.[69]

In our new system we recorded the noise generated by a semiconductor component called a Zener diode, a source of electronic noise used in most commercial RNGs. We constructed thirty-two separate devices that we called "quantum noise generators" (QNGs) and recorded the noise in each QNG at 1,000 samples per second. Then we ran the thirty-two QNGs starting one day before the election to four days afterward. The QNGs were powered by a battery, so the array was completely "off the grid," and data were collected in a quiet garage in a house near Lucasfilm's Skywalker Ranch in a rural area in Marin County, California. We thought that would be an especially appropriate place to see if we could detect a disturbance in the Force.

What we found is shown in Figure 12 (see page 144). The top graph indicates the relationship between successive samples of noise (this is known as an autocorrelation analysis). Truly random data shouldn't show any systematic relationships between one sample and the next, but what we observed was a visually obvious spike in the data a few minutes after midnight Pacific time on November 9. This spike was within minutes of when news outlets around the world were calling the election for the Republican candidate.[70] The odds against chance of observing a peak value of that magnitude within an hour of the final results of the election, as compared to all of the data recorded over six days, was calculated to be 226 million to 1.

What this implies is consistent with the idea that when millions of minds intently focus on the same event it causes a ripple in the fabric of space-time. In this case it explicitly suggests a wrinkle in *time*, because an autocorrelation is a measure of self-similarity in time.[71]

The bottom graph in Figure 12 shows the result of analyzing dependencies among the outputs of QNGs (this is known as a *mutual information analysis*).[72] Just as there shouldn't be any dependencies in the temporal sequence of data produced by truly random systems, there also shouldn't be any dependencies *between* the outputs of separate random systems. But what we see is a spike at midnight associated with odds against chance of 81,000 to 1. This again suggests a wrinkle in space-time, but in this case it's a wrinkle in *space*, because it indicates that the QNG devices were no longer acting like separate objects. By

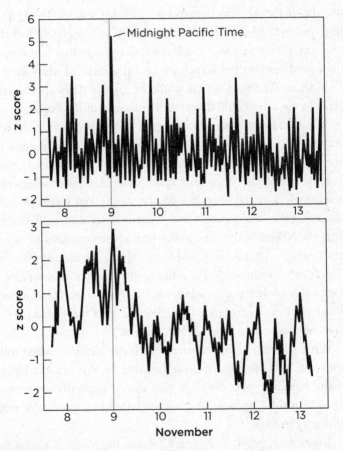

Figure 12. U.S. presidential election results announced just after midnight on November 9, 2016. Top: Autocorrelation analysis, with the spike at midnight associated with odds against chance of 226 million to 1. Bottom: Mutual information analysis, with the peak value associated with odds against chance of 81,000 to 1. See text for explanation.

analogy, the QNGs were floating like a collection of buoys in the ocean. Normally the motion of such buoys would be independent, but for a short period of time on election night, when the news media focused the attention of millions of viewers, the buoys moved together like a single object.[73]

In the context of magic, what this and other field consciousness studies suggest is that rituals designed to draw and focus the attention of a group may accomplish more than simply produce a psychological sense of group coherence. They may also, as the magical traditions suggest, literally distort the fabric of reality.

LAW OF CORRESPONDENCES

The Law of Correspondences is a principle underlying many magical practices. Based on the assumption of an interconnected reality, this law proposes that inner and outer experience, or mind and matter, intermingle and interact. It's the principle behind the practice of sigils and writing magic. What you sustain in your mind is reflected in the world at large. This idea, popularized in one form as the Law of Attraction, has been tested in psi research primarily in mind-matter interaction or psychokinetic experiments. But it exists in many forms. Here we'll consider how it manifests in mind-body interactions where the mind is associated with one person and the body with another, distant person.

The Feeling of Being Stared At

Many people have reported the "feeling of being stared at." A scenario in everyday life is when a man (typically) stares at a woman (typically) whom he finds attractive. To avoid appearing boorish, ideally the man doesn't stare like a drooling lunatic, but rather gazes obliquely from a location where he thinks she can't see him. After a minute or so, the woman suddenly looks up, as though something caught her attention, and more often than not she turns directly toward the man and either glares at him with contempt or, if the man is more fortunate, smiles.

British biologist Rupert Sheldrake's book on this topic, *The Sense of Being Stared At*, describes many experiments he and others have conducted to test if these anecdotal reports are due to sensory cues, peripheral vision, or a genuine psi sense.[74]

In a simple form of this experiment, one person of a pair is assigned to be the starer (let's call him Mulder); the other is the staree (let's call her Scully). They sit within a few yards of each other, with Scully's back to Mulder. To begin the experiment, Mulder flips a coin to decide if he should stare or not stare at the back of Scully's neck. If the assignment is to stare, Mulder intensely gazes at Scully for ten seconds. Then he alerts her with a "cricket clicker" (a handheld device that makes a cricket sound) to respond either yes if she thinks Mulder is staring at her or no if she thinks he isn't.

Sheldrake popularized experiments of this type, some involving trial-by-trial feedback under informal conditions such as tests conducted by pairs of children in classrooms, and under more controlled conditions such as designs using blindfolds without trial-by-trial feedback, and under even more secure conditions such as having Mulder stare at Scully through a window and from a far distance.[75]

In the published literature, I found sixty of these experiments reporting a total of 33,357 trials by Sheldrake and others. The overall success rate was 54.5 percent, where chance expectation was 50 percent—a rather small effect in absolute terms. But the overall odds against chance for seeing this small effect over thousands of repeated trials is a staggering 202 octodecillion (that's 2×10^{59}) to 1.[76] This is so far from a chance outcome that it should have settled the existence of this phenomenon once and for all. But of course it didn't.

Critics have suggested that this result is due to one or more design flaws, or even to blatant fraud. Many of the suggested flaws, like inadvertent cuing, peripheral vision, collusion, cheating, or misrecording the responses, have been tested. Some of those flaws might indeed explain a proportion of the results. But no one flaw or combination of flaws has been identified that can credibly account for the overall results, including fraud, because many independent groups have successfully replicated these results. In addition, the subset of studies conducted where Mulder and Scully were separated by windows and at far distances from each other still ended up with astronomical odds against chance.

We were curious to see if we could get similar results in our lab. We used a computer to randomly assign the staring condition of each trial and automatically record the results. We ran twelve pairs of people in the test, including five pairs of children ages eight to fourteen. The data were collected in thirty-one sessions of twenty trials each. The overall hit rate was 53 percent, which is not quite significant given the number of trials run in the experiment, but consistent with what others have reported using a similar experimental design. We also found that after the first six trials in a run of twenty trials the odds against chance were about 1,000 to 1. After the sixth trial, performance began to decline, suggesting that the participants found the test tiring or boring, so their ability to sense distant staring dropped off.[77]

The Unconscious Feeling of Being Stared At

A more rigorous form of this experiment involves isolating Mulder and Scully by both distance and shielding, and where the measure of interest is Scully's physiological condition (heart rate, blood pressure, etc.) when Mulder is staring at her over a one-way video circuit, as compared to when the video display is turned off and Mulder's attention is withdrawn. Over a period of years, we conducted studies using this basic design and involving several hundred pairs of people. In our lab, Scully was isolated from Mulder by placing her inside a 2,800-pound electromagnetically shielded chamber constructed out of double-walled, solid steel walls, floor, and ceiling, and Mulder was located behind a wall in a room about twenty meters away.[78]

Before we conducted these tests, we experimented with loud sounds, cellphones, walkie-talkies, and jumping on the floor to see if there were any normal ways that the two parties in these experiments could communicate. No such methods were found. One day, while testing loud sounds, we blasted a Coast Guard air horn in the "sender's" room and measured the sound level in the "receiver's" shielded room. There were no detectable changes in sound level in the shielded room when the blasts occurred. But we did accidentally summon the local fire department. We didn't realize that the sound a Coast Guard horn makes is similar to a fire alarm. Nor did we know that the horn blast could be heard five miles away.

Among the studies that we conducted using this setup, we found that being stared at affected one's "gut feelings," as measured by changes in electrical activity in the belly.[79] We also found in long-term emotionally bonded couples, one of whom was being treated for cancer, that when the healthy partner gazed at the image of the patient, it affected the patient's physiology. We also found that if the healthy partner had been trained in a meditation technique called *tonglen* (a Tibetan word for "giving and receiving"), which focuses on cultivating and sending compassionate intention, the patient had a larger and more sustained physiological response.[80]

Meta-analysis

As noted earlier in this chapter, a meta-analysis of laboratory experiments involving pairs of participants who were strictly isolated, and where physiological measures were used to detect distant staring, showed strong overall evidence that this effect was real. German psychologist Stefan Schmidt, who conducted the meta-analysis, conservatively concluded, "The existence of some anomaly related to distant intentions cannot be ruled out."[81]

Many of these studies were conducted in the usual abstract, white-coat, emotionally neutral manner. Such experiments have the advantage of being able to safely study aspects of human behavior and performance, but they also have a disadvantage, namely, that the dispassionate design is unlike real life. It is especially unlike the provocative rituals and extreme motivations often involved in magical practices. But that doesn't mean experiments can't use more alluring designs.

Voodoo

In the 1990s, Dutch researcher Rens Wezelman was a visiting scholar in my lab when I was at the University of Nevada. Rens proposed that we use a magical principle to try to enhance the outcome of a feeling-of-being-stared-at experiment.[82] We euphemistically called the study a test of a "traditional magical healing ritual," but it was really about voodoo.

The term *voodoo* comes from Voudon, an Afro-Caribbean religion that originated in Haiti.[83] Formed from a mixture of West African traditions and Roman Catholicism, it shares the magical belief in the Law of Correspondences. In this case, the correspondence under test was the relationship between an effigy of a person and the actual person.

To begin, each of us molded an effigy of ourselves out of Play-Doh, a modeling clay. Around the effigy we put personal belongings, messages, nail clippings, bits of hair, and whatever else we felt would make the effigy "alive." With the effigy we included our own photo, a watch or other object we'd habitually carry, and a one-page autobiography.

During the experiment—again calling the sender Mulder and the receiver Scully—we had Mulder kindly gaze at the Scully doll and mimic giving it a neck or back rub. We explicitly prohibited sticking pins in the Scully doll or doing anything spooky to the doll that we wouldn't normally do with Scully herself. We wanted to discourage the clichéd negative connotation of voodoo and encourage the feeling that the doll *was* the distant person.

Mulder and Scully were located in rooms on different floors of adjacent buildings, separated by about 100 meters, with several concrete walls and a staircase between the buildings. There were no electronic connections or other means of ordinary communication between the rooms.

Scully was located in the receiver's room, wired up with a physiological monitor to continuously record her heart rate, electrodermal activity (small changes in the activity of her sweat glands), and blood volume pulse (a measure of blood flow) in one of her fingers.[84]

To begin a test session, the experimenter synchronized Mulder's laptop computer with the computer used to collect Scully's physiological data; then she gave the laptop and the Scully doll to Mulder and asked him to go to the sender's chamber in the building next door. This was a dimly lit acoustically and electromagnetically shielded chamber. Black fabric was placed on the walls and the ceiling of the chamber, and the effigy and other ritual objects were placed on a black cloth on a small table in the center of the chamber. A candle on the table was the main source of illumination. A laptop computer was also on the table; it was used to present instructions to Mulder. The idea of this eerie-sounding setup was to create the stereotype of a magical ritual space. After settling in, Mulder started the instruction program on the laptop. Meanwhile the experimenter started to record Scully's physiology and waited quietly until the session was over.

Mulder prepared for the session by reading Scully's autobiography, gazing at her doll effigy, and trying to make a mental connection with her. During the intentional influence periods, Mulder used any mental strategies that he thought would help Scully to calm down. They included sending nurturing thoughts toward the doll or the photographs, or mentally massaging areas over the doll where Scully said she was especially responsive to relieving stress, like the shoulders or the back. Play-Doh is a soft material, so we thought it best to not handle the doll itself, lest it fall apart.

Each session consisted of ten intentional influence periods and ten resting periods, each one minute in length. A counterbalancing scheme for the influence and rest periods was used to avoid biases due to natural cycles and drifts in physiological states. The laptop program in the sender's chamber instructed Mulder when it was time to influence Scully, to relax, or to prepare for a change in instructions. It also indicated when the test session was finished, upon which Mulder left the ritual sender's chamber and returned to the lab where Scully and the experimenter were waiting. A single session in this experiment took about a half hour from start to finish. Three sessions were usually completed in a day, with the three participants (sender, receiver, experimenter) taking turns in each of the three roles. Incidentally, all of the individuals in this study (as in all of our experiments) understood the point of the experiment, all agreed to participate, and all were free to opt out of the study at any time and for any reason.

Results

The results, shown in Figure 13, indicate that Mulder's intention periods successfully influenced Scully's physiology. Her fingertip blood volume increased significantly and her heart rate decreased significantly. Each of these measures took about half of the one-minute influence period to reach its peak deviation from the baseline. Both of these changes were consistent with a relaxation response, because an increase in fingertip blood volume means the capillaries in the hands are dilating, associated with warmer hands and a "blushing" response, and heart rate slows down when relaxing.

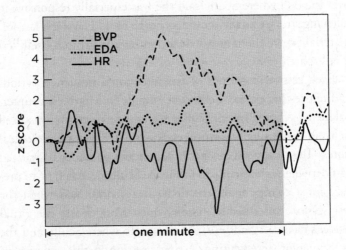

Figure 13. Results of voodoo test showing average changes in electrodermal activity (EDA), heart rate (HR), and blood volume pulse (BVP) during active sending intention versus control periods.

However, the modest rise in electrodermal activity was unexpected. Normally when a person relaxes, electrodermal activity progressively declines; it doesn't increase. So this outcome—a sort of relaxed arousal state—was puzzling. Still, the bottom line was that controlled use of a magical technique caused two measures of physiology to significantly change in ways that were unexpected from a conventional perspective, but in alignment with the Law of Correspondences.

We repeated the same experiment with two new participants and a different physiological monitoring system. We ran a total of sixteen sessions, and as in the original experiment, the results again showed that blood volume pulse significantly increased and heart rate significantly decreased. But this time electrodermal activity also significantly increased. The successful replication provided confidence that the experimental technique had worked, but it also increased our confusion about why electrodermal activity increased, and in this case significantly so. To investigate this puzzle, we asked each participant to describe how they had interacted with the effigy doll. It turned out that in this study they rubbed the shoulders of the dolls to give the patient a "remote massage," and they all also stroked the hair and/or face of the dolls. That is, unlike in the first experiment, they *touched* the effigies.

Based on the Law of Correspondences, we speculated that what we were seeing in Scully's physiology might be similar to what happens in the human body during an actual hands-on massage. So we measured what happened physiologically when one member of our team directly massaged another member's shoulders and stroked his hair. We ran a session using the same timing and measurements used in the voodoo experiment.

What we found was that during the actual massage electrodermal activity increased, heart rate decreased, and blood volume increased. In other words, this was the same pattern observed in the voodoo experiment, suggesting that during the ritual the actions and thoughts of the distant healer were indeed mimicked in the patient, as though the healer and patient *were actually touching each other*. In the first experiment the doll wasn't touched, which may be why the electrodermal activity in that test did not rise as much as it did in the replication study.

This test suggested that psi research could benefit by paying closer attention to magical principles. However, I also felt that adding voodoo to our experimental repertoire would be sociopolitically explosive. So we didn't try it again. One can push the envelope only so far in a university setting without causing administrators to faint. I've met a few who were tough and capable of withstanding the heat generated by controversy. But others? Well, let's just say that they tend to spook easily.

THEURGY

Theurgy involves communication with disembodied entities, also known as spirits, angels, fairies, phantoms, shades, and ghosts. Some magicians are inclined to evoke entities with darker connotations, known as demons, imps, gremlins, jinn, specters, wraiths, and banshees. Another type of traditional magical entity is a *servitor*, a thought-form created to serve (hence the name) a specific purpose.[85] In Tibetan lore, such creatures are known as *tulpas*.[86] In Jewish lore, a similar mind-made creature is called a *golem*. These creatures apparently have a penchant for making up their own minds after a while, so they're not always benign or trustworthy.

Do such spirits actually exist? From a scientific perspective the jury is still out. Some of the ghost-busting shows on television are, like all "reality TV" programs, scripted and carefully edited to generate ghostly excitement; otherwise no one will watch the show. Most of the time, genuine haunting expeditions encounter nothing unusual at all. Sometimes credible investigators do report anomalous events, and I've investigated several purportedly haunted sites, including an eight-hundred-year-old castle with a long history of things that go bump in the night, and during those expeditions there were a few odd moments. But drawing firm conclusions from field studies is difficult.[87]

Fortunately, there are a few phenomena amenable to scientific study that suggest the independent existence of disembodied entities. One involves near-death experiences, the other mediumship. There are other bodies of evidence, such as stories suggestive of reincarnation, but those are not suitable for experimental work, unless you'd like to volunteer and are willing to risk being reincarnated as a manatee.

Disembodied Minds

Nobel laureate Francis Crick (1916–2004) famously quipped that the mind—the self-aware, subjective aspect of the brain—is "nothing but a pack of neurons." Crick asserted that all mental activity, all of "your joys and your sorrows, your memories and your ambitions, your sense of identity and free will, are in fact no more than the behavior of a vast assembly of nerve cells and their associated molecules."[88] That proposal, which is now a central tenet of the neurosciences, suggests that near-death experiences (NDEs) are best understood as hallucinations caused by distortions in neural activity as the brain shuts down.[89] No other explanation is possible because from the "pack of neurons" perspective mind and brain are identical. In that case, the NDE's visions of distant environments or discussions with disembodied entities are examples of bizarre dreams.

But there are problems with the assumption that consciousness is generated by the brain. The main problem is that the neurosciences demonstrate *correlations* between brain activity and different states of cognition and consciousness. That is, when we look at images or we think about things, brain activity varies in predictable ways. These relationships are quite real in the sense that they can be repeatedly demonstrated, but as any student of elementary statistics will tell you, correlation does not imply causation. In other words, just because a flower reliably turns toward the sun during the day, it's not valid to jump to the conclusion that the flower is *causing* the sun to move or the Earth to turn. As esoteric scholar Gordon White writes:

As for the contention that the brain "creates" these experiences—and somehow emanates consciousness itself—

this is entirely without proof. The brain is a dark place. It contains no sounds or colours. When viewed with high-end medical devices, the human brain will treat us to a largely unpredictable fireworks show of electrochemical reactions. But so will dead salmon when you put them in an MRI. To say these electrical signals are creating experience is to say that Rihanna lives in your radio. She doesn't.[90]

Another counterargument to a brain-based explanation for consciousness is the observation that NDEs are reported even when the brain's electrical activity, as reflected in an electro-encephalogram (EEG), has flatlined.[91] This would seem to rule out hallucinations and dreams, because if the brain is completely inactive, then the mind must also be inactive. So NDEs could not be reported, but ipso facto they are.

At face value, this line of reasoning seems to be persuasive, but it's been challenged by recent discoveries that brains continue to show activity well below what was once considered to be flatline conditions, such as in deep coma or the dying brain. In 2013, Daniel Kroeger and his colleagues at the University of Montreal reported that a "novel brain phenomenon is observable in both humans and animals during coma that is deeper than the one reflected by the isoelectric EEG."[92] The same year, scientist Jimo Borjigin and his colleagues at the University of Michigan found evidence indicating that the brain is not completely quiescent during cardiac arrest, and in particular that "high-frequency neurophysiological activity in the near-death state exceeded levels found during the conscious waking state. . . . The mammalian brain can, albeit paradoxically, generate neural correlates of heightened conscious processing at near-death."[93] Based on such findings, if NDEs consisted only of dream-like images, then however vivid, convincing, or unusual they may seem, brain-oriented explanations could not be completely excluded. In other words, maybe all of those awesome experiences about seeing the light, speeding through a tunnel, and meeting deceased relatives really are due to brain-generated hallucinations.

But hallucinations do not cover the full phenomenology of NDEs. Some experiences also include perceptions from *outside the body*, like floating near the ceiling above an operating table, or witnessing events happening beyond the reach of the ordinary senses. When such perceptions are verifiably accurate, they are far more difficult to explain away as brain illusions.[94] These types of perceptions are not reported very often, but that they *ever* happen challenges the criticism that NDEs can only be figments of a dying brain, or that those reporting these experiences are psychologically dissociated.[95]

Other studies indicate that memories of NDEs remain crystal clear and are not embellished even after two decades.[96] NDE memories are also significantly different from imagined events. At a neural level, NDE memories resemble ordinary memories of everyday events; they don't look like memories of imagined events.[97] Dutch cardiologist Pim van Lommel summarized the state of the science about NDEs in a 2011 article in the *Annals of the New York Academy of Sciences*:

> The NDE is an authentic experience that cannot be simply reduced to imagination, fear of death, hallucination, psychosis, the use of drugs, or oxygen deficiency. Patients appear to be permanently changed by an NDE during a cardiac arrest of only some minutes' duration. . . . Our consciousness, with the continuous experience of self, does not always coincide with the functioning of our brain: enhanced or nonlocal consciousness, with unaltered self-identity, apparently can be experienced independently from the lifeless body.[98]

Theoretical explanations for these experiences still lag far behind the empirical data, but that's common in the history of science. Herbal preparations containing salicylates were used for thousands of years before it was understood why acetylsalicylic acid (better known as aspirin) worked.[99] And even with robust effects that were easy to demonstrate, like magnetism, it took centuries before useful explanatory theories were devised.[100] Given that no one knows how consciousness can arise out of matter, it isn't surprising that science has to yet provide a satisfactory explanation for these experiences.

Theoretical quibbles aside, how does the existence of psi influence our understanding of NDEs? The main implication is that it falsifies the theory that reports of distant perceptions during NDEs can be due only to confabulation or coincidence. Does distant perception imply the persistence of consciousness after bodily death? In my opinion, so far the evidence is insufficient to give a confident answer. Everything we know about psi from a scientific perspective to date comes from tests involving living persons. In addition, there is abundant anecdotal and experimental evidence that non-ordinary states of consciousness (e.g., dreaming, meditating, being under the influence of entheogenic compounds) are conducive to enhanced psi phenomena.[101] Given that near-death is a prime example of a non-ordinary state of consciousness, it may be that some of the strikingly vivid aspects of NDEs arise because clearer forms of psi perception are suppressed by a normally functioning brain. That is, from an evolutionary point of view, for our species to survive we had to pay very close attention to the here and now. We need to sense the tiger stalking us right now, not a tiger a thousand miles away or two weeks from next Tuesday. That evolutionary pressure made ordinary conscious awareness exceptionally adept at detecting danger, but at a cost of excluding naked reality—awareness of events distant in space or time.

So when normal brain functions are incapacitated through brain injury, brain surgery, or an NDE, it's possible that the neurological and psychological filters that ordinarily prevent us from perceiving naked reality might also begin to subside. In that case, some people might report significant *increases* in feelings of self-transcendence, unexpected enhancements in consciousness, and improved cognitive skills. And that is exactly what happens. It doesn't happen all the time, or for everyone suffering a brain insult. But that it *can* happen is sufficient to counter the idea that consciousness—especially more refined states of consciousness—is completely dependent on a normally functioning brain.[102]

The largest experimental test of NDEs to date appeared in 2014 in the journal *Resuscitation*. In a multi-site, four-year study, physician Sam Parnia from the Stony Brook Medical Center of the State University of New York, along with colleagues at hospitals around the United States and Britain, studied cardiac arrest patients to see how many would report NDEs. For those who did, they asked how many would be able to report awareness while their heart was verifiably stopped and their brain was flatlined. In some sites the study also involved a shelf that held a hidden photographic target above the hospital operatory that could be seen only by someone floating near the ceiling. If a patient went out of his or her body and hovered near the ceiling, and could remember seeing the target, then that would provide objective evidence that the out-of-body state was real and not an illusion.[103]

After several years, the experiment included 2,060 cardiac arrest patients, of whom 330 survived. Of the survivors, 140 were eligible for the test (they responded to the request for an interview, signed informed consents, and so on) and were subsequently interviewed. Of them, 101 completed all of the surveys and were eligible for the second phase of the investigation. Of the eligible group, 55 reported some sense of awareness or memories during the cardiac arrest. Only 9 of the 55 had experiences consistent with an NDE, and of them only *two* had auditory or visual awareness during episodes of ventricular fibrillation.

Unfortunately, both of those cases occurred in locations

where the shelves and target photographs had not been placed. One of the two candidates could not participate in the follow-up survey due to ill health. The one remaining case, according to the article, was a 57-year-old man who

> described the perception of observing events from the top corner of the room and continued to experience a sensation of looking down from above. He accurately described people, sounds, and activities from his resuscitation. . . . His medical records corroborated his accounts and specifically supported his descriptions and the use of an automated external defibrillator (AED). Based on current AED algorithms, this likely corresponded with up to 3 min of conscious awareness during [cardiac arrest] and CPR.

The bottom line is that NDEs suggest that one or more of today's assumptions about the mind-brain relationship is probably wrong. A better understanding of these experiences might well find that *some* features of an NDE are associated with an impaired brain. But it also seems likely given the independent evidence for psi and other bodies of survival research that an adequate explanation will also include glimpses of realities that are presently beyond the grasp of today's science.

For a journalist's review of the evidence for disembodied forms of consciousness, I recommend Leslie Kean's 2017 book, *Surviving Death*.[104] And for a discussion of NDEs from a medical perspective, I recommend John Hagan's 2017 book, *The Science of Near-Death Experiences*.[105]

Dead or Alive

Another line of research that probes the theurgic domain are studies of mediumship. Mediums are people who claim to be able to communicate with the deceased. Double and triple-blinded studies show that some mediums can gain accurate information about the deceased under conditions that strictly exclude all conventional explanations.[106] Mediums' *experience* is that the information they've obtained comes from the deceased. But where it actually comes from is not yet certain.

Some mediums claim that they can just glance at a photograph of a person and immediately tell if the person is alive or deceased. To test this claim, we invited twelve professional mediums to our lab to look at photos.[107] All of the photos used in the experiment were first transformed into a uniform grayscale and then the photos were counterbalanced across eight categories: gender, age, gaze direction, glasses, head position, smile, hair color, and image resolution. For each image of, say, a middle-aged, dark-haired man who was gazing at the camera, wore glasses, and was smiling with his head tilted to one side, one photo fitting that same description would be of a living person and another would be of a deceased person. This counterbalancing method was used to avoid giving the medium any clues about whether the person was alive or dead.

The mediums examined 404 of these photos displayed in a random order on a computer monitor, one photo at a time. Each was shown for a maximum of eight seconds. Half of the people in the photos were deceased, and half were alive at the time the experiment was conducted. The mediums were asked to press one button if they thought the person in a photo was living, a second button if they thought the person was deceased, and a third button if they didn't know.

The mediums' overall average accuracy on this task was 53.8 percent, where 50 percent was expected by chance. That's associated with modest odds against chance of 250 to 1. Five of the twelve mediums independently obtained statistically significant results, and nine of the twelve mediums obtained results in a positive direction.

Besides demonstrating that the mediums could statistically

discern who was alive or dead based on a fast glance at a photograph, their performance showed an unexpected outcome. We used photos of people from three time periods: many decades ago, a few decades ago, and recently. The mediums' performance was much more accurate with the "newly deceased" (56.8 percent correct) than with the "older deceased" (51.7 percent) or the "long deceased" (50.2 percent). This result, which surprised us, suggests a possible way to experimentally explore the idea of reincarnation, because mediums sometimes report that a person who passed away long ago no longer "feels" dead, presumably because that person (or some aspect of that person's spirit) has gone on to another incarnation. This finding was unexpected, so we'll have to see if it's repeatable in future experiments.

We also collected electrical brain activity from the mediums as they performed the task. We observed a robust effect while they were looking at the photos. At 100 milliseconds after the photo was displayed on the monitor, which is before the mediums could consciously decide how they were going to respond, their brains showed different patterns of activity when they correctly decided if the person was alive or dead, as compared to when their decision was incorrect. This suggests that the mediums were unconsciously sensitive to *something* that gave them a clue about the status of the people in the photos. We published the results of this experiment, and then something unexpected happened.

The Other Scarlet Letter

Our study was peer-reviewed and appeared in one of the highest-impact academic psychology journals. Within four months of it being published it had been viewed thousands of times and was rated among the top 5 percent of the millions of papers tracked by a company that measures the scientific impact of journal articles. The journal's public relations office even featured it on their Facebook account as an item of special interest.

Then, one day we were informed that the article was going to be retracted. This means it would be ceremoniously stricken from the journal's website and marked forever after with the word "retracted," in large red letters. This practice ensures that the article is eternally shamed, just like the scarlet *A* shames its wearer in Nathaniel Hawthorne's novel *The Scarlet Letter*. Retraction of a journal article is rare and serious, because it implies that the reported results were found to be fraudulent, seriously mistaken, plagiarized, or unethical.

My colleagues and I were of course alarmed to learn about the retraction. So we immediately asked the editor who informed us about the retraction to tell us what was going on. In cases involving retractions, authors are supposed to be given a chance to correct any misconceptions or mistakes. The editor replied that the article would be retracted whether or not we agreed to it, nor would we be given the opportunity to respond. That was an egregious breach of editorial ethics, so we asked if any concerns about fraud had been raised or if someone had found a methodological problem that we overlooked. The editor replied that it wasn't about fraud or mistakes. So again we asked why the article was being retracted.

We received no response and the article was retracted. The woo-woo taboo dies hard.

Six months later, we submitted another article for publication. It reported a survey of psi experiences reported by meditators, which I briefly mentioned in Chapter 5. Our paper discreetly proposed that because psi experiences were so commonly reported by meditators, surely these reports were worthy of further investigation.

The article was rejected even before it was sent out for review. The rejection used wording similar to the notice of retraction for our mediumship paper, providing a clue as to why the earlier article had been retracted. The rejection read: "The content of this manuscript does not meet the standards of rigor required by the journal to be considered for publication." Fortunately, this time the editor provided an explanation of what he meant by "standards of rigor."

In a nutshell, the editor was unhappy because we were too open to the mere *possibility* that the meditators' experiences might be due to genuine psi. He wanted us to state that the meditators' experiences were "psychological illusions or delusions," and not to imply that such experiences might be real. He agreed that it was important in science to be tolerant of phenomena thought to be improbable, but it wasn't proper to be sympathetic to *impossible* ideas, like—in his terms—that "pigs can fly" or "water can be turned into wine."

Encountering this sort of prejudice is common in psi research, but we weren't prepared for his next statement. The editor was so confident in his belief that psi effects are literally impossible that he added: "I will do everything in my power to avoid any public research grant money being spent in that direction." Then, to add insult to injury, he added that he might reconsider publishing a revised paper, but *only if we explicitly denied the possibility that psi exists.*

This editor's position was quite clear, but it was also flagrantly wrong. It was based on the false equivalency that the study of commonly reported human experiences is like trying to prove that pigs can fly. It ignored 150 years of empirical literature and numerous meta-analyses demonstrating that some psi phenomena are real. And it blithely dismissed the history of science, which has repeatedly shown that today's most cherished scientific concepts will eventually be replaced by unimaginable new discoveries.

When a scientist or journal editor declares that something is impossible *and must be stopped*, even in the face of supporting experimental evidence, then we're no longer dealing with science. This is a sign of scientism, the dogmatic belief that a narrow interpretation of today's scientific worldview is infallibly correct. Enforcing dogma was the purpose of the Inquisition, whose motto was, essentially, "Eliminate heretical ideas. Resistance is futile."[108] If drawing an analogy with the Inquisition seems too harsh, then consider the editor's closing offer. It was exactly the same as the Inquisition's most effective strategy for extracting confessions: recant your heretical beliefs, and maybe—just maybe—we'll spare you.

As a practice, science aspires to be rigorous, open, and humble in the face of the great unknown. But scientists are also human, so the same tendencies that spawned the Inquisition are still very much present today, and virtually every scientific and scholarly discipline struggles against the tendency to collapse into dogmatic thinking.[109] As a 2017 editorial in *New Scientist* said, "To advance science we need to think about the impossible. Science sets out what we think is true—but when it gets stuck, it's time to explore what we think isn't."[110] When dealing with consciousness and its far capacities, exploring the unthinkable is absolutely necessary.

Medium Brains

Setting aside the worries of those who fear the impossible, we decided to investigate if mediums were in a unique brain state when they said they were communicating with the deceased, or if they were just imagining those communications. In this test, we recruited six professional mediums who were previously vetted for accuracy by the Windbridge Institute.[111] Each medium came to our lab and performed two tasks. In the first task, she was given the first name of a deceased person—say, Bob—and then asked twenty-five questions about Bob. The questions included Bob's physical appearance when he was alive, his personality, hobbies, cause of death, favorite foods, occupation, and so on. After each question, the medium was asked to silently gain information relevant to the question for twenty seconds and then talk about that information.

At no time did the mediums or experimenters know who Bob was, nor did they interact with the "sitter"—the individual who had requested information about Bob. This prevented the possibility that the mediums could have used "cold reading" techniques to fish for information. There are many methods used by performers who fake mediumship readings to extract information in normal ways, but they work only if the mentalist or a confederate has the opportunity to speak to the sitter.[112] For example:

> The original "Classic Reading" is a list of twelve truisms that can be said to apply to almost anyone. Dating back to the 1940's, these "stock" lines can be used to either supplement an already known reading system such as palmistry, or to add interest to a mentalist effect where there is a need to "say something" appropriate to give the impression that more is known about a person than is otherwise apparent.[113]

During our experiment, to avoid the possibility of methods such as cold reading, an experimenter who did not know any of the deceased individuals served as a *proxy* for the sitter, and she posed the questions to the mediums. Each medium was asked to "read" two people, known only by their first name. Let's call them Bob and George. The medium's responses were transcribed, any reference to Bob and George by name was removed, and then both transcripts were sent to the two sitters. The sitter who knew Bob, sitter B, had to score both transcripts for accuracy, and the sitter who knew George, sitter G, had the same task. If the medium gained accurate information during the reading we would expect that sitter B would rate the Bob transcript better than the George transcript, and just the opposite for sitter G.

Sitter ratings were returned for four of the six mediums. All four scored positively, and three of four scored significantly above chance. One of the mediums was highly accurate, scoring with odds against chance of 20,000 to 1.

Then we asked the mediums to experience four different mental states: (1) recollection, meaning thinking about a living person they knew; (2) perception, listening to an experimenter describe a person unknown to them; (3) fabrication, imagining a person; and (4) mediumship, interacting mentally with a deceased person. Each of these mental states was sustained for one minute and each state was repeated three times. While the mediums performed these tasks we recorded their brains' electrical activity. The results showed that their brain activity while they were performing a mediumship reading was significantly different than during the other three states: recollection, perception, or fabrication. We concluded that "the experience of communicating with the deceased may be a distinct mental state that is not consistent with brain activity during ordinary thinking or imagination."[114]

Incidentally, this article, which was published in the top-ranked journal *Frontiers in Psychology*, was viewed over 20,000 times as of mid-2017. That places it in the upper 1 percent of articles read in that journal and in the upper 5 percent of the millions of articles tracked by Altmetric, a company that measures the impact of scientific publications. This reflects the intense interest in psi and related phenomena, including magic. As we've already discussed, magic has been suppressed for centuries, making it strictly taboo within today's academic mainstream. But the underlying phenomena and interest haven't diminished a whit.

THE BOTTOM LINE

This brief review of the scientific evidence for psi and its relationship to magical practices shows that scientific methods can be used to explore the three categories of magical practice, and that doing so has the potential to advance the state of the art.

This evidence won't budge those who've bet their careers on the belief that magic is primitive nonsense or is literally impossible. A personal experience of psi, or magic, might cause one to question such beliefs, but as we've seen in the opening chapter, Michael Shermer's startling story softened his long-established position for only a little while. Then it hardened up again. Personal experience is not likely to change a rigidly held position, especially if one has a reputation as a professional skeptic.[115] As author and social activitist Upton Sinclair once quipped, "It is difficult to get a man to understand something when his salary depends upon his not understanding it."

To neopagans, occultists, witches, and others who are regularly engaged in magical practices, this same evidence may be perceived as obviously true but also as abstract and unbearably dry. Those who subscribe to a deep religious faith may find the same evidence frightening or heartening, depending on the tenets of their particular faith. For fans of magical fiction, this evidence won't seem like Harry Potter at all. It portrays magic as weak and the arguments are overly technical.

We know that magic as portrayed in the movies and in books is an exaggeration. But if real magic is *this* subtle, then why should we care about it? The answer is that if we see real psi in average people as well as in those with natural talent, then we know we're dealing with an inherent human capability. That means we can safely assume that psi abilities are distributed among the general population, just like virtually all other talents. And in that case, what would we find if we examined people at the upper end of the talent curve? People with *exceptional* talent? Are there any genuine Merlins out there?

Chapter 7

MERLIN-CLASS MAGICIANS

In a way, we are magicians. We are alchemists, sorcerers and wizards. We are a very strange bunch. But there is great fun in being a wizard.

—BILLY JOEL

HERE WE'LL CONSIDER THREE REAL-WORLD EXAMPLES OF magical power far beyond anything that we typically see in the laboratory. All three of these individuals were observed to do mind-blowing things by dozens to thousands of multiple, credible witnesses. Evidence based on eyewitness testimony can never be as certain as measurements taken in controlled experiments, and there is always the problem that history embellishes a good story. But as you'll see, there are persuasive reasons to pay attention to the documented evidence in these cases. Each involved many witnesses over long periods of time. In such instances the mundane explanations boil down to mass hallucinations, collusion, or blatant fraud. My take on these individuals is that they probably had genuine talents.

ST. JOSEPH OF COPERTINO

The first case is Joseph Desa, born in Copertino, Italy, in 1603. Like most ordinary people in the seventeenth century, Joseph was poor and born during a time of widespread poverty, plague, hunger, and war. The Catholic Church was the principal authority among European nations, and its power was enforced with an iron hand in the form of the Inquisition. The general population was constantly on the edge of desperation, quickly inflamed by rumors, and easily spooked. It was a time when the mass mind vacillated between moments of panic, dismay, and fanaticism.

Within this context, when Joseph was nine years old he fell ill from an infection, which led to gangrene. It crippled him for five years, much of it spent bedridden and in pain. Without access to the Internet (Wi-Fi would not arrive for another four hundred years) or even a book, Joseph escaped the prison and pain of his body through daydreams, reveries, and fantasies. In some of those states he was spontaneously transported into states of ineffable bliss.

Finally, a hermit with a reputation as a surgeon operated on the boy, and Joseph encountered his first miracle: he survived the surgery. But without schooling and stunted in social skills, Joseph was perceived as dimwitted. He easily fell into trances and gained the nickname "Boccaperta" (Gaping Mouth) for his tendency to look up with his mouth open when entranced by Church music. Hired and fired from many workaday jobs, he felt attracted to the contemplative life of the Church. After a harrowing series of failures and near misses, he was ordained when he was twenty-five years old.

The Church suited Joseph, but his special talents soon became a problem. Early in his career, if a member of the town displeased him, there were consequences. For example:

> A certain Count don Cosimo Pinelli had an ongoing sexual liaison with the daughter of Martha Rodia; Joseph said that if the count didn't desist from his amours, he would go blind.

This turned out to be what happened, and Joseph bragged about his prediction, but later restored the man's sight, this time getting him to leave the girl alone and pay reparations to the family! Before long nobody in Copertino dared enter the company of the friar unless their conscience was squeaky-clean; otherwise they shrank in terror from the gaze of the black-bearded friar.[1]

Fortunately, Joseph's tendencies toward becoming Lord Voldemort were suppressed.[2] But as he grew older his abilities became stronger, more frequent, and more difficult to hide. He gained a reputation as a prophet and a miracle healer, and he exhibited telepathy, precognition, the odor of sanctity, power over animals and natural forces, and—the icing on the cake—when giving Mass he spontaneously levitated, not just once but hundreds of times in front of many startled congregations.[3] This became a big problem, because living miracle-makers threatened to deflect the public's attention away from Church authority. And that was strictly forbidden.

Church officials kept moving Joseph from town to town and tried to keep him away from people by prohibiting him from doing priestly duties. The strategy didn't work. Besides hordes of ordinary people wanting to witness his feats, stories about him began to attract nobles, clergy, and royalty. And that in turn led to unwanted attention from the Inquisition. While on trial by the Inquisition in Rome, Joseph was ordered to say Mass in public to see if the rumors about him were true.

They were. He lifted off the ground in the presence of the inquisitors.

You can imagine how freaked out they must have been. But Joseph experienced another miracle that day. He was just given a stern warning to stop all this levitating nonsense, and somehow he escaped being burnt as a witch. But his abilities were not completely under his control and continued to persist, attracting more and more attention, until a second encounter with the Inquisition put him under house arrest for the rest of his life. Still, given his history, he was extremely fortunate, for this was during the peak years of the witch-burning craze.

A century after his death Joseph was canonized by Pope Benedict XIV as St. Joseph. Pope Benedict, born Prospero Lorenzo Lambertini, had previously served as the Church's Advocatus Diaboli, or "Devil's Advocate." This position was charged with arguing why a person nominated for sainthood was not worthy of that position. Any suggestion of fraud, exaggeration, or collusion regarding miracles attributed to the nominee was thoroughly examined. The materials amassed in the case of Joseph amounted to thirteen volumes housed in the Vatican Archives (they are still there today). They include the Inquisition's trial records, biographies written over the years, diaries, letters, and official Church documents from the different cities and convents Joseph lived in or visited.

Joseph lived for sixteen years at Grotella Convent near Copertino, one of the longest stretches he spent in one location. During that time it was documented that he levitated at least seventy times in front of multiple witnesses. I'll give just one example of the kinds of documented reports involving Joseph's levitations:

April 30, 1639: After stepping inside the Church, Giuseppe [St. Joseph] glanced at a painting of the Holy Virgin located in the vault above the wooden frieze of the altar of the Immaculate Conception, a Madonna painted with the Baby Jesus in her arms in a way that strikingly resembled the Madonna of the Grotella [convent where Joseph had spent many years]. At the sight of her, Padre Giuseppe gave a huge scream and flew about thirty meters in the air and, embracing her, said, "Ah, Mamma mia! You have followed me!" It all happened so quickly that those present were filled with sacred terror, marveling to each other, and remaining in a stupor over the Padre's performance.[4]

For many more details about St. Joseph, I recommend philosopher Michael Grosso's 2016 book, *The Man Who Could Fly*. Grosso reviewed the evidence for Joseph's abilities and compared his case with similar instances of miraculous behavior recorded throughout history. Grosso concluded that Joseph was for real, basing his judgment on the written historical record: thirty-five years of multiple eyewitness testimonies from ordinary people as well as popes, cardinals, ambassadors, dukes, and kings from all over Europe. And that was just the formal written testimonies. An untold number of congregants, probably numbering in the thousands, had also witnessed Joseph's abilities.[5]

DANIEL DUNGLAS HOME

Two centuries after St. Joseph, Daniel Dunglas Home was born near Edinburgh, Scotland, in 1833. He was one of eight children of Elizabeth McNeill, a descendant of a Scottish Highland family said to have the gift of "second sight." Today we'd call that gift clairvoyance, or remote viewing.

Unless you've read about the history of psychic phenomena, you may never have heard of Home (it's pronounced "hume"). But his psychic feats—including levitation—were just as prodigious and in some ways even more startling than St. Joseph's.

The case of Home is especially interesting because his abilities were subjected to scientific tests. The testimony of Home's abilities is also better than St. Joseph's because the former's performances were extensively covered in the newspapers of the day, and they were repeatedly observed by the most accomplished illusionists and conjurers (stage magicians) of the day, who naturally assumed he was cheating.

When he was nine years old, Home was adopted by his aunt

and her husband and they emigrated to America, landing in a town near Norwich, Connecticut. Like St. Joseph, Home was an unusually sensitive child. As an infant he was so weak he wasn't expected to survive, and he had a lifelong highly nervous temperament. Also like St. Joseph, the "feats Home performed were so extraordinary that when witnesses described what they had seen, they were dismissed as foolish, even insane."[6] That quote is from a 2005 biography of Home by University of Edinburgh historian Peter Lamont, entitled *The First Psychic*. The title of Lamont's book refers to the first time that the word *psychic* was used in the popular press to describe someone with Home's abilities.

Lamont's book is especially useful in assessing Home's feats because Lamont is a historian of psychology, an experienced illusionist, and a member of the Inner Magic Circle, a special branch of the London-based organization for magicians called the Magic Circle. One becomes a member of the Inner Magic Circle by invitation only, based on proven expertise and other significant contributions to the art of conjuring. Being a member of that fraternity, Lamont naturally regarded Home with a practiced, skeptical eye. But despite a strong inclination to regard magic solely in terms of tricks and illusions, that's not what Lamont concluded about Home. He was just as puzzled as everyone else:

What are we to make of Daniel Dunglas Home? It is true that there were many accusations of fraud, but most of them were entirely without base, and actual evidence for fraud was both rare and inconclusive. He might have been a cheat, but if he was, then he cheated successfully for two decades, before hundreds of witnesses in thousands of séances. Many of the witnesses were hostile to spiritualism, and many remained unconvinced by what they had seen, yet time and again they admitted that they were unable to explain what had happened.[7]

The best conjurers of the day tried, and failed, to explain Home's feats. Scientists investigating Home, including one of the most prominent chemists and physicists of the day, Sir William Crookes (1832–1919), reported evidence in support of Home's claims. Crookes's critics were reduced to making ad hominem attacks and misrepresenting the nature of his research.[8]

The phenomena produced by Home were in the context of a rising cultural interest in spiritualism, especially in the form of physical mediumship. These performances involved speaking to spirits via rapping sounds, levitating tables, invisible spirits playing musical instruments, sitters at the séances being touched by spirits, and so on. Many of these séances were conducted in rooms that were completely dark, or dimly lit by candles or gaslight. Demand for such performances was high, and because of supply and demand, many mediums were only too happy to perform séances for tidy sums. Many of them were subsequently unmasked as frauds.

It was in this context that Home was performing his séances throughout Europe, both for secular and scientific people highly skeptical of the claimed phenomena and for spiritually inclined people sympathetic to it.

Lamont's book provides a full accounting of the kinds of phenomena associated with Home and the settings of his performances. To give a flavor of that history, I'll recount one episode involving a group of highly skeptical Dutch rationalists who were openly hostile to spiritualism. They were members of the Dutch Radical School of Modern Protestantism, which virulently denied all biblical miracles, miraculous divine intervention, and the concepts of spirits. Like other skeptics, they had loudly dismissed Home's claims without having seen them. But

Home wasn't intimidated by skepticism, so he agreed to perform a series of séances for them.

Home arrived in the Netherlands on January 31, 1858. The following day he conducted a séance for Queen Sophie of the Netherlands. A few days later in a hotel in Amsterdam, Home held a séance for ten of the Dutch rationalists, none of whom he had previously met. The group included a doctor of philosophy, a physician, a lawyer, an optician, and a Dr. Gunst, who reported the setup:

> [The skeptics] sat round a large mahogany table, which they examined sufficiently to note that the top, column and base were "directly and immovably fixed" together. . . . On top of the table were four [bronze] candelabras, with two more below, which "made it possible to obtain an undisturbed view of what was happening under the table."[9]

The group placed their fingertips on the table in plain view, and Home told them that if they wished to remove their hands they could do so. They tested themselves to make sure they weren't being manipulated by suggestion, were allowed to talk freely among themselves, and "laughed mockingly concerning the matter at hand."[10]

Within this context one would not expect much to happen. But then:

> These expressions stopped soon enough. For as they mocked, "the table started to make a sliding movement," and those towards whom it was moving "were requested to try to stop this movement; this, however, they could not do." When the table stopped, raps began, and when raps were requested "in a certain manner, and as many times as we should indicate, [t]his wish was carried out to the full." As Daniels' skeptical witnesses watched in characteristic disbelief, the table

"started to rise up on one side . . . so high that all of us were very much afraid that [the candelabras] would fall off."[11]

Two more séances were held with this group, with increasingly inexplicable phenomena. Dr. Gunst later reviewed the normal interpretations that critics had offered as an explanation for Home's effects. The first was that Home was using some sort of conjuring trick or gimmick. This was dismissed because, according to Dr. Gunst, the "Amsterdam séance room was well illuminated all the time the sittings lasted. Furthermore, the skeptical observers were crowded around Home (the performer) and not restricted in any movement or observation they desired to make."[12]

The second explanation, that the table movements were due to unconscious motor movements by the sitters, was dismissed because the séance table was large and sturdy enough to seat fourteen people, and besides the thickness of the wood it had a very heavy central column. Despite the weight of the table, it was observed by multiple witnesses to levitate at least twelve inches off the floor.

The third explanation, regarding faked "spirit hands" touching the sitters, was deemed insufficient because the séance room was well lighted, so they were able to keep Home under constant surveillance and the sitters were still touched in quick succession, as they had requested, with one person being correctly touched after making requests *mentally*.

The fourth explanation, hallucination, was dismissed because, unlike claims that Home could perform only in front of "believers" who might be inclined to imagine things, these séances were conducted for a group of avowed skeptics, none of whom Home knew.

Other common interpretations, such as Home deflecting attention while using his feet to perform the trick, were excluded because the skeptics could easily see under the table and noted that Home had not moved. Still other objections asserted that the room must have been prepared by confederates in advance, using hidden wires and gimmicks. That too could be ruled out because "the séances were conducted in a hotel where Home had never been before and where he arrived only a few hours before the commencement of the first sitting."[13]

Dr. Gunst concluded that strange things really had happened but could not be explained. He added, "And nothing could be observed that could give rise to even the slightest suspicion that Mr. Home was acting in a fraudulent manner."[14] This was consistent throughout Home's career. No one ever brought forth evidence of fraud, nor was there any evidence that the effects were due to hallucination. In sum, Home, like St. Joseph, remains a genuine mystery.

So far we've discussed people who lived centuries ago. In such cases, even with excellent documentation it's difficult to know with any certainty what happened back then. What about a modern Merlin?

TED OWENS

Ted Owens (1920–1987) was born in Bedford, Indiana.[15] His case is not as well known as those of St. Joseph or Home. But he's an example of a twentieth-century American who apparently performed remarkable feats with still-living witnesses to his abilities. If even a fraction of his claimed abilities were real, then Owens could be considered on par with St. Joseph and Home.

Owens grew up poor and couldn't get along with his mother. As a youth, he lived with his grandparents who, like many during the Depression in 1930s America, often engaged in popular psychic games like the Ouija board. His grandmother was known for finding lost objects and predicting deaths, and his grandfather was a dowser.[16]

Owens's specialty was affecting the weather and "calling in" UFOs. He was described as a difficult character, angry, dark, egotistical, and chronically frustrated that the U.S. government did not seek his assistance as a psychic. He was anxious to demonstrate his gifts to anyone who would pay attention, and many such examples are provided in Jeffrey Mishlove's book, *The PK Man: A True Story of Mind over Matter*. Mishlove followed Owens for years, documenting and testing his claims. As an example, in 1976 Owens pronounced:

> In the interest of science, I am going to give a demonstration of my psi force abilities to the people who live in the San Francisco area 100 miles in circumference, using San Francisco as the bull's-eye of my target. As of today, and daily for the following ninety days, I will telepath to living entities in another dimension for them to appear in the above target area, so that they may be seen by police, scientists, or other responsible observers who are qualified to report the sightings, also for them to cause electromagnetic and magnetic anomalies within the above-described area. It is my intent to produce not one, but at least three major UFO sightings, as described above, within the above-named time period . . . to be reported in the newspapers in order for the experiment to be a valid one.[17]

As if that wasn't enough, he further predicted that the San Francisco area would suffer "power blackouts, perhaps massive ones, small and large power failures," and to put the icing on the cake, that "alien life-forms would be seen in the target area."[18]

A ninety-day period and a hundred-mile radius leave a lot of leeway for something odd to happen with the weather. But a mass sighting of UFOs and "alien life-forms"? That would be rare, especially around large cities. Mishlove describes what happened next:

The San Francisco experiment began formally on November 7, 1976. The first anomaly to strike the Bay Area came about two and one-half weeks later when a wind storm struck the city, resulting in a massive blackout.

According to a November 27 *San Francisco Examiner* story, the winds "gusting up to 60 to 70 miles per hour—the fiercest in years—created havoc and widespread damage within the Bay Area . . ." The story went on to relate that over 200 burglar alarms had been activated by the winds and that power outages had darkened as many as 100,000 homes. The winds had struck at an inopportune time as well. Since it was Thanksgiving weekend, many of the Pacific Gas and Electric's workers were out of town, making immediate repair work difficult to accomplish.[19]

Within the ninety-day period: check. In the San Francisco Bay Area: check. Massive blackout: check. Mishlove continues:

On December 3, [Owens] told me over the phone that one of his predicted UFO sightings was about to occur within the next few days. He made a point of reminding me that the sighting would be seen by many reputable witnesses and even be reported on the front page. The fulfillment of this specific prediction came on December 8, when the best documented UFO sighting ever reported from the Bay Area startled hundreds of onlookers.[20]

The story of the sighting made front page headlines in the *Berkeley Gazette* on December 10 [1976]. The accompanying [photo and caption] read: Stephan Poleskie, who, wind permitting, creates aerial art by flying a stunt plane overhead while leaving trails of colored smoke, was startled Wednesday while performing over Cal-State Sonoma. Poleskie suddenly became aware of a circular white object only 1,000 feet away. The event was also captured on Channel 9 TV cameras, and

Poleskie said videotape reruns check out and confirm the existence of a curious copilot in the sky.[21]

A UFO reported on the front page of a newspaper: check. Many witnesses and a bonus video: check. But what about the prediction of other UFOs and "alien life-forms"? Mishlove continues:

> Just a few days before Owens' February 7 [1977] deadline, a second major UFO case came to light in the San Francisco area, one that indeed involved the sighting of an alien life-form. On February 2, the *Concord Transcript* announced that a bizarre UFO abduction had been reported by a local resident. Concord, a quiet little city east of Berkeley, is well within the fifty mile target radius centering on San Francisco.[22]

Aliens: check.

Mishlove followed up on the police report and found that the Oakland center of the Federal Aviation Administration had no reports of UFOs that morning, and the abductee was an ordinary married salesman who lived in the Concord area who had no previous psychic experiences and had claimed to have read nothing about UFOs.

Mishlove cites many other examples of Owens's predictions about extreme weather, directing lightning strikes, power blackouts, UFO sightings, unexpected outcomes of football games, plane crashes, and even a specific warning a month before the space shuttle *Challenger* blew up in January 1986. The outcomes of many of these events confirmed part or all of Owens's predictions. Owens was confident about his predictions because he, or "Space Intelligences" from a "higher dimension" he was in contact with, had actually *caused* those events. That is, he wasn't just predicting these events.

It isn't possible to judge Owens's claims with any certainty, because he would sometimes take credit for strange events after the fact. But enough of his low-probability predictions did come true, so that leaves us with a modern record not unlike the magical feats associated with tales of St. Joseph and D. D. Home.

These three individuals were rare but not absolutely unique. I suspect, based on laboratory tests, that psi abilities are like many other human abilities, and as such, they would be distributed as a normal curve. Merlin-class magicians would fall to the far right side of that curve, where such talents can be found in perhaps one in a million people. That means we would be dealing with potentially seven thousand people in the early twenty-first century with these kinds of abilities.

Who are they? What are they up to? Are these the "invisible adepts" that Blavatsky and others insisted were real? There are many tales of shamans, gurus, and other adepts who have displayed remarkable abilities. How do we even begin to understand them?

Chapter 8

TOWARD A SCIENCE OF MAGIC

> *I regard consciousness as fundamental. I regard matter as derivative from consciousness. We cannot get behind consciousness. Everything that we talk about, everything that we regard as existing, postulates consciousness.*

> —Nobel laureate physicist Max Planck,
> father of quantum theory

BASED ON THOUSANDS OF PSI EXPERIMENTS PUBLISHED over the last century by researchers around the world, many properties of psychic phenomena have been discovered.[1] In order of scientific confidence, meaning the degree to which the evidence has been successfully and independently repeated, six conclusions may be drawn:

1. We have the capacity to gain information unbound by the everyday limitations of space or time, and without the use of the ordinary senses. In the vernacular, psi is a genuine "sixth sense." Based on the available scientific evidence, this is a virtual certainty.

2. Psi capacities are widely distributed among the general population. Extreme levels of psi talent are rare, but laboratory tests indicate that most people have some discernible ability, whether they're aware of it or not.

3. These effects arise from the unconscious.[2] Psi abilities can be

observed during conscious awareness, but more reliable effects can be detected below the level of awareness via physiological measurements and other techniques used to study "implicit" and unconscious responses.

4. Psi effects are stronger during non-ordinary states of consciousness, such as during meditation, while dreaming, or while under the influence of psychedelic compounds.

5. We have the capacity to mentally influence the physical world, probably not through application of the four known physical forces, but perhaps through as yet unidentified principles that either affect the probabilities of events or "warp" the fabric of space-time.

6. We can gain information from sources purported to be nonphysical entities.

There have been many attempts to account for psi using existing scientific models. These theoretical efforts have yet to persuade the broader scientific community, largely because psi is deeply related to consciousness in some way, and we're still far from understanding what consciousness *is*, never mind what its capabilities may be. But there are signs that science is headed toward a major shift in worldview. When that transformation is complete, the evidence for psi, and its close association with magic, will become far more palatable.

To begin, we'll briefly review what is meant by the "Western scientific worldview," as this is held by most people around the world who've been exposed to a standard secular education. What is that worldview, and why is it in need of repair?

THE SCIENTIFIC WORLDVIEW

The term "Western scientific worldview" is actually a misnomer. It's not as though each point of the compass has different sciences. The term "Western" refers to a Eurocentric development that began around the Age of Reason in the seventeenth century. It consists of three key assumptions:

- *Realism.* The physical world consists of objects with real properties that are completely independent of observation. This means that your double-shot, extra-hot, no-foam, skinny latte from your local coffee shop has real properties, like a certain taste, warmth, flavor, and aroma. It also means that those properties exist even when you're not paying attention to your drink. In the everyday world, this assumption is just a matter of common sense.
- *Locality.* Objects are completely separate. "Action at a distance" is impossible. For object A to affect object B, you have to shove A and make it collide into B. In the realm of deep physics, this collision might involve infinitesimally tiny particles or force fields, but the general idea still holds.
- *Causality.* The arrow of time is a consequence of the second law of thermodynamics, so it's against the law to try to get information from the future. There are no exceptions. Try to reverse time and you'll go directly to jail.

Combine those three core assumptions and you end up with four principles that form the scientific worldview: mechanism, physicalism, materialism, and reductionism.

- *Mechanism* says that everything can be understood like the gears of a clock. Events unfold forward in time in a strictly orderly, tit-for-tat, cause-and-effect fashion.
- *Physicalism* says that everything can be described with real properties that exist in ordinary space and time, and that any meaningful statement is provable by logic or mathematics or can be demonstrated by easily verifiable experimental facts.
- *Materialism* says that everything, including mind and consciousness, consists of matter and energy. It doesn't make

sense to call something "spiritual," "nonphysical," or "immaterial." This is why some scientists are quick to label such ideas nonsense or woo-woo.

- *Reductionism* says that everything is made up of a hierarchy of ever-smaller objects, with subatomic particles at the bottom. Causation flows strictly upward, from the microscopic to the macroscopic.

Those principles and assumptions are very powerful. After they were adopted, it took humanity only a few hundred years to advance from staring slack-jawed at the moon as the most exciting form of evening entertainment to asking the voice recognition feature of your smart home controller to dim the lamp, turn up the thermostat, make a cup of coffee, and play an on-demand movie on your tablet computer while you video-chat with a friend on the other side of the planet.

So it isn't sensible to throw away what demonstrably works. If we had based our worldview solely upon religious texts or esoteric lore, we wouldn't be enjoying the wonders of streaming movies and emoji texting. It took a dedicated interest in what was long regarded as "natural magic" by generations of proto-scientists, many at risk of their lives and careers, to establish today's scientific worldview. That worldview has advanced so far and so fast that it has practically eliminated the need to talk to each other. Anything that takes more than 140 characters to tweet is probably not worth saying anyway.[3]

But does the reigning worldview account for everything? Or does it create blinders that allow only certain ideas and exclude others? Does a powerful worldview make it a little too easy to decide what is or is not supposed to be possible, and in so doing inhibit our imagination?

You can guess where I'm headed. It is well known that the assumptions of realism, causality, and locality *do not hold in all circumstances.* From quantum mechanics we know that elementary objects, such as electrons and photons, do not have fully determined properties before they are observed. So the commonsense understanding of reality is a special case of a more comprehensive worldview. From Einstein's general relativity, we know that a fixed arrow of time is an illusion. So the everyday experience of causality is a special case of a more comprehensive worldview. And from quantum theory we also know that "spooky action at a distance" definitely exists, so the commonsense meaning of locality is a special case of a more comprehensive worldview. Given that what we thought were fundamental assumptions are not so fundamental after all, then what is that more comprehensive worldview?

THE PERENNIAL PHILOSOPHY

A clue is provided by a theme that spans all of the esoteric cosmologies—the Perennial Philosophy. This idea was popularized in modern times by British novelist Aldous Huxley in a 1945 book by that title.[4] It says that there is a single, underlying mystical cosmology from which all of the tremendously diverse religious traditions of the world have emerged. This same idea has been called the primordial tradition, the secret wisdom, the forgotten truth, the ancient theology, the *prisca theologia*, and so on.[5]

There are, of course, many nuances among these traditions due to idiosyncratic differences in cultural, sociopolitical, and linguistic factors. If a mystic lives in a culture that hasn't advanced to the point where, say, schoolchildren casually chat about the latest black hole found in the galaxy, then she will be limited to describing her subjective experience of a black hole using concepts that are within her language. In pre-scientific times, those descriptions would be limited to metaphors and parables, like the allegory of Plato's cave. A mystic's contemporaries, awed by her otherworldly wisdom, may take her metaphors literally. And that's the beginning of a slippery slope that heads toward dogma and away from the essence of the mystic's actual experience.

Scholars interested in magic and esotericism tend to focus on the differences among these cultural and historical variations. But when we focus on the *similarities*, we find that three simple ideas keep popping up:

1. *Consciousness is fundamental,* meaning it is primary over the physical world.
2. *Everything is interconnected.*
3. *There is only one Consciousness.*

That's it. Those three ideas are the basis of real magic.[6]

Those same ideas are also expounded in the various philosophies that assume there's ultimately just one "substance" underlying reality. Historically that substance has been called by many names: Spirit, Advaita, Brahman, Tao, Nirvana, Source, Yahweh, God, and numerous others. A 2017 book that examines this substance from a scientific viewpoint is *You Are the Universe: Discovering Your Cosmic Self and Why It Matters*, by Deepak Chopra and physicist Menas Kafatos. The "cosmic self" they refer to is this ever-present essence of all existence. In recent times, to avoid religious connotations, the more neutral term *consciousness* is sometimes used.

By *consciousness* I mean awareness—that which allows us to enjoy subjective experience and *know* that we've experienced it.[7] If we bite into a lemon, we know what it tastes like. But if we attempt to trace *how* we know based on the signals that travel to the brain from electrochemical sensors on the tongue, nowhere do we find what the subjective *taste* of a lemon is actually like.

That's because the experience we're seeking is inside the brain-body machinery in a way that cannot be observed from the outside. Science is exceptionally adept at studying features of the external world, but so far it has just barely scratched the surface at developing ways to study the "inner world."

Part of the failure is due to the method that gives science its power. The origin of the word *science* is from the Latin for "to know," "to distinguish by separating," rooted in the Latin *scindere*, "to cut." These meanings capture the essence of the scientific application of reductionism. That is, if you want to understand an old-fashioned wind-up watch, you disassemble it into pieces, and you'll soon discover lots of interlocking gears that completely determine how the watch works. You could do the same with a digital watch, or even a computer-based smartwatch. Once the parts are identified, the whole can be understood, at least in principle. This technique works remarkably well for all sorts of things in the everyday world.

But reductionism only works for objects that can be cleanly separated, and that doesn't include the set of all possible things, especially at the quantum scale. We also have no idea how to take awareness apart. Philosophers would call such an attempt a "category mistake," like trying to take the square root of an orange. In other words, the way that the neurosciences approach the problem of consciousness, as a form of intricate brain machinery, may be misconceived from the get-go. As cosmologist Jude Currivan says, "Its fallacy is the assumed duality between the apparent immateriality of mind and the seeming materialism of the physical world."[8]

Recognition of this problem has sparked a revival of interest among scientists and scholars toward the philosophical notion of *idealism*—the idea that reality is fundamentally of, and in, the mind. Related ideas include *panpsychism*—the idea that matter at all levels, including fundamental particles, has an inherent property of sentience, or mind. And *neutral monism*—the idea that mind and matter are actually complementary aspects of the same "stuff," like two sides of the same coin.

KASTRUP'S BALONEY

Computer scientist Bernardo Kastrup provides a clear explanation of idealism in his 2014 book, *Why Materialism Is Baloney*.[9] His claim is that the neuroscience assumption that the physical brain gives rise to subjective experience is full of holes (or perhaps baloney), and he takes great pains to explain why.

He cites a 2007 article in one of the top scientific journals, *Nature*, which showed that realism—remember, this is the commonsense assumption that there is an external reality with real properties that exist independently of observation—is not compatible with quantum theory, nor with experimental results.[10] The authors of that *Nature* paper concluded their discussion with a statement that, when you really grok it, should make your hair stand up: "We believe that our results lend strong support to the view that any future extension of quantum theory that is in agreement with experiments must abandon certain features of realistic descriptions."[11]

What that means is that holding fast to any simple form of realism is headed in the wrong direction. Or in simpler terms: *reality depends on observation*.[12] But who or what is doing the observation? This too was addressed in a 2005 article in *Nature* by John Hopkins University physicist Richard Henry. In a paper entitled "The Mental Universe," Henry wrote:

> Physicists shy from the truth because the truth is so alien to everyday physics. A common way to evade the mental Universe is to invoke "decoherence"—the notion that "the physical environment" is sufficient to create reality, independent of the human mind. Yet the idea that any irreversible act of

amplification is necessary to collapse the wave function is known to be wrong. . . . The Universe is entirely mental.

The import of such articles appearing in a journal such as *Nature* cannot be overstated. *Nature* is the orthodox voice of the scientific mainstream. This is telling us that from a trusted, mainstream perspective it is now acceptable to discuss ideas that would have caused a medieval esotericist to scowl and whisper, "Hush! The Inquisition will hear you!"

While it's acceptable to publish interpretations of physics in *Nature*, it's not acceptable to directly confront what some regard as the metaphysical foundations of science (even though that's *exactly* what those articles are doing).[13] You're not likely to find *Nature* publishing studies about magic anytime soon. Indeed, in 1980 when a minor miracle occurred and *Nature* published a positive study on remote viewing, it raised such a firestorm that academics were fainting in the street.[14] The following year, British biologist Rupert Sheldrake's first book, *A New Science of Life*, was reviewed by John Maddox, then the editor of *Nature*. Maddox wrote, "This infuriating tract . . . is the best candidate for burning there has been for many years." Then, with righteous indignation, he added, "Sheldrake is putting forward magic instead of science, and that can be condemned in exactly the language that the Pope used to condemn Galileo, and for the same reason. It is heresy."[15]

The definition of *heresy* in the Merriam-Webster dictionary is "adherence to a religious opinion contrary to church dogma."[16] Maddox's church was science, which isn't supposed to have a dogmatic set of acceptable beliefs. But such is the fear of magic. It caused the editor of one of the most prestigious scientific journals in the world to forget that science is not a religion.

Mainstream science does not take kindly to the resurrection of magical concepts, but that is what we are seeing in experimental tests of quantum theory. Those papers are not thought of as being supportive of magic because they aren't viewed from an esoteric perspective. But the underlying concepts point firmly toward the Perennial Philosophy. As Bernardo Kastrup writes,

> If idealism is true and all reality is indeed in mind, then the simplest hypothesis is that there is but one mind; one irreducible medium in which the dance of existence unfolds. Otherwise, one would have to postulate that mind has arisen irreducibly countless times in nature, once for every conscious being. This is, of course, a tremendously inflationary postulate. So we will stick to the most parsimonious alternative: there is but one irreducible medium of mind, the sole ontological primitive of all reality.[17]

There is a growing number of books that dive deeply into the historical, philosophical, experimental, and theoretical support for the notion that consciousness is fundamental. Three that I recommend for those who'd like to study this topic in detail are *Irreducible Mind*, a comprehensive review of the many challenges to prevailing mechanistic ideas about consciousness;[18] *One Mind*, which lays out in exquisite detail why the notion of a single, collective mind has been taken very seriously by many scientists and scholars;[19] and *Beyond Physicalism*, which makes a persuasive case that today's neuroscience assumption that consciousness is a meaningless side effect of "meat machines" (that is, us), is evidently wrong.[20] These books don't mention magic per se, but they do discuss the type of worldview that is completely compatible with the reality of magic.

CONSCIOUSNESS AND MAGIC

Let's assume that the esoteric traditions are correct and that personal consciousness [c] and Universal Consciousness [C] are made out of the same "stuff." Personal consciousness [c] may be thought of not as a tiny piece of [C] that has been broken off and is separate from the rest of the universe, but rather as the tip of an extremely large "iceberg" of consciousness. With this idea in mind, then:

- *Divination* works because [C] is more fundamental than the physical concepts of time and space, so [c] too can perceive what is ordinarily experienced as past, present, and future. Most people, most of the time, don't identify with [C], but when that happens—in the magical state of *gnosis,* or the yogic state of *samadhi*—then divination is perfectly normal. What [c] can *express* about [C] is severely limited because [C] is inconceivably "larger" than everyday reality. As such, [C] is also beyond ordinary concepts and language. That's why mystics are always frustrated when asked to describe their experience. The moment we step beyond the ordinary, language fails.

- *Force of will* works because the physical world emerges from and is modulated by [C]. Our personal will, expressed by [c], can also create and modulate physical reality, but not to a great extent; this may be due to what might be called "reality inertia." That is, when an elephant shakes its body, the tip of its tail will whip around wildly, but if the tail swats a fly the elephant's body won't budge. Force-of-will effects observed in the laboratory and in everyday life are generally small because you're like the tail trying to push the elephant.

  The relationship between personal intention and [c] may be thought of in this way: [c] is like a battery and intention is like an electrical circuit. The circuit is a design that's poised to act, but without the power of [c] the circuit won't accomplish anything. Intention, the urge to accomplish a goal, might be an entirely human-centric concept, but it might also be an inherent property of [c]. At this point in our understanding of consciousness we don't know what it's capable of without immediately assuming that "it" is necessarily human. While

[c] is mainly interested in our personal universe, [C] in some enigmatic way may well be involved with the workings of the rest of the cosmos. Perhaps as we enjoy playing a video game, [C] may delight in directing the path of the Andromeda galaxy as part of a universal pinball game.

- *Theurgy* works because the human physical form is just one of a potentially infinite number of ways that consciousness can be embodied. There is no reason for the "body" that hosts [c] to necessarily be physical, at least not in the way that we currently understand physicality.

A SKETCH OF REALITY

Figure 14 is a sketch of reality suggested by the Perennial Philosophy. Above the horizontal line we find ordinary conscious awareness and the everyday world of large, stable objects. This "high" reality is where we live most of the time. It's also the domain of common sense and where science has focused upon. Note the parallels between ordinary awareness, classical physics, and the natural and counting integers (1, 2, 3 . . .).

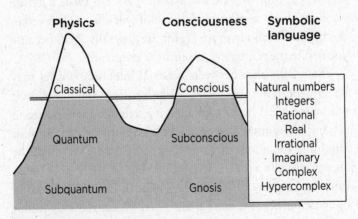

Figure 14. Model of reality.

Just below the horizontal line in Figure 14 is the human unconscious, quantum reality, and a list of increasingly abstract numbers, the symbolic language of physics. To describe physical reality below the level of everyday awareness, physics requires the use of mathematics that are more abstract than simple integers. We know that a mental domain exists below conscious awareness from research in psychotherapy, psychology, the neurosciences, and meditation. Our conscious life emerges from the unconscious, and likewise, the classical physical world emerges from the quantum domain.

From our vantage point "above" this sketch we can see that what appears to be two separate islands is actually two peaks of the same mountain, most of which resides under the surface. The separations experienced in the everyday world are similarly an illusion based on our limited perspectives. The esoteric traditions can be understood as attempting to describe this mountain from the bottom up.

Until the beginning of the twentieth century, scientists studying the physical world did not realize that there was anything below the "surface." Nor did scientists, psychiatrists, and psychologists studying the mind realize that the mind too existed in layers below the surface. As science advances, it continues to probe progressively deeper levels of reality. At some point, a threshold may be reached where further dives may not be possible without a tighter integration of consciousness and physics, because those two apparently different topics are probably an illusory separation as well. As eminent neuroscientist Christof Koch has said, "Consciousness is really physics from the inside. Seen from the inside, it's experience. Seen from the outside, it's what we know as physics, chemistry, and biology."[21]

Eventually we may reach the domain that the esoteric traditions call gnosis. At that stage, gnosis is not just a state of awareness, nor is it a state of physics. Such dualistic distinctions only appear at higher levels. Instead, ultra-deep layers of reality may be more like physicist David Bohm's concept of what he called an "implicate order," an inherently mental, *potential* domain, from which physical reality emerges.[22] This emergence is what we've been calling force-of-will magic, for want of a more accurate term. At that stage, as Gregory Dawes writes in *Parergon*, the journal of the Australian and New Zealand Association for Medieval and Early Modern Studies,

> the distinction between magic and science [becomes] difficult. It cannot be found in magic's invoking of occult powers, for modern science also invokes powers that remain occult (that is to say, "hidden") even when they can be demonstrated experimentally and described in precise, mathematical terms. Modern science differs from magic in its understanding of the powers involved.[23]

HIERARCHIES OF KNOWLEDGE

Sketches of reality can be instructive as metaphors, but how do we actually get from today's halting understanding of deep reality to some future time when we have a scientifically testable understanding?

Consider Figure 15 as a model of today's hierarchy of knowledge (see page 197). It assumes that the foundations of reality are physical: matter and energy. From that domain elementary particles and energies combine in complex ways and emerge into the realm we call chemistry. From there biology emerges, and then psychology.

In each of these hierarchical stages, higher levels emerge from lower levels. The higher levels often contain new properties that the lower levels do not share, and that could not be predicted from the lower levels. The elements hydrogen and oxygen can be combined to form H_2O, the water molecule. But neither hydrogen nor oxygen is wet.

Somehow at the top of this hierarchy a new property emerges. We call it consciousness. But this property is radically different from all of the other properties emerging from lower levels, because consciousness no longer has ordinary physical properties. Philosophers call subjective experience *qualia* because experience is an internal *quality*, rather than a measurable external *quantity*. It is sometimes argued that the brain must be generating consciousness because an anesthesiologist can apply a drug cocktail to your bloodstream and reliably switch off conscious awareness. But that doesn't mean the awareness was *caused* by brain activity. For example, about 1 in 1,000 people undergoing surgery discover to their distress that they're fully conscious while under general anesthesia.[24]

We call emergence of a new property into a higher level an instance of "upward causation," because the arrow of causation seems to point upward in this knowledge hierarchy. But higher

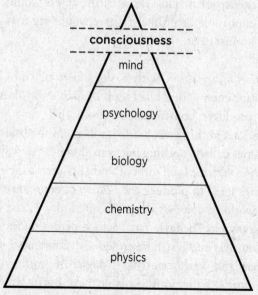

Figure 15. Today's hierarchy of science.

levels can also influence levels below. Nobel laureate Roger Sperry called this property "downwards causation."[25] As an example, if a person picks up a pencil and begins to write, the electrons that compose that pencil will all start to move in ways that, from the electrons' perspective, they'd have no way of predicting or (in an anthropometric sense) understanding.

Deep confusion over what philosophers have called the "mind-body problem" has persisted for millennia without resolution ever since philosophers first identified it as a problem. Consciousness remains a problem even with the fancy neuroimaging tools available today. The impasse has led to a growing sense that radically new approaches to understanding consciousness may be required. We increasingly find such proposals in philosophy, physics, the neurosciences, and psychology.

Here are seven common ways proposed to understand the relationship between consciousness—pure awareness—and physical reality.[26] These interpretations lead to different likelihoods of the existence of magic. Three of the seven would say that magic is impossible or unlikely. Three would say it is possible. One says it must exist.

1. *Reductive materialism*, with a side order of consciousness. Matter (or energy) organizes itself in such a way that it eventually produces consciousness. From this view subjective awareness is nothing but recursive loops in the brain. This is sometimes called "nothing but-ism." Magic? No way.

2. *Reductive materialism*, without added consciousness. Matter organizes itself to produce the *illusion* of consciousness. This is the world of zombies, long a favored idea in the eccentric view known as "behaviorism," which denies the existence of consciousness and is still taken seriously by some zombie philosophers and neuroscientists.[27] Magic? Impossible.

3. *Soft idealism*. Consciousness is primary but matter emerges

out of consciousness, as do the brain-based activities that we call cognition and perception. Magic? Possible.

4. *Hard idealism.* Consciousness is primary and matter exists only as an appearance within consciousness. In other words, at fundamental levels the world is not made of matter and energy. It consists of something much more abstract: pure awareness. This is what Bernardo Kastrup argues and what other hardcore idealists propose. Magic? Obvious.

5. *Straight-up dualism.* Both consciousness and matter exist, but neither arises from the other. They are separate, primitive "substances," like the warp and woof of the fabric of reality. This idea is most famously associated with French philosopher René Descartes's famous quip, "I think therefore I am." It is vaguely similar to the yoga theory called *samkhya*. I discuss this in more detail later. Magic? Possible.

6. *Wishy-washy monism.* Consciousness and matter are two different ways of looking at the same reality, like the two sides of the same coin or the two apparent sides of a Möbius strip. Magic? Possible.

7. *Cynical nihilism.* Neither consciousness nor matter exists. Everything's a pointless illusion. This is the refuge of suicidal philosophers, nihilistic skeptics, and a majority of college sophomores. *No magic for you.*

REALITY AND INFORMATION

With these seven interpretations in mind, an interesting scientific trend is emerging. It used to be that we'd expect only philosophers enthusiastic about Eastern or Western versions of idealism to talk openly about reality emerging from consciousness. But now we see an increasing number of mainstream scientists and scholars openly proposing this idea. Some suggest that reality literally *is* information, like a cosmic conscious hologram.[28] Others talk about reality as a mathematical or a supercomputer-based simulation. A 2016 article in the online magazine *BBC Earth* cites technology entrepreneur Elon Musk, MIT cosmologist Alan Guth, MIT physicist Seth Lloyd, University of Oxford philosopher Nick Bostrom, Nobel laureate astrophysicist George Smoot, and others, as fans of the idea that we're living inside a simulation.[29]

These themes have been extensively explored since the 1940s in science fiction literature, television programs, and movies, perhaps most famously as the central theme in the *Matrix* movie trilogy. The connection between these ideas and magic is obvious, at least to magicians. As Patrick Dunn, a magician specializing in semiotics (signs and symbols), wrote in his 2005 book, *Postmodern Magic*:

> Information does everything we claim energy or spirits do: it is nonphysical yet interacts with matter; it is manipulated with the human mind and stored in symbols; it can be copied, transported, and transformed instantly; and science even studies it. So, the information paradigm is a splendid model for what we're doing when we do magic. After all, the brain deals with information in quantities far greater than the miniscule electrical impulses passing between its neurons. If my mind can cause change on a symbolic level, perhaps it really can cause change. Perhaps the information passing through my mind also passes through the world at large—everything being connected to the same matrix.[30]

Let's examine this trend in more detail. In 2013, the Foundational Questions Institute held an essay contest on John Wheeler's famous question, "It from bit or bit from it?"[31] The contest attracted 170 entries. The institute's 2015 contest was on the topic "The mysterious connection between physics and mathematics." In 2017, the theme was "How can mindless mathematical laws give rise to aims and intention?" The director of the Foundational Questions Institute, MIT physicist Max Tegmark, described the burgeoning interest in these questions in his 2014 book, *Our Mathematical Universe*:

> There's something very mathematical about our Universe, and . . . the more carefully we look, the more math we seem to find. So what do we make of all these hints of mathematics in our physical world? Most of my physics colleagues take them to mean that nature is for some reason described by mathematics, at least approximately, and leave it at that. But I'm convinced that there's more to it.[32]

Tegmark assumes that "there exists an external physical reality completely independent of us humans." But as we've already discussed, there are good reasons to believe that reality is actually *not* completely independent of observation. So what Tegmark is getting at is that the abstract structures provided by mathematics seem to have a life of their own. They don't just describe it; in some sense, he believes, the purely symbolic language of mathematics literally *is* the universe.

This resonates with an earlier consideration by Nobel laureate physicist Eugene Wigner, who marveled over the astonishing ability of mathematics to accurately describe the behavior of the physical world. He noted that in spite of the baffling complexities of the world some features are stable enough, and we've been clever or lucky enough to identify them as "laws of nature." Without those regularities science never would have developed. Wigner believed it was neither natural nor expected that such laws of nature should exist, much less that we've been able to discover some of them.

Like Wigner, mathematician Sir Roger Penrose also noted

that "some of the basic physical laws are precise to an extraordinary degree, far beyond the precision of our direct sense experiences or the combined calculational powers of all conscious individuals within the ken of mankind."[33] Penrose cited Newton's gravitational theory as applied to the movements of the solar system. The theory is precise to one part in 10 million. Einstein's theory of relativity improved on Newton's by another factor of 10 million, and it also predicted bizarre new effects such as black holes and gravitational lenses. When astrophysicists went looking for these unexpected phenomena, to everyone's astonishment (except maybe Einstein's) they found them.

Penrose suggested that the amazing accuracy of these mathematical predictions "was not the result of a new theory being introduced only to make sense of vast amounts of new data. The extra precision was seen only *after* each theory had been produced."[34] One way to interpret these astounding coincidences is that pure math is in contact with Plato's concept of primordial Forms or Ideas. This again implies that we live within a symbolic reality.

For those who insist that mind and consciousness are nothing more than bioelectrical circuits in the brain, then mathematics too must be nothing more than the brain's representation of a preexisting, independent, external physical world. That seems reasonable enough until we realize that the symbols generated by three pounds of neural tissue somehow describe not only vast swatches of the physical universe to an unbelievably precise degree, but they also predict phenomena that strongly contradict common sense, such as quantum entanglement and black holes.

How is it possible for a hunk of warm, wet tissue to not only describe itself in exquisite detail but also describe exotic realms that the human body and brain cannot access through its ordinary senses, and that must have been around for billions of years before we developed methods of detecting them. And do all this with mind-boggling accuracy? That puzzling question suggests that maybe the brain didn't dream up these ideas after all. Rather, *the ideas dreamed up the brain.*

If that's the case, then, as magic proposes, we really do shape the world based on our expectations. Think of the thousands of physicists and engineers at CERN's Large Hadron Collider near Geneva, Switzerland, all working feverishly for years to detect the Higgs boson. In 2012, they rejoiced at finally seeing something that looked like the Higgs.[35] But some viewed that success as a little too convenient, as Harriet Kim Jarlett posted on the CERN website in October 2016:

> When researchers discovered the Higgs boson in 2012, it was a huge moment of achievement. It showed theorists had been right to look towards the Standard Model for answers about our Universe. *But then the particle acted just like the theorists said it would, it obeyed every rule they predicted.* If it had acted just slightly differently it would have raised many questions about the theory, and our universe. Instead, it raised few questions and gave no new clues about to where to look next. In other words, the theorists had done too good a job.[36]

A SYMBOLIC REALITY

Mathematics is the language of physics, and Max Tegmark thinks that mathematics *is* the universe. But despite the appeal of symbolic and informational models of reality, there's a big problem: Gödel's incompleteness theorems. Mathematician Kurt Gödel *proved*—that's a word not to be taken lightly—that no system of mathematics can be considered complete. Any non-trivial mathematical or logic system will be either incomplete or inconsistent.

And that in turn means the universe cannot be completely modeled with mathematics. Said another way, a symbolic language *by itself* can describe physical reality amazingly well, but something will always be left out. Is that something "outside" the physical world, meaning nonphysical? Could the missing element be consciousness?

From a religious perspective, a theist may enthusiastically agree and point to biblical scripture such as John 1:1: "In the beginning was the Word, and the Word was with God, and the Word was God." That poetic phrase is intriguing, but poetry doesn't provide much explanatory power. For that we'll have to turn to science, but it's not going to be easy. As physicists Sara Walker and Paul Davies explained:

> We propose that the hard problem of life is the problem of how "information" can affect the world. . . . [W]e suspect that a full resolution of the hard problem *will not ultimately be reducible to known physical principles*. . . . If we are so lucky as to stumble on a new fundamental understanding of life, it could be such a radical departure from what we know now that it might be left to the next generation of physicists to reconcile the unification of life with other domains of physics.[37]

What the trend in information physics suggests is illustrated in Figure 16 (see page 205). The hierarchical structure of science remains exactly the same as before, except that now the "bottom" of the hierarchy is Universal Consciousness [C]. The physical world emerges from [C], and the top of the pyramid is the mind, meaning the brain's machinery involved in information processing, cognition, and perception. From this perspective we enjoy conscious awareness not because the brain generates it, but because [C] permeates every layer of the physical world, just like electrons permeate every layer "above" the discipline of phys-

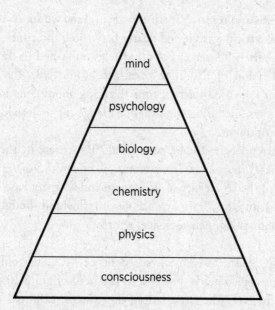

Figure 16. A more comprehensive knowledge hierarchy.

ics. Based on this hierarchy, *which maintains everything currently known in science*, so we don't have to throw away any of our textbooks, magic is no longer an impossible anomaly. It's now a predictable consequence of understanding reality from a more comprehensive perspective.

CONSCIOUSNESS AS FUNDAMENTAL

Scholarly interest in consciousness as a fundamental property of reality has always existed, mainly among philosophers. But now it's increasingly appearing within science, and unlike in times past, scientists today are far more open to this possibility. In 2014, the online journal *Frontiers in Human Neuroscience*, the #1 most-cited journal in academic psychology, published an article entitled "A Call for an Open, Informed Study of All Aspects of Consciousness."[38] It was signed by 101 scientists from universities and research institutes around the world. As of mid-2017 this article was viewed nearly fifty thousand times, which is greater than 99 percent of all articles published in the *Frontiers* collection of fifty-nine open-access journals. The article called for increased tolerance for thinking about consciousness in new ways, including ways that challenge the materialistic scientific worldview.

This trend can also be seen in a 2015 article in the ultra-orthodox *Philosophical Transactions of the Royal Society*. Giulio Tononi of the University of Wisconsin and Christof Koch of the Allen Institute for Brain Science, both influential thought leaders in mainstream neuroscience, wrote:

> Is consciousness—subjective experience— . . . not only in other people's heads, but also in the head of animals? And perhaps everywhere, pervading the cosmos, as in old panpsychist traditions and in the Beatles' song? While these kinds of questions may seem scientifically inappropriate, we argue below that they can be approached in a principled and testable manner.[39]

The long-held taboo that once prohibited scientists from even mentioning the word *consciousness*, especially the heretical idea that consciousness might "pervade the cosmos," required that Tononi and Koch add an apology to their proposal. But in a less formal publication, Koch was more forthcoming. In a 2014 article in *Scientific American*, entitled "Is Consciousness Universal?," he wrote:

> The mental is too radically different for it to arise gradually from the physical. This emergence of subjective feelings from physical stuff appears inconceivable and is at odds with a basic precept of physical thinking, the Ur-conservation law—*ex nihilo nihil fit* [out of nothing comes nothing]. . . .

The phenomenal hails from a kingdom other than the physical and is subject to different laws.[40]

We've already discussed Max Tegmark's ideas and the essay contest of the Foundational Questions Institute. But we also find statements like this in 2005, offered by the eminent quantum physicist Anton Zeilinger, of the University of Vienna: "Reality and information are the same. We need a new concept which encompasses both. In a sense, reality and information are the two sides of the same coin. I feel that this is the message of the quantum."[41] Or this by New York University science writer Charles Siefe in his 2007 book, *Decoding the Universe*: "Information appears, quite literally, to shape our universe."[42] Or an idea by physicist Vlatko Vedral, in his similarly titled 2012 book, *Decoding Reality*:

Information (and not matter or energy or love) is the building block on which everything is constructed. Information is far more fundamental than matter or energy. . . . Information can also be used to explain the origin and behaviour of microscopic interactions such as energy and matter. . . . Information, in contrast to matter and energy, is the only concept that we currently have that can explain its own origin.[43]

Entire journal issues are now devoted to the mathematics and physics of consciousness.[44] And post-materialistic ideas are appearing in new journals dedicated to consciousness studies, including *Psychology of Consciousness*, published by the voice of mainstream academic psychology, the American Psychological Association (APA).[45] In 2016, the APA also published a book entitled *Transcendent Mind*, by psychologist Imants Barušs of King's University College in Canada and neuroscientist Julia Mossbridge of the Institute of Noetic Sciences. Barušs and Mossbridge emphasized this growing movement:

We are in the midst of a sea change. Receding from view is materialism, whereby physical phenomena are assumed to be primary and consciousness is regarded as secondary. Approaching our sights is a complete reversal of perspective. According to this alternative view, consciousness is primary and the physical is secondary. In other words, materialism is receding and giving way to ideas about reality in which consciousness plays a key role.[46]

The same trend can be found in biology. Physician Neil Theise and physicist Menas Kafatos propose in a 2016 article in the journal *Communicative and Integrative Biology* that "non-dual awareness is foundational to the universe, not arising from the interactions or structures of higher level phenomena. . . . The cosmos . . . can be understood to derive *from* awareness rather than being suffused by it or giving rise to it."[47]

Medical researchers too are sensing a shift from solely materialistic models of health and healing. This can be seen as an exponential rise of publications on the role of spirituality in health and healing. Based on a search on PubMed, the U.S. government's online National Library of Medicine, we find that from 1940 to 2016 some 2,645 articles were published on the topic of "spirituality in medicine." Nearly all of those articles were published since 2000. Before 1980, a grand total of two articles were published, indicating that until the twenty-first century mainstream medicine had little interest in nonmaterial concepts like spirituality.

The same trend is evident in complexity theory. Stuart A. Kauffman, one of the principals at the famed Santa Fe Institute and a pioneer in the study of complex systems, writes in his 2016 book, *Humanity in a Creative Universe*:

From Newton we achieved and are now trapped by the view that there is a "theory of everything," reductive materialism, whose laws will "govern" and logically "entail" all that can or does become since the Big Bang, but are themselves somehow "outside of the universe." This is the Pythagorean dream of a mathematizable world. I aim to show that this view is surely false for the living world and perhaps aspects of the abiotic world. . . .

To solve the enigma, I will propose that we are conscious and so are quantum variables such as electrons and protons exchanging photons measuring one another, where measurement is mediated, I claim, by consciously observing one another. I cannot see any way of showing that electrons consciously measure one other, but [Dean] Radin's experiments are a first hint that we can show how human consciousness can "mediate" measurement, perhaps even nonlocally. . . .

This all leads to a vast panpsychism, in which all quantum measurement is mediated by Mind, conscious and freewilled, as part of the furniture of the entire universe! It is the enigma all the way down. Mind is part of the actual becoming of the universe.[48]

In philosophy, the discipline that has been struggling to understand the nature of reality thousands of years before science appeared, we increasingly find opinions like those of philosopher Philip Goff, of the Central European University in Budapest. Goff's position in a 2017 essay was bluntly entitled, "Panpsychism is crazy, but it's also most probably true."[49]

Philosophers Robert Koons, of the University of Texas at Austin, and George Bealer, of Yale University, write in their 2010 book, *The Waning of Materialism*,

Materialism is waning in a number of significant respects— one of which is the ever-growing number of major philosophers who reject materialism or at least have strong sympathies with anti-materialist views. It is of course commonly thought that over the course of the last sixty or so years materialism achieved hegemony in academic philosophy. . . . It is therefore surprising that an examination of the major philosophers active in this period reveals that a majority, or something approaching a majority, either rejected materialism or had serious and specific doubts about its ultimate viability.[50]

One of those "major philosophers" is Jerry Fodor from Rutgers University, who wrote, "I think it's strictly true that we can't, as things stand now, so much as imagine the solution of the hard problem [of explaining subjective awareness]. . . . I would prefer that the hard problem should turn out to be unsolvable if the alternative is that we're all too dumb to solve it."[51] And in case his position was not clear enough, Fodor emphasized that "nobody has the slightest idea how anything material could be conscious. Nobody even knows what it would be like to have the slightest idea about how anything could be conscious."[52] In a similar vein, the distinguished philosopher Thomas Nagel from New York University writes in his 2012 book, *Mind and Cosmos,*

It is prima facie highly implausible that life as we know it is the result of a sequence of physical accidents together with the mechanism of natural selection. . . . My skepticism is not based on religious belief, or on a belief in any definite alternative. . . . I realize that such doubts will strike many people as outrageous, but that is because almost everyone in our secular culture has been browbeaten into regarding the reductive research program as sacrosanct.[53]

The bottom line is this: Throughout science and scholarship a basic principle of the Perennial Philosophy—that consciousness is fundamental—is slowly becoming acceptable to talk about. Within science this notion tends to be cast into the more conventional language of information and mathematics, but the connection with consciousness is undeniable. After centuries of life-threatening suppression, the societal shift that now allows scientists and scholars to publicly discuss consciousness in a new light might seem like a trifling matter. But it's a positively *astounding* transformation.

In the world of academia, the primary currency is *ideas*. And like any form of currency, ideas are fervently protected. This makes acceptable currents in the mainstream move like molasses. Fortunately, given current trends, this particular molasses is beginning to heat up and pour like a fine maple syrup. If that flow continues to accelerate, then formerly esoteric concepts such as magic, and scientifically challenging phenomena such as psi, may soon be poised to transform into new, modernized forms.

Chapter 9

CONCLUDING THOUGHTS

The universe is full of magical things patiently waiting for our wits to grow sharper.

—EDEN PHILLPOTTS

WHY CAN'T I CREATE MY OWN REALITY?

If magic is real, then why can't I use it to solve big, intractable problems, such as poverty, disease, and war? Why can't I use it to make my personal dreams come true, every time?

You can, sort of.

For most fledgling magicians, most of the time, magic will be fragile and subtle. That's because three factors are working against you: reality inertia, lack of talent, and the unconscious. The first, as discussed briefly in Chapter 8, is that reality appears to be highly reactive to intention, but it's also elastic and fully interconnected. So when your intention warps the universe a bit here, then somewhere else a distortion is going to appear, and someone (or something) may not like it. So they (or it) will push back to repair the warp and maintain the status quo. Such rebound effects have been repeatedly observed in psi experiments studying the force of will. They've been variously labeled a "balancing" effect, a "differential" effect, a "release of effort" effect, and a "statistical equilibrium" effect.[1] The fabric of reality seems to prefer stability over chaos, and it's apparently highly adept at self-repair.

The second factor is that it isn't easy to achieve the state of gnosis, which is where magic happens. Yogis who diligently practice their craft for decades are not guaranteed to achieve the siddhis, the Eastern version of Western magic. Most dedicated practitioners are likely to spontaneously experience various powers occasionally, but for magic to work reliably under conscious control requires both steadfast practice *and* natural talent. Practice can be managed with persistence. Talent—you either have it or you don't.

The third factor is that consciously you might strongly desire something, but unconsciously you may not. This conflict leads to self-defeating behaviors that can neutralize or even reverse a magical effort. The unconscious is, by definition, hidden, below your awareness. The only way to unveil what's going on in the depths of your unconscious mind is through practices such as meditation, where you slowly peel away deeper and deeper layers of the mind, or by working with a psychotherapist who can more objectively sense what's going on, or by taking the right psychedelic drug in a supportive context. You say you're serious about losing weight, and yet every morning you have two buttered croissants with your coffee, and every evening you manage to eat an entire chocolate pie. Really? Let's talk about that.

Don't feel disappointed that magic isn't as strong as it's portrayed in fiction. It's actually fortunate that magic is fairly weak. It prevents us from accidentally blowing up the universe with our momentary whims. This danger is a perennial theme in folktales that warn us of the thrill of unleashing a genie from a bottle. As a reward, the genie gives us three wishes. What could go wrong? Basically, everything. These stories hardly ever end well. They are cautionary tales about the consequences of releasing our uncontrolled or unthinking desires.

PSYCHIC ROBOTS

The human brain and body are a superb host for Universal Consciousness [C]. This living form offers many paths for personal consciousness [c] to realize it's the same as [C]. But there could be countless other ways that [C] might be expressed, especially in systems that are sufficiently complex for [c] to become self-reflective. There's no reason, for example, that a suitably constructed robot brain and body couldn't also host a self-aware form of [c]. If that turns out to be the case, then it's a good bet that not only will robots eventually make humans redundant, as Bill Gates, Elon Musk, and Stephen Hawking have been warning us, but conscious robots may also be profoundly psychic wizards.[2]

That's because in principle a robot would have much better control over the psychological and brain-oriented factors (like the hyperanalytical frontal lobes) that seem to be particularly effective in blocking psychic awareness in humans. That is, we've been shaped by evolution to be highly effective at personal and social survival, which means we're exceptionally adept at avoiding predators, outwitting prey, and cooperating with others in our tribe. But we gained those skills at a price.

Our brains are very good at making snap judgments, quickly forming stereotypes, and responding to our needs here and now. We rarely need to know what's happening elsewhere. So everyday awareness has become a highly refined form of mental myopia, and this is exactly the opposite of the kind of expansive consciousness required to roam throughout the galaxy, peer deep into the past or future, or perform magic. When it's safe to set aside ordinary awareness and we dream, meditate, or take an entheogenic compound, we may momentarily escape the hardwiring that tightly binds us to the mundane present. But a robot mind with more refined control over its states of awareness won't have to worry about being eaten by a tiger. It will be able to skip over eons of evolutionary shaping. So it may quickly come to realize that [c] and [C] are identical, and that in turn suggests that a robot not only will be able to do everything you can do faster, better, and cheaper, it will also know everything you're thinking and will be able to perform incredibly powerful magic.

Levitating robot wizards . . . yet another reason to worry about the coming *singularity*—the day the robots become conscious.[3]

THE FUTURE OF MAGIC

Assuming we're smart enough to avoid a robot wizard Armageddon, imagine a future when we've developed a rational, scientific basis for magic, along with an applied technology. We'll be able to shape the fabric of reality at will, we'll know the far past and the far future, and we can enlist the assistance of nonhuman forms of intelligence.

Imagining such a future is a challenge because it requires a civilization unlike anything we've ever known. It would be more similar to stories about Atlantis or the mythological realm of the Olympian gods than to any of the scenarios based on projections of today's technologies. Most "realistic" visions of the future typically start with our present technologies, make them smaller and more ubiquitous, add a few genetically enhanced features, and then explore the deep consequences of everyone wearing identical silver jumpsuits.

It's probably fortunate that we won't have a robust science-based magic at our command in the short term. If a breakthrough technique allowed magic to appear overnight, it would very likely destroy the world. Think of a time when you've been waiting in a line at the Department of Motor Vehicles for two hours, and just as you finally reach the clerk she goes on a break and never returns. Now, multiply your flash of anger by seven billion. Two minutes after the switch is turned on that unleashes magic around the world, our world would end. Magician Peter Carroll agrees:

> If science ever did begin to make serious enquiry into magic, the result would be disaster. Humanity has proved itself totally incapable of handling even a moderately dangerous substance like plutonium with responsibility. Imagine what it would do with machine-enhanced sorcery or even simple, reliable telepathy. It is in the interests of the survival of the species that occultists continue to ridicule and discredit their own arts in the eyes of orthodox science.[4]

In light of the potential dangers, then what do I hope to achieve by writing a book like this? My goal is modest. I'd like to help dissolve the woo-woo taboo and its "paranormal" baggage. Many scientists and scholars, like the majority of the general public, are fascinated by esoteric topics. But very few are willing to risk the sociopolitical penalties of openly revealing their interests. It sounds crazy, but for some people the mere *idea* that psi or magic might be real can evoke violent reactions, just as the prejudices of race, gender, sexual identity, religion, or ethnicity evoke them. Humans are hardwired to quickly reject people and ideas that are different from us; "others" are dastardly and dangerous. These common tendencies must be identified and forcefully countered.

To sidestep expected prejudices, magic can be reframed as the academic study of the full capacities of consciousness in light of the rising interest in informational descriptions of reality. This would be a careful, deliberate, non-hysterical, rational process, and it would be wonderful if we can avoid feeling compelled to build the magical equivalent of an atomic bomb because we're afraid that someone else is going to win the magical arms race. If humanity has any chance of maturing beyond its barely controlled adolescence, we're going to need a much better understanding of what consciousness is, and what it—and by association all of us—are really capable of.

WHERE'S THE ALIEN?

We're not going to discover intelligent extraterrestrials (ETs) by scanning the heavens for the alien equivalent of Top 40 pop hits wafting out of the Andromeda galaxy on radio waves. Electromagnetic broadcasts are extremely primitive means of communication. We've been beaming them in the open for only about fifty years, and most communications are now carried digitally underground by fiber optics. Using giant radio telescopes in hopes of spotting signals from ETs is like trying to talk to star people using smoke signals. It's not impossible, but I wouldn't suggest you hold your breath waiting for a reply.

Imagine an intelligent species a few thousand or a few million years more advanced than us. They are likely to know far more about consciousness and what it can do than what we currently understand. What we crudely call magic they may understand to an exquisitely fine degree. They won't need physical rockets to traverse the universe. They won't even need science-fiction-style warp-drive ships, or for that matter any ships at all. If we can already see tiny space-time warps in our little laboratory psi experiments, then they'd be able to manipulate huge chunks of space-time like slabs of soft butter. They would be able to spy on us, perhaps even *embody* us, from the dark side of distant galaxies, far better than we're able to spy on friends and enemies with today's aerial drones.

If extraterrestrials are watching, they may well have decided that as a species, we're still basically infants, spending most of our time sleeping, pooping, or crying. We haven't reached out to say hello via humanity's global telepathic mind because we're still enthralled with the cowboy myth of rugged individualism.[5] What other than our planet-sized ego makes us think that the conscious universe of galactic minds would be interested in engaging with infants?

SECRET ADEPTS

What may be easier to imagine than a future magic-based civilization is a magic developed behind the scenes and used by secret cabals on behalf of humanity. The Marvel comic book series and 2016 movie *Dr. Strange* offer a popular representation of that enduring esoteric fantasy. That scenario is more likely to manifest in the short run than a widespread public application of rational magic. In fact, we know it's more than just likely. It's also true.

Psychics have been employed by police departments, governments, and businesses throughout history.[6] From the 1970s through 1990s, the United States and the Soviet Union each maintained highly classified programs of psi research and applications.[7] Government interest in the use of psi remained strong for a purely pragmatic reason—it provided useful information when no other sources were available.

In December 1979, a ninety-four-page classified report was issued by the U.S. Army. The report contained an assessment of one of the U.S. government's early top-secret psi programs, which was code-named Grill Flame.[8] That report, stamped "SECRET / CLOSE HOLD / HAND CARRY," was declassified in 2003 by a Freedom of Information Act request. The Grill Flame review committee consisted of nine experts representing expertise in psychiatry, biostatistics, psychology, physics, engineering, and operations research. These individuals were prescreened to ensure that they had no preconceived opinions about psi, either for or against. The purpose of the review, one of many conducted over the two decades of the U.S. government's involvement, was as follows:

> The prime motivation for the professional commitment invested by the committee members was based on the high potential payoff which the parapsychological phenomena could have for the military and intelligence communities, if, indeed, such effects could be harnessed, controlled, and further advanced.

Their assessment of the evidence was stated in careful, measured terms:

> On balance, the Committee has indeed been persuaded that there is some probability that effects attributed to the [remote viewing] phenomena exist under unexplained circumstances and in conjunction with particular individuals.

Another classified review nearly two decades later, issued by the Defense Intelligence Agency, concluded that progress had been made:

> The evidence for a valid information transfer anomaly [a euphemism the committee used for remote viewing] meets all recognized statistical and methodological criteria. This means the anomaly cannot be explained by poor experimental design, incorrect protocols, faulty analyses, or fraud. The magnitude of this anomaly is considered to be medium-to-large when compared to other known human behaviors.[9]

It's important to appreciate that these reports were not intended for public consumption. The government agencies seeking these reviews were charged with two no-nonsense questions:

Do reports of psi phenomena represent a threat to national security? And can these abilities, assuming they exist, be used for espionage? The answers were in the affirmative. The same conclusions were reached by many other U.S. government reviews, both classified and in the public domain.

If this is so, then why, when you surf the Internet looking for answers, does the question of the *existence* of psi remain so controversial? The simple truth is that people believe what they want to believe. And now that you've read this book, you also know that the controversy persists because psi implies magic, and nearly everyone within Western culture, especially those in academia, and even more so those who hold strong religious beliefs, have been influenced by thousands of years of negative propaganda. Thus, to maintain comfort, we've collectively agreed to relocate real magic into entertainment and fiction, where it happily earns billions of dollars.

SPIRITUAL MATERIALISM

A proportion of those who are sincerely dedicated to esoteric practices, especially meditation, will at some point come to a fork in the road. Are they interested in transcending the tribulations of being human and go for enlightenment? Or would they rather go for power? Both paths are possible.

Enlightenment occurs when personal consciousness realizes that it is identical with Universal Consciousness. This is not just an appreciation of the abstract idea that I've summarized as $[c] = [C]$, but a direct, tangible, certain realization of this identity. This is the principal truth described by mystics throughout history, and individuals who glimpse that truth often describe it as the most profound transformational event in their lifetime. Or, if they believe in reincarnation, then it's the culmination of all of their lifetimes. Defining *precisely* what enlightenment means is not a simple matter because the experience itself is so far from the everyday world. As meditation teacher Shinzen Young puts it,

> You can think of enlightenment as a kind of permanent shift in perspective that comes about through direct realization that there is no thing called "self" inside you.[10]

To be clear, it's not that [c] isn't *real*, but rather that it misidentifies itself with the brain and the body. That misapprehension is what maintains the sense of personal ego and separateness, and that's why magic and the esoteric principle of interconnectedness clash so violently with common sense. Bodies are separate, and minds certainly seem to be locked inside them. So how could my intentions affect anything outside of me? How can I know what someone else is thinking? How can I tell what will happen tomorrow?

As we've seen, based on the current scientific worldview, *you can't*.

But within the esoteric worldview there is no outside world, no separation, no time. Everything is already *within* consciousness, which is beyond ordinary space-time. Said another way, when the Indian sage Ramana Maharshi was asked, "How are we to treat others?" his reply was simple: "There are no others."

As personal consciousness [c] draws closer to Universal Consciousness [C] the sense of separateness begins to decrease and incidents of psychic perception, synchronicities, and manifested intentions begin to increase. These powers can be intoxicating and seductive, which is why in most meditation traditions the student is advised to just regard these phenomena as yardsticks along the path to enlightenment. Don't dwell on them. By contrast, within the magical traditions these powers are exactly what you're attempting to achieve.

Compared to the lofty goals of enlightenment, magic is more commonly associated with the acquisition of egotistical power.

But that's just a stereotype. Magic can also be used for healing, counseling, enhancing survival, and reducing suffering. The range of possibilities spanning the spiritual-material axis is vast.

THE BOTTOM LINE

Many scientific and scholarly disciplines are slowly coming around to the idea that consciousness is far more important than previously imagined. This shift of opinion, combined with the idea that reality is a form of information, provides a renewed appreciation of ancient esoteric legends about magic. If we can get past the supernatural connotations, the religious fears and prohibitions, and the occult baggage, then through the scientific study of magic we have the potential to make rapid progress in gaining a better understanding of who and what we are. If we can't escape our past, then we may be running headlong into extinction.[11]

Magic is real.

Let's deal with it.

NOTES

CHAPTER 1: BEGINNING

1. Douthat, R. (December 24, 2016). Varieties of religious experience. *New York Times*.

2. Alexander, E. (2012). *Proof of Heaven: A Neurosurgeon's Journey into the Afterlife*. Simon & Schuster.

3. Douthat, R. (December 24, 2016). Varieties of religious experience. *New York Times*. Also Friedkin, W. (October 2016). The Devil and Father Amorth: Witnessing "the Vatican Exorcist" at work. *Vanity Fair*.

4. Shermer, M. (September 1, 2016). Is it possible to measure supernatural or paranormal phenomena? *Scientific American*.

5. This quote by Twain is doubly instructive. Besides suggesting in Twain's charming style that "what everyone knows" ain't necessarily so, there's no evidence that Twain ever wrote or spoke this quip. See Shephard, A. (2015). "It ain't what you don't know that gets you in trouble," which must be why *The Big Short* opens with a fake Mark Twain quote. *New Republic*. newrepublic.com/minutes/126677/it-aint-dont-know-gets-trouble-must-big-short-opens-fake-mark-twain-quote.

6. Shermer, M. (September 1, 2016). Is it possible to measure supernatural or paranormal phenomena? *Scientific American*.

7. Shermer, M. (October 1, 2014). Anomalous events that can shake one's skepticism to the core. *Scientific American*.

8. Loftus, E. F. (1993). The reality of repressed memories. *American Psychologist*, 48, 518–537.

9. Carroll, P. J. (1987). *Liber Null & Psychonaut: An Introduction to Chaos Magic*. Red Wheel Weiser. Kindle ed., 162.

10. From Sartre's 1943 play, *No Exit*.

11. Brayton, E. (October 20, 2016). Wiles prayed for God to confuse Hillary's mind so she'd lose debate. *Patheos*.

12. Hughes, M. M. (February 16, 2017). A spell to bind Donald Trump and all those who abet him: February 24th. *ExtraNewsfeed*.

13. "Notes: Black Magic." Faust.com. faust.com/legend/black-magic/notes.

CHAPTER 2: SCIENCE AND MAGIC?

1. Birch, H., Stuart, C., & Looi, M. K. (August 31, 2013). The 20 big questions in science. *Guardian*.

2. Churchland, P. (1989). *Neurophilosophy: Toward a Unified Science of the Mind-Brain*. Bradford. Also Dennett, D. C. (1992). *Consciousness Explained*. Back Bay Books.

3. I'm avoiding the use of technical jargon as much as possible. If this were an academic paper, I'd use the phrase "neural correlates of consciousness." When I think it's useful to elaborate on technical issues, I'll put them here in the endnotes.

4. Psi is simply the letter *p* in Greek. It refers to the first letter of the word *psyche*, a term that encompasses all aspects of the mind, including cognition, perception, awareness, and metaphysical concepts such as soul and spirit. It is not an acronym, nor is it pronounced "P-S-I."

5. I've attended many private scientific meetings on parapsychological topics, including one held at the U.S. National Academy of Sciences. Based on what I've seen, and the inquiries I regularly receive, my impression is that the *majority* of scientists and scholars are personally interested in psi, but they've learned to keep their interests quiet. The same is true for many government, military, and business leaders I've met. The taboo is much stronger in the Western world (e.g., United States, Europe, Australia) than it is in Asia and South America.

6. Newport, F., & Strausberg, M. (June 8, 2001). Americans' belief in psychic and paranormal phenomena is up over last decade. Gallup. Moore, D. W. (June 16, 2005). Three in four Americans believe in paranormal. Gallup. Cosgrover-Mather, B. (April 29, 2002). Poll: Most believe in psychic phenomena. CBS News.

7. A list of affiliates of the AAAS is at www.aaas.org/aaas-affiliates.

8. The Parapsychological Association was founded in 1957 and has been an elected affiliate of the American Association for the Advancement of Science since 1969.

9. Moore, D. W. (June 16, 2005). Three in four Americans believe in paranormal. Gallup.

10. Winkelman, M. (1982). Magic: A theoretical reassessment. *Current An-*

thropology, 23(1), 37–66. Roney-Dougal, S. (1991). *Where Science and Magic Meet*. Element Books.

11. Bonewits, I. (1989). *Real Magic: An Introductory Treatise on the Basic Principles of Yellow Magic*. Red Wheel Weiser. Kindle ed.

12. Bonewits used terms like *clairgustance*, meaning "sensing a taste from a distance," and *psychopyresis*, meaning "mentally causing fire."

13. Dunn, P. (2005). *Postmodern Magic: The Art of Magic in the Information Age*. Llewelyn. Kindle ed., 385–386.

14. White, G. (2016). *Pieces of Eight: Chaos Magic Essays and Enchantments*. Amazon Digital Services. Kindle ed.

15. Johns Hopkins Archaeological Museum. (n.d.) An unpublished magic spell from late antiquity. archaeologicalmuseum.jhu.edu/the-collection /object-stories/an-unpublished-magic-spell-from-late-antiquity.

16. Gardiner, P. (2006). *Gnosis: The Secret of Solomon's Temple Revealed*. Career Press, 207.

CHAPTER 3: MAGICAL POTPOURRI

1. Google search on *magick*, as of April 10, 2017.

2. List of bestselling books. (Accessed July 19, 2017). *Wikipedia*. Also see Moore, J. (Accessed July 19, 2017). The bestselling books of all time. Ranker.com. ranker.com/list/best-selling-books-of-all-time/jeff419.

3. List of highest-grossing movies. (Accessed July 19, 2017). *Wikipedia*. Also see All time worldwide box office grosses. (Accessed July 19, 2017). *Box Office Mojo*.

4. Ortal-Paz, S. (Fall 2010). Some observations on Jewish love magic: The importance of cultural specificity. *Societas Magica Newsletter*.

5. Gideon, B. (2008). *Ancient Jewish Magic: A History*. Cambridge University Press.

6. It's unlikely that a Roman magician would have used a Yiddish word in a love spell. But this book is rated PG.

7. Okay, this is an exaggeration to highlight the cultural differences.

8. Eneborg, Y. M. (2013). *Ruqya shariya*: Observing the rise of a new faith healing tradition amongst Muslims in east London. *Mental Health, Religion & Culture*, 16(10), 1080–1096.

9. Hanegraaff, W. J. (2013). *Western Esotericism: A Guide for the Perplexed*. Bloomsbury. Kindle ed., 45–46.

10. Georgetown University, Center for Applied Research in the Apostolate. (Accessed July 19, 2017). Frequently requested church statistics. georgetown.edu/frequently-requested-church-statistics.

11. Catechism of the Catholic Church. Part 3, Section 3, Chapter 1, Article I.III, 2116–2117. www.vatican.va/archive/ENG0015/__P7E.HTM.

12. Brunner, B. (Accessed July 19, 2017). Banned books: From *Harriet the Spy* to *The Catcher in the Rye*. *InfoPlease*.

13. Ross, S. (Accessed July 19, 2017). Harry Potter banned? *InfoPlease*.

14. American Library Association. (Accessed July 19, 2017). Top ten most challenged books list. ala.org/bbooks/frequentlychallengedbooks/top10.

15. Gerson, M. (October 26, 2007). Harry Potter's secret. *Washington Post*.

16. Barrett, T. (October 29, 2007). More proof that Harry Potter harms kids. *Conservative Truth*.

17. Hanegraaff, W. J. (2013). *Western Esotericism: A Guide for the Perplexed*. Bloomsbury. Kindle ed., 64.

18. Bailey, M. D. (April 2006). The disenchantment of magic: Spells, charms, and superstition in early European witchcraft literature. *American Historical Review*, 111(2), 383–404.

19. Bogdan, H. (2012). Modern Western magic. *Aries: Journal for the Study of Western Esotericism*, new series, 12, 1–16.

20. Davies, O. (2012). *Magic: A Very Short Introduction*. Oxford University Press, 16, citing Tylor, E. B. (1920). *Primitive Culture: Researches into the Development of Mythology, Philosophy, Religion, Language, Art, and Custom*. 6th ed. John Murray.

21. Davies, O. (2012). *Magic: A Very Short Introduction*. Oxford University Press, 1.

22. Frazer, J. G. (1922). *The Golden Bough*. Macmillan, 222.

23. Kroeber, A. L. (1923). *Anthropology*. Harcourt, Brace, 298.

24. University of Chicago Press website description of Betz, H. D. (1992). *The Greek Magical Papyri in Translation, Including the Demotic Spells*, vol. 1. University of Chicago Press. press.uchicago.edu/ucp/books/book/chicago/G/bo3684249.html.

25. Davies, O. (2012). *Magic: A Very Short Introduction*. Oxford University Press, 32.

26. Betz, H. D. (1992). *The Greek Magical Papyri in Translation, Including the Demotic Spells*, vol. 1. University of Chicago Press, xlviii.

27. Winkelman, M. (1982). Magic: A theoretical reassessment. *Current Anthropology*, 23(1), 37–66.

28. Luke, D. (2010). Anthropology and parapsychology: Still hostile sisters in science? *Time and Mind: The Journal of Archaeology, Consciousness and Culture*, 3(3), 245–266.

29. Eliade, M. (1964). *Shamanism: Archaic Techniques of Ecstasy*. Translated by W. R. Trask. Routledge and Kegan Paul, 87.

30. Lyon, W. S. (2016). The necessity to rethink magic. *Journal for the Study of Religion, Nature and Culture*, 10(2), 214.

31. Grove, S. (September 12, 2011). Africa's modern day witch hunt, *Newsweek*.

32. Onyulo, T. (February 27, 2015). Witch hunts increase in Tanzania as albino deaths jump. *USA Today*.

33. Horowitz, M. (July 4, 2014). The persecution of witches, 21st-century style. *New York Times*.

34. Mullick, M. S. I., Khalifab, N., Nahara, J. S., & Walker, D.-M. (2013). Beliefs about Jinn, black magic and evil eye in Bangladesh: The effects of gender and level of education. *Mental Health, Religion & Culture*, 16(7), 719–729.

35. Schlier, B., et al. (2015). The community assessment of psychic experiences measures nine clusters of psychosis-like experiences: A validation of the German version of the CAPE. *Schizophrenia Research*, 169(1–3), 274–279.

36. Williams, L. M., & Irwin, H. J. (1991). A study of paranormal belief, magical ideation as an index of schizotypy and cognitive style. *Personality & Individual Differences*, 12(12), 1339–1348.

37. Subbotsky, E. (January–March 2014). The belief in magic in the age of science. *SAGE Open*, 1–17. Lipka, M. (November 4, 2015). Americans' faith in God may be eroding. Pew Research Center. www.pewresearch.org/fact-tank/2015/11/04/americans-faith-in-god-may-be-eroding. Hutson, M. (2012). *The 7 Laws of Magical Thinking: How Irrational Beliefs Keep Us Happy, Healthy, and Sane*. Penguin. Kindle ed., 72–73. Mohr, C., et al. (2014). Priming psychic and conjuring abilities of a magic demonstration influences event interpretation and random number generation biases. *Frontiers in Psychology*, 5, 1542. Stavrova, O., & Meckel, A. (2017). The role of magical thinking in forecasting the future. *British Journal of Psychology*, 108(1), 148–168. Streuli, J. C., et al. (2017). Children's left-turning preference is not modulated by magical ideation. *Laterality*, 22(1), 90–104.

38. Risen, J. L. (2016). Believing what we do not believe: Acquiescence to superstitious beliefs and other powerful intuitions. *Psychological Review*, 123(2), 182–207.

39. Suttie, J. (November 13, 2012). What's so magical about magical thinking? *Greater Good Magazine*. Greater Good Science Center. University of California, Berkeley.

40. Valdesolo, P. (October 19, 2010). Why "magical thinking" works for some people. *Scientific American*.

CHAPTER 4: ORIGINS OF MAGIC

1. *Entheogenic*, meaning "God- or divine-generating," is a word used more often now than earlier terms with negative connotations, like *hallucinogenic*.

2. Smith, H. (2000). *Cleansing the Doors of Perception: The Religious Significance of Entheogenic Plants and Chemicals*. Jeremy P. Tarcher/Putnam.

3. Walsh, R. (2007). *The World of Shamanism: New Views of an Ancient Tradition*. Llewellyn.

4. Jaspers, K. (1953). *The Origin and Goal of History*. Translated by Michael Bullock. Yale University Press. Stefon, M. (Accessed July 19, 2017). The Axial Age: 5 fast facts. List: Philosophy & Religion. *Encyclopaedia Britannica*.

5. Cook, G. (October 4, 2011). History and the decline of human violence. *Scientific American*.

6. Underhill, E. (2002). *Mysticism: A Study in the Nature and Development of Spiritual Consciousness*. Dover, 235.

7. Conway, D. (1985). *Secret Wisdom: The Occult Universe Explored*. Jonathan Cape, 136–157.

8. Mark, J. J. (January 18, 2012). The Eleusinian Mysteries: The Rites of Demeter. *Ancient History Encyclopedia*. Keller, M. L. (2009). The ritual path of initiation into the Eleusinian Mysteries. *Rosicrucian Digest, 2*.

9. Mark, J. J. (January 18, 2012). The Eleusinian Mysteries: The Rites of Demeter. *Ancient History Encyclopedia*.

10. Burkert, W. (1987). Themistios fragment 168, translation. *Ancient Mystery Cults*. Harvard University Press, 91–92.

11. Valencic, I. (1994). Has the mystery of the Eleusinian Mysteries been solved? *Yearbook for Ethnomedicine and the Study of Consciousness*, 3, 325–336.

12. Voltaire (1694–1778) once quipped that the Holy Roman Empire was neither holy, nor Roman, nor an empire.

13. James, W. (1902). *The Varieties of Religious Experience*. Modern Library, 380–381.

14. Carroll, P. J. (1987). *Liber Null & Psychonaut: An Introduction to Chaos Magic*. Red Wheel Weiser. Kindle ed., 122–124.

15. Heinlein, R. A. (1961). *Stranger in a Strange Land*. Penguin, 213.

16. Lewis, B. (2008). The Arab destruction of the library of Alexander: Anatomy of a myth. In el-Abbadi, M., & Mounir, O. (eds.), *What Happened to the Ancient Library of Alexander?* Brill.

17. El-Abbadi, M. (January 3, 2017). Library of Alexandria. *Encyclopaedia Britannica*. Chesser, P. (n.d.). The burning of the library of Alexandria. eHistory. ehistory.osu.edu/articles/burning-library-alexandria.

18. Pliny the Elder. (1963). *Natural History*. Vol. 8. Translated by W. H. S. Jones. Harvard University Press, Book 30, II. Given that the roots of magic are often traced to the Middle East, one may wonder why the historical genealogy of esoteric lore seems to hover mostly around European scholars. Many scholars from the Middle East, Asia, and India were deeply involved with magic, including Muslim scholars al-Kindi and Suhrawardi. I'm just restricting the scope of what I can cover in a single chapter because the focus is on science and magic, and not on the enormously rich history of esotericism in general.

19. Pliny the Elder. (1963). *Natural History*. Vol. 8. Translated by W. H. S. Jones. Harvard University Press, Book 30, I.

20. Pliny the Elder. (1963). *Natural History*. Vol. 8. Translated by W. H. S. Jones. Harvard University Press, Book 30, XI.

21. Singla, S., & Kaur, S. (2016). Biological activities of cow urine: An Ayurvedic elixir. *European Journal of Pharmaceutical and Medical Research*, 3(4), 118–124.

22. Marrone, S. P. (2015). *A History of Science, Magic and Belief: From Medieval to Early Modern Europe*. Palgrave, xvi, 317.

23. About the Nag Hammadi Library (The Nag Hammadi Scriptures). (n.d.). The Gnostic Society Library. gnosis.org/naghamm/nhl.html.

24. Pagels, E. (1979). *The Gnostic Gospels*. Vintage Books.

25. Hanegraaff, W. J. (2013). *Western Esotericism: A Guide for the Perplexed*. Bloomsbury. Kindle ed., 19–20.

26. Hauck, D. W. (1999). *The Emerald Tablet: Alchemy for Personal Transformation*. Penguin Compass, 381. Also see "Kill them all and let God sort them out." (July 22, 2015). *This Day in Quotes*. thisdayinquotes.com /2011/07/kill-them-all-and-let-god-sort-them-out.html.

27. Headsman. (July 22, 2009). 1209: Massacre of Beziers, "kill them all, let God sort them out." ExecutedToday.com. executedtoday.com/2009 /07/22/1209-albigensian-crusade-cathars-beziers.

28. Hauck, D. W. (1999). *The Emerald Tablet: Alchemy for Personal Transformation*. Penguin Compass, 9.

29. Laszlo, E. (2006). *Science and the Reenchantment of the Cosmos: The Rise of the Integral Vision of Reality*. Inner Traditions, 25.

30. Hauck, D. W. (1999). *The Emerald Tablet: Alchemy for Personal Transformation*. Penguin Compass, 60. Fernandes, J., & Armada, F. (2005). *Heavenly Lights: The Apparitions of Fatima and the UFO Phenomenon*.

EcceNova. Vallee, J., & Aubeck, C. (2010). *Wonders in the Sky: Unexplained Aerial Objects from Antiquity to Modern Times*. TarcherPerigee.

31. Hermetic Fellowship online, hermeticfellowship.org.

32. Moses factoid: Moses is the most frequently mentioned prophet in the Quran, at 136 times. Muhammad is mentioned by name only 5 times. In Knight, M. M. (2016). *Magic in Islam*. TarcherPerigee, 34.

33. Hanegraaff, W. J. (2013). *Western Esotericism: A Guide for the Perplexed*. Bloomsbury. Kindle ed., 28.

34. Hauck, D. W. (1999). *The Emerald Tablet: Alchemy for Personal Transformation*. Penguin Compass, 25. *The Sepher Yetzirah*. (1887). Translated by W. W. Westcott. Available at hermetic.com/texts/yetzirah.

35. Hauck, D. W. (1999). *The Emerald Tablet: Alchemy for Personal Transformation*. Penguin Compass, 32.

36. Dawes, G. W. (2013). The rationality of Renaissance magic. *Parergon* 30(2), 33–58.

37. Hanegraaff, W. J. (2013). *Western Esotericism: A Guide for the Perplexed*. Bloomsbury. Kindle ed., 90.

38. Van Helden, A. (1995). Giordano Bruno (1548–1600). The Galileo Project, Rice University, galileo.rice.edu/chr/bruno.html.

39. Davies, O. (2012). *Magic: A Very Short Introduction*. Oxford University Press, 47.

40. Hanegraaff, W. J. (2013). *Western Esotericism: A Guide for the Perplexed*. Bloomsbury. Kindle ed., 33.

41. Hanegraaff, W. J. (2013). *Western Esotericism: A Guide for the Perplexed*. Bloomsbury. Kindle ed., 34.

42. White, M. (1997). *Isaac Newton: The Last Sorcerer*. Addison-Wesley, 122.

43. Ibid, 128.

44. Ibid.

45. Crabtree, A. (1993). *From Mesmer to Freud: Magnetic Sleep and the Roots of Psychological Healing*. Yale University Press.

46. From whom Ehrich Weiss, better known as "Houdini," later adopted his stage name.

47. Beloff, J. (1993). *Parapsychology: A Concise History*. Athlone Press, 30–31.

48. Huxley, A. (1945). *The Perennial Philosophy*. Harper.

49. Goodrick-Clarke, N. (2008). *The Western Esoteric Traditions: A Historical Introduction*. Oxford University Press. Kindle ed., 193.

50. Society for Psychical Research. (2014–). *Psi Encyclopedia*. spr.ac.uk/publications/psi-encyclopedia.

51. Gottschalk, S. (2006). *Rolling Away the Stone: Mary Baker Eddy's Challenge to Materialism.* Bloomington and Indianapolis: Indiana University Press.

52. Regardie, I. (2002). *The Golden Dawn: The Original Account of the Teachings, Rites & Ceremonies of the Hermetic Order.* 6th ed. Llewellyn.

53. Blavatsky, H. P. (1888) *The Secret Doctrine.* 2 vols. Theosophy Trust.

54. Hanegraaff, W. J. (2013). *Western Esotericism: A Guide for the Perplexed.* Bloomsbury. Kindle ed., 91.

55. Goodrick-Clarke, N. (2008). *The Western Esoteric Traditions: A Historical Introduction.* Oxford University Press. Kindle ed., 211–212.

56. Goodrick-Clarke, N. (2008). *The Western Esoteric Traditions: A Historical Introduction.* Oxford University Press. Kindle ed., 213–214.

57. Tillet, G. (2012). Modern Western magic and Theosophy. *Aries,* 12, 17–51.

58. Asprem, E. (2008). Magic naturalized? Negotiating science and occult experience in Aleister Crowley's scientific illuminism. *Aries,* 8, 139–165.

59. Pasi, M. (2011). Varieties of magical experience: Aleister Crowley's views on occult practice. *Magic, Ritual, and Witchcraft,* 6(2), 123–162.

60. Magicians often adopted pseudonyms as a pragmatic strategy to prevent the Inquisition from identifying them. That tradition remains popular among modern magicians.

61. Fortune, D. (2011). *Psychic Self-Defense: The Classic Instruction Manual for Protecting Yourself Against Paranormal Attack.* Rev. ed. Weiser Books.

62. Steiner, R. (1947). *Knowledge of the Higher Words and Its Attainment.* Translated by George Metaxa. Anthroposophic Press, 1–2.

63. Needleman, J. (1992). G. I. Gurdjieff and his school. In Faivre, A., & Needleman, J. (eds.), *Modern Esoteric Spirituality,* vol. 21, 360. Crossroad. Also Needleman, J. (1999). G. I. Gurdjieff and his school. *Gurdjieff International Review,* 3(1).

64. Hanegraaff, W. J. (2013). *Western Esotericism: A Guide for the Perplexed.* Bloomsbury. Kindle ed., 67.

65. Faivre, A., & Needleman, J. (eds.). *Modern Esoteric Spirituality,* vol. 21, 382. Crossroad.

66. At the time, chaos mathematics was a new approach to understanding the behavior of complex systems. Carroll's other influence was quantum theory, which suggests that reality is fundamentally probabilistic. Thus Carroll interpreted magic as a means of mentally nudging probabilities. The same idea has been proposed in psi research by physicists such as Evan Harris Walker, as an explanation for psychokinetic effects.

Walker, E. H. (2008). *The Physics of Consciousness: The Quantum Mind and the Meaning of Life.* Basic Books.

67. Carroll, P. J. (1987). *Liber Null & Psychonaut: An Introduction to Chaos Magic.* Red Wheel Weiser. Kindle ed., 112–113.

68. Klimo, J. (1987). *Channeling: Investigations on Receiving Information from Paranormal Sources.* Jeremy P. Tarcher. Auerbach, L. (1993). *Reincarnation, Channeling and Possession: A Parapsychologist's Handbook.* Warner, 188.

69. Hastings, A. (1991). *With the Tongues of Men and Angels.* Holt, Rinehart & Winston.

70. Katz, M. (2011). *Tibetan Dream Yoga.* Bodhi Tree Publications.

71. Roberts, J. (2011). *The Nature of Personal Reality: Specific, Practical Techniques for Solving Everyday Problems and Enriching the Life You Know.* A Seth Book. Amber-Allen. Kindle ed., 248–250.

72. Roberts, J. (2011). *The Nature of Personal Reality: Specific, Practical Techniques for Solving Everyday Problems and Enriching the Life You Know.* A Seth Book. Amber-Allen. Kindle ed., 315–317.

73. James, A. (2017). *As a Man Thinketh.* Amazon Digital Services LLC, 4, 17.

74. Top 20 lists in books. (Accessed July 19, 2017). Amazon.com. amazon.com/b?ie=UTF8&node=11913537011.

75. Positive Psychology Center, University of Pennsylvania. ppc.sas.upenn.edu.

76. Dunn, P. (2005). *Postmodern Magic: The Art of Magic in the Information Age.* Llewelyn. Kindle ed., 432–433.

77. White, G. (2016). *Pieces of Eight: Chaos Magic Essays and Enchantments.* Amazon Digital Services. Kindle ed., 48–49, 68–70.

CHAPTER 5: PRACTICE OF MAGIC

1. Sala, L. (2014). *Ritual: The Magical Perspective.* Nirala.

2. Young, S. (2016). *The Science of Enlightenment: How Meditation Works.* Sounds True. Kindle ed., 1861–1862.

3. Wallace, B. A. (2007). *Hidden Dimensions: The Unification of Physics and Consciousness.* Columbia University Press, 103.

4. With a nod to Douglas Adams's wonderful phrase from his book *The Hitchhiker's Guide to the Galaxy.*

5. R. H. J. (1991). *It Works!* 31st ed. DeVorss.

6. This idea is based on a creative suggestion by Patrick Dunn in his 2008

book, *Magic, Power, Language, Symbol: A Magician's Exploration of Linguistics*. Llewelyn. Kindle ed., 926–930.

7. British artist and occultist Austin Osman Spare (1886–1956) is credited with devising the modern version of a sigil. Grant, K. (1961). Austin Osman Spare: An introduction to his psycho-magical philosophy. Available at pastelegram.org/e/126.

8. Wheeler, J. A. (1989). Information, physics, quantum: The search for links. *Proceedings of the Third International Symposium on the Foundations of Quantum Mechanics*, Tokyo, 310.

9. Tegmark, M. (2014). *Our Mathematical Universe: My Quest for the Ultimate Nature of Reality*. Knopf Doubleday. Kindle ed., 5538–5539.

10. Redd, N. T. (July 12, 2016). Einstein's theory of general relativity. Space.com. space.com/17661-theory-general-relativity.html.

11. The Golden Gate Bridge, north of San Francisco, California.

12. How remote viewing and remote influencing are taught. Biblioteca Pleyades. bibliotecapleyades.net/vision_remota/esp_visionremota_9e.htm. The Firedocs website has information about remote viewing: firedocs .com/remoteviewing. See especially Gaenir, P. J. (1998). *The Controlled Remote Viewing Manual*. firedocs.com/remoteviewing/answers /crvmanual/CRVManual_FiredocsRV.pdf.

13. For an introduction and free online course on remote viewing, I recommend Greg Kolodziejzyk's website, remote-viewing.com. For seminars, workshops, and other training opportunities, the International Remote Viewing Association website, www.irva.org, is a good place to begin.

14. White, R. A. (1964). A comparison of old and new methods of response to targets in ESP experiments. *Journal of the American Society for Psychical Research*, 58(1).

15. Of hundreds of such books, here are three I recommend: Arcangel, D. (2005). *Afterlife Encounters: Ordinary People, Extraordinary Experiences*. Hampton Roads. Giesemann, S. (2011). *Messages of Hope: The Metaphysical Memoir of a Most Unexpected Medium*. One Mind Books. Swedenborg, E. (1996). *Conversations with Angels: What Swedenborg Heard in Heaven*. Chrysalis Books. There are also many organizations for people interested in these ideas, such as eternea.org.

16. Vallee, J., & Aubeck, C. (2010). *Wonders in the Sky: Unexplained Aerial Objects from Antiquity to Modern Times*. TarcherPerigee. Strieber, W., & Kripal, J. J. (2016). *The Super Natural: A New Vision of the Unexplained*. TarcherPerigee.

17. Cardoso, A. (2010). *Electronic Voices: Contact with Another Dimension?* O Books. Also see itcjournal.org. And see Cardoso, A. (2012). A two-

year investigation of the allegedly anomalous electronic voices or EVP. *NeuroQuantology*, 10(3), 492–514. Available at itcjournal.org/PDF /Report—571-1451-1-PB.pdf.

18. Two of hundreds of possible examples: Moura, A. (2003). *Grimoire for the Green Witch*. Llewellyn. Buckland, R. (2010). *Buckland's Complete Book of Witchcraft*. Llewellyn.

CHAPTER 6: SCIENTIFIC EVIDENCE

1. Bauer, H. H. (2012) *Dogmatism in Science and Medicine: How Dominant Theories Monopolize Research and Stifle the Search for Truth*. McFarland.

2. I met Jessica Utts in 1985 when we were both working on a top-secret psi research program conducted for the U.S. government. That and other projects performed as part of that research effort are now commonly known as "Stargate," which was the last of many code names used over the years.

3. The talk at the 2016 Joint Statistical Meetings in Chicago can be found at ww2.amstat.org/meetings/jsm/2016/webcasts/index.cfm or youtu.be /hEFaUg0roKw starting at the 40-minute mark. The talk is also available as an article: Utts, J. (2016). Appreciating statistics. *Journal of the American Statistical Association*, 111(516), 1373–1380.

4. See, e.g., May, E. C., Rubel, V., McMoneagle, J. W., & Auerbach, L. (2015). *ESP Wars: East & West: An Account of the Military Use of Psychic Espionage as Narrated by the Key Russian and American Players*. Crossroad Press.

5. Utts, J. (2016). Appreciating statistics. *Journal of the American Statistical Association,* 111(516), 1373–1380.

6. Schwartz, S. (July/August 2015). Six protocols, neuroscience, and near death: An emerging paradigm incorporating nonlocal consciousness. *Explore*, 11(4), 252–260.

7. For those interested in more details, see the discussions about these experiments in my 2006 book *Entangled Minds* (Simon & Schuster) and my 2013 book *Supernormal* (Random House).

8. Tressoldi, P. E. (2011). Extraordinary claims require extraordinary evidence: The case of non-local perception, a classical and Bayesian review of evidences. *Frontiers in Psychology*, 2, 117. Also Williams, B. J. (2011). Revisiting the ganzfeld ESP debate: A basic review and assessment. *Journal of Scientific Exploration*, 25(4), 639–661.

9. Radin, D. (2013). *Supernormal*. Random House. Radin, D. (2006). *En-*

tangled Minds. Simon & Schuster. Radin, D. (1997). *The Conscious Universe*. HarperOne. Tressoldi, P. E. (2011). Extraordinary claims require extraordinary evidence: The case of non-local perception, a classical and Bayesian review of evidences. *Frontiers in Psychology*, 2, 117.

10. Mossbridge, J., Tressoldi, P. E., & Utts, J. (2012). Predictive physiological anticipation preceding seemingly unpredictable stimuli: A meta-analysis. *Frontiers in Psychology*, 3, 390.

11. Bem, D., Tressoldi, P., Rabeyron, T., & Duggan, M. (2016). Feeling the future: A meta-analysis of 90 experiments on the anomalous anticipation of random future events. *F1000Research*, 4, 1188.

12. Bosch, H., Steinkamp, F., & Boller, E. (2005). Examining psychokinesis: The interaction of human intention with random number generators—a meta-analysis. *Psychological Bulletin*, 132, 497–523. Radin, D. I., Nelson, R. D., Dobyns, Y., & Houtkooper, J. (2006). Reexamining psychokinesis: Commentary on the Bösch, Steinkamp and Boller meta-analysis. *Psychological Bulletin*, 132, 529–532.

13. Nelson, R. D., Radin, D. I., Shoup, R., & Bancel, P. A. (2002). Correlations of continuous random data with major world events. *Foundations of Physics Letters*, 15, 537–550. Also see global-mind.org/results.html.

14. There is no question that this experiment has demonstrated a statistical anomaly. Analysis of non-event times shows that the data conforms as expected to a random binomial distribution. There are ongoing debates about how to interpret this anomaly. One leading hypothesis, the one that launched the experiment in the first place, is that movements of global mind are correlated with, or perhaps *create*, a negentropic "disturbance in the force." Another is that the effect is due to the experimenters, who select the events to study and the time courses of the analyzed data. For this latter explanation it's important to realize that these types of decisions are made *in advance* of analyzing the data, so the results are not due to "data snooping." I personally lean toward the mind-matter interaction hypothesis.

15. Schmidt, S., Schneider, R., Utts, J. M., et al. (2004). Distant intentionality and the feeling of being stared at: Two meta-analyses. *British Journal of Psychology*, 95, 235–247.

16. Schmidt, S. (2012). Can we help just by good intentions? A meta-analysis of experiments on distant intention effects. *Journal of Alternative and Complementary Medicine*, 18(6), 529–533.

17. Ball, P. (February 16, 2017). The strange link between the human mind and quantum physics. *BBC Earth*. Also Kent, A. (2016). Quanta and qualia. arXiv:1608.04804v1 [quant-ph].

18. Freedman, M., Jeffers, S., Saeger, K., Binns, M., & Black, S. (2003). Effects of frontal lobe lesions on intentionality and random physical phenomena. *Journal of Scientific Exploration*, 17, 651–668.

19. Radin, D., Michel, L., & Delorme, A. (2016). Psychophysical modulation of fringe visibility in a distant double-slit optical system. *Physics Essays*, 29(1), 14–22. Radin, D., Michel, L., & Delorme, A. (2015). Reassessment of an independent verification of psychophysical interactions with a double-slit interference pattern. *Physics Essays*, 28(4), 415–416. Radin, D., Michel, L., Pierce, A., & Delorme, A. (2015). Psychophysical interactions with a single-photon double-slit optical system. *Quantum Biosystems*, 6(1), 82–98. Radin, D. I., Delorme, A., Michel, L., & Johnston, J. (2013). Psychophysical interactions with a double-slit interference pattern: Experiments and a model. *Physics Essays*, 26(4), 553–566. Radin, D. I., Michel, L., Wendland, P., Rickenbach, R., Delorme, A., & Galdamez, K. (2012). Consciousness and the double-slit interference pattern: Six experiments. *Physics Essays*, 25(2), 157–171. Radin, D. I. (2008). Testing non-local observation as a source of intuitive knowledge. *Explore*, 4(1), 25–35.

20. There are many interpretations of the observer effect. The description here is simplified to provide the gist of this puzzling phenomenon.

21. Rosenblum, B., & Kuttner, F. (2011). *Quantum Enigma: Physics Encounters Consciousness*. 2nd ed. Oxford University Press.

22. Baer, W. (2015). Independent verification of psychophysical interactions with a double-slit interference pattern. *Physics Essays*, 28(4), 47–54. Radin, D., Michel, L., & Delorme, A. (2015). Reassessment of an independent verification of psychophysical interactions with a double-slit interference pattern. *Physics Essays*, 28(4), 415–416.

23. Guerrer, G. (August 25, 2017). Consciousness-related interactions in a double-slit optical interferometer. OSFPrePrints. https://osf.io/zsgwp/, as of August 2017.

24. Radin, D. (June 7, 2016). New experiments show consciousness affects matter. YouTube. youtu.be/nRSBaq3vAeY.

25. Gissurarson, L. R. (1997). Descriptive analysis of mentations on volitional tasks. *Journal of the Society for Psychical Research*, 62(848), 22–35.

26. PEAR was an acronym for Princeton (University) Engineering Anomalies Research.

27. Jahn, R., & Dunne, B. J. (1987). *Margins of Reality: The Role of Consciousness in the Physical World*. Harcourt Brace Jovanovich, 142.

28. Nelson, L. A., & Schwartz, G. E. (2006). Consciousness and the anomalous organization of random events: The role of absorption. *Journal of Scientific Exploration*, 20(4), 523–544.

29. United States Conference of Catholic Bishops, Liturgy of the Eucharist, http://www.usccb.org/prayer-and-worship/the-mass/order-of-mass /liturgy-of-the-eucharist/the-real-presence-of-jesus-christ-in-the-sacrament -of-the-eucharist-basic-questions-and-answers.cfm.

30. Mead, P. S., Slutsker, L., Dietz, V., et al. (1999). Food-related illness and death in the United States. *Emerging Infectious Diseases*, 5(5), 607–625.

31. Radin, D. I., Hayssen, G., & Walsh, J. (2007). Effects of intentionally enhanced chocolate on mood. *Explore: The Journal of Science and Healing*, 3(5), 485–492.

32. For research design aficionados: neuroticism was used as a covariate.

33. See articles at tillerinstitute.com. Also Tiller, W. A., et al. (2001). *Conscious Acts of Creation: The Emergence of a New Physics*. Pavior. Tiller, W. A., et al. (2004). Towards general experimentation and discovery in "conditioned" laboratory spaces, Part I: Experimental pH-change findings at some remote sites. *Journal of Alternative and Complementary Medicine*, 10(1), 145–157.

34. Shiah, Y-J, & Radin, D. I. (in press, 2017). A randomized, controlled trial of the effects of intentionally treated water on growth of *Arabidopsis thaliana* seeds with cryptochrome mutations. *Explore: The Journal of Science and Healing*.

35. Maeda, K., Robinson, A. J., Henbest, K. B., et al. (2012). Magnetically sensitive light-induced reactions in cryptochrome are consistent with its proposed role as a magnetoreceptor. *Proceedings of the National Academy of Sciences*, 109(13), 4774–4779.

36. Theoretical and Computational Biophysics Group, University of Illinois at Urbana-Champaign. (2014). Cryptochrome and magnetic sensing. www.ks.uiuc.edu/Research/cryptochrome. Solov'yov, I. A., et al. (2014). A chemical compass for bird navigation. In Mohseni, M., et al. (eds.). *Quantum Effects in Biology*, 218–236. Cambridge University Press.

37. Gardiner, J. (2012). Insights into plant consciousness from neuroscience, physics and mathematics: A role for quasicrystals? *Plant Signaling & Behavior*, 7(9), 1049–1055. For a popular article about "plant intelligence," see Pollan, M. (December 23–30, 2013). The intelligent plant. *New Yorker*.

38. Strauss, L. L. (March 29, 1959). Eminent scientist reports how far a baseball curves. National Institute of Standards and Technology. nist.gov news-events/news/1959/03/eminent-scientist-reports-how-far-baseball -curves.

39. I am grateful to Tom Etter and Richard Shoup for many stimulating discussions that led to this experiment.

40. The experiment actually consisted of six repetitions of 100 trials each, but to avoid confusing the reader I'm mentioning that here rather than in the main text. The full paper is reported in Radin, D. I. (2006). Experiments testing models of mind-matter interaction. *Journal of Scientific Exploration*, 20(3), 375–401.

41. It could be also argued that what this outcome suggests is a phenomenon with no temporal direction at all, that is, a fully time-symmetric effect. It's *interpreted* as a retrocausal influence because it seems, from our limited perspective in time, to flow backward in time.

42. Mihailović, D. T., et al. (2016). Time in philosophy and physics. In Mihailović, D. T., Balaž, I., & Kapor, D. (eds.), *Developments in Environmental Modelling*, 29. Elsevier. Ivanovs, J. (August 2017). Splitting and time reversal for Markov additive processes. *Stochastic Processes and Their Applications*, 127(8), 2699–2724. Jørgensen, S. E., & Svirezhev, Y. M. (2004). Teleology and extreme principles: A tentative fourth law of thermodynamics. In *Towards a Thermodynamic Theory for Ecological Systems*. Pergamon, 301–323.

43. Merali, Z. (August 26, 2010). Back from the future. *Discover*.

44. Radin, D. I. (2006). Psychophysiological evidence of possible retrocausal effects in humans. In D. Sheehan (ed.)., *Frontiers of Time: Retrocausation Experiment and Theory*. American Institutes of Physics. Radin, D. I. (2011). Predicting the unpredictable: 75 years of experimental evidence. In D. P. Sheehan (ed.), *Quantum Retrocausation: Theory and Experiment*. American Institute of Physics.

45. Schmeidler, G., & Murphy, G. (1946). The influence of belief and disbelief in ESP upon individual scoring levels. *Journal of Experimental Psychology*, 36(3), 271–276. Schmeidler, G. (1994). ESP experiments 1978–1992. In Stanley Krippner (ed.), *Advances in Parapsychological Research*, vol. 7, 104–197. McFarland.

46. Walsh, K., & Moddel, G. (2007). Effect of belief on psi performance in a card guessing task. *Journal of Scientific Exploration*, 21(3), 501–510.

47. Lawrence, T. (1993). Bringing in the sheep: A meta-analysis of sheep/goat experiments. Paper presented at the Parapsychological Association Annual Conference, Toronto, Canada.

48. Storm, L., & Tressoldi, P. (2017). Gathering in more sheep and goats: A meta-analysis of forced-choice sheep-goat ESP studies, 1994–2015. *Journal of the Society for Psychical Research*, 81(2), 79.

49. Shiah, Y.-J., & Radin, D. (2013). Metaphysics of the tea ceremony: A

randomized trial investigating the roles of intention and belief on mood while drinking tea, *Explore*, 9(6), 355–360.

50. Used for stratified random sampling.

51. Johnson, D. (November 19, 1977). PLATOnic parapsychology. *Daily Illini*, 2.

52. Known as the PLATO system, an acronym for Programmed Logic for Automatic Teaching Operations. See Jones, S. (November 23, 2015). PLATO: Computer-based education system. *Encyclopaedia Britannica*.

53. People were allowed to contribute more or less trials or sessions in a given day, but we chose this uniform criterion, one session of 25 trials per person, to avoid biases that can be introduced by optional stopping artifacts.

54. The result of each trial in this test is associated with a p-value, which is transformed by an inverse normal transform into a standard normal deviate, i.e., z score.

55. Bem, D. (2011). Feeling the future: Experimental evidence for anomalous retroactive influences on cognition and affect. *Journal of Personality and Social Psychology*, 100(3), 407–425.

56. Carey, B. (January 5, 2011). Journal's paper on ESP expected to prompt outrage. *New York Times*.

57. Lehrer, J. (November 15, 2010). Feeling the future: Is precognition possible? *Wired*.

58. Radin, D. (2013). *Supernormal*. Random House, 175.

59. Bem, D., Tressoldi, P. E, Rabeyron, T., & Duggan, M. (2016). Feeling the future: A meta-analysis of 90 experiments on the anomalous anticipation of random future events [version 2; referees: 2 approved]. *F1000Research*, 4:1188 (doi: 10.12688/f1000research.7177.2).

60. Personal correspondence from Prof. Daryl Bem.

61. Clark, S. (March 1, 2017). Cosmic uncertainty: Does time go both ways? *New Scientist*.

62. For example: Honorton, C., & Ferrari, D. C. (1989). Future telling: A meta-analysis of forced-choice precognition experiments, 1935–1987. *Journal of Parapsychology*, 53, 281–308. Radin, D. I. (2006). Psychophysiological evidence of possible retrocausal effects in humans. In D. Sheehan (ed)., *Frontiers of Time: Retrocausation Experiment and Theory*. American Institutes of Physics. Radin, D. I. (2004). Electrodermal presentiments of future emotions. *Journal of Scientific Exploration*, 18, 253–274. Radin, D. I., & Borges, A. (2009). Intuition through time: What does the seer see? *Explore*, 5(4), 200–211. Radin, D. I., & Lobach, E. (2007). Toward understanding the placebo effect:

Investigating a possible retrocausal factor. *Journal of Alternative and Complementary Medicine*, 13, 733–739. Radin, D. I., Vieten, C., Michel, L., & Delorme, A. (2011). Electrocortical activity prior to unpredictable stimuli in meditators and non-meditators. *Explore*, 7, 286–299. Mossbridge, J. A., Tressoldi, P., Utts, J., Ives, J. A., Radin, D., & Jonas, W. B. (2014). Predicting the unpredictable: Critical analysis and practical implications of predictive anticipatory activity. *Frontiers in Human Neuroscience*, 8, 146. Mossbridge, J. A., & Radin, D. I. (in press). Precognition as a form of prospection: A review of the evidence. *Psychology of Consciousness: Theory, Research, and Practice.*

63. Barlett, T. (March 17, 2017). Spoiled science. *Chronicle of Higher Education*.

64. Engber, D. (May 17, 2017). Daryl Bem proved ESP is real, which means science is broken. *Slate*.

65. Of course this doesn't mean that all seers are legit. Throughout history many so-called fortune tellers have been fraudulent. As always, caveat emptor.

66. The outlier was identified as a residual greater than two sigma from the linear regression line. Of course, post-hoc analyses don't carry the same evidential strength as planned analyses, but they can be instructive.

67. Williams, B. J. (November 9, 2016). Field RNG exploration review: 2016 U.S. presidential race. Facebook. www.facebook.com/notes/bryan -j-williams/field-rng-exploration-review–2016-us-presidential-race/101 53949359522050. This method of analysis is called a *cumulative deviation,* which is useful for detecting slow trends in the data. But it can overlook faster-moving events.

68. Barret, J. (December 21, 2016). How many votes did Trump and Clinton get? The final vote count. *Daily Wire*.

69. This is due to the exclusive-or (XOR) logic used in RNGs. This logic technique ensures that small drifts or cycles in electronic noise or due to environmental influences will not bias the random bits that are generated. If the logic gate isn't used, it's extremely difficult to construct an RNG that predictably generates 1s and 0s with a 50/50 likelihood. Unfortunately, the XOR also masks what the noise levels were inside the RNG before the noise was converted into bits.

70. Two of the thirty-two channels did not record properly, so data from thirty channels were analyzed. All of the QNGs ran off a battery to avoid possible glitches from the electrical power grid. The analysis followed four steps. First, for each minute of data in each of the thirty QNGs we determined the median autocorrelation across lags 1 to 10

milliseconds. Second, we formed a trimmed mean across the thirty QNGs for each minute of data. Third, we determined a thirty-minute sliding window of the variance of the mean formed in step two. And fourth, we evaluated the joint probability of the magnitude and timing of the observed peak value within one hour of midnight Pacific Time. That probability was converted into the odds figure reported in the text.

71. I use the word *cause* with hesitation because, as we've already seen, psi effects do not seem to operate as simple causal influences. In any case, with this type of experiment what we measure is a *correlation* between the output of the QNG and world events.

72. This was like the previous analysis except for two changes: the second step determined the average mutual information across all thirty QNGs per minute, and then the third step used a six-hour moving window. Otherwise the rest of the analysis was the same. Use of different sliding window lengths was useful in revealing different temporal and spatial characteristics of the phenomenon. These results should be considered exploratory and as not a formal experiment.

73. There is a close relationship between quantum entanglement and mutual information. See, e.g., Lombardi, O., Holik, F., & Vanni, L. (2016). What is quantum information? *Studies in History and Philosophy of Science Part B: Studies in History and Philosophy of Modern Physics*, 56, 17–26.

74. Sheldrake, R. (2013). *The Sense of Being Stared At: And Other Unexplained Powers of Human Minds*. 3rd ed. Park Street Press.

75. Sheldrake, R. (1998). The sense of being stared at: Experiments in schools. *Journal of the Society for Psychical Research*, 62, 311–323. Sheldrake, R. (1999). The "sense of being stared at" confirmed by simple experiments. *Biology Forum*, 92, 53–76. Sheldrake, R. (2000). The "sense of being stared at" does not depend on known sensory clues. *Biology Forum*, 93, 209–224. See this webpage for other articles: www.sheldrake.org/research.

76. Radin, D. I. (2005). The sense of being stared at: A preliminary meta-analysis. *Journal of Consciousness Studies*, 12(6), 95–100.

77. Radin, D. I. (2004). On the sense of being stared at: An analysis and pilot replication. *Journal of the Society for Psychical Research*, 68, 246–253.

78. As an example of just one these studies: Radin, D. I., Stone, J., Levine, E., et al. (2008). Compassionate intention as a therapeutic intervention by partners of cancer patients: Effects of distant intention on the patients' autonomic nervous system. *Explore*, 4(4), 235–243.

79. Radin, D. I., & Schlitz, M. J. (2005). Gut feelings, intuition, and emotions: An exploratory study. *Journal of Alternative and Complementary Medicine*, 11(4), 85–91. This study used an electrogastrogram to measure electrical activity associated with peristalsis.

80. Radin, D. I., Stone, J., Levine, E., et al. (2008). Compassionate intention as a therapeutic intervention by partners of cancer patients: Effects of distant intention on the patients' autonomic nervous system. *Explore*, 4(4), 235–243.

81. Schmidt, S. (2012). Can we help just by good intentions? A meta-analysis of experiments on distant intention effects. *Journal of Alternative and Complementary Medicine*, 18(6), 529–533.

82. Rebman, J. M., Wezelman, R., Radin, D. I., Hapke, R. A., & Gaughan, K. (1995). Remote influence of human physiology by a ritual healing technique. *Subtle Energies and Energy Medicine*, 6, 111–134.

83. Radford, B. (October 30, 2013). Voodoo: Facts about misunderstood religion. *LiveScience*.

84. Fingertip blood flow was measured with a photoplethysmograph, which measures vasoconstriction, a correlate of blood pressure.

85. Kreiter, J. (2014). *Create a Servitor: Harness the Power of Thought Forms*. Amazon Digital Services. Kindle ed., 171.

86. David-Neel, A. (2012). *Magic and Mystery in Tibet*. Dover. Kindle ed., 278–279.

87. Auerbach, L. (2004). *Hauntings and Poltergeists: A Ghost Hunter's Guide*. Ronin.

88. Crick, F. (1994). *The Astonishing Hypothesis: The Scientific Search for the Soul*. Touchstone.

89. McNamara, J. (2012). *Brain Facts: A Primer on the Brain and Nervous System*. 7th ed. Society for Neuroscience.

90. White, G. (2016). *Pieces of Eight: Chaos Magic Essays and Enchantments*. Amazon Digital Services. Kindle ed., 224–227.

91. van Lommel, P. (2010). *Consciousness Beyond Life: The Science of the Near-Death Experience*. HarperOne.

92. Kroeger, D., Florea, B., & Amzica, F. (2013). Human brain activity patterns beyond the isoelectric line of extreme deep coma. *PloS One*, 8(9), e75257.

93. Borjigin, J., Lee, U., Liu, T., Pal, D., Huff, S., Klarr, D., Sloboda, J., Hernandez, J., Wang, M. M., & Mashour, G. A. (2013). Surge of neurophysiological coherence and connectivity in the dying brain. *Proceedings of the National Academy of Science*, 110(35), 14432–14437.

94. Greyson, B. (2007). Consistency of near-death experience accounts over

two decades: Are reports embellished over time? *Resuscitation*, 73(3), 407–411.

95. French, C. C. (2005). Near-death experiences in cardiac arrest survivors. *Progress in Brain Research*, 150, 351–367.

96. Greyson, B. (2007). Consistency of near-death experience accounts over two decades: Are reports embellished over time? *Resuscitation*, 73(3), 407–411.

97. Palmieri, A., et al. (2014). "Reality" of near-death-experience memories: Evidence from a psychodynamic and electrophysiological integrated study. *Frontiers in Human Neuroscience*, 8, 429.

98. van Lommel, P. (2011). Near-death experiences: The experience of the self as real and not as an illusion. *Annals of the New York Academy of Science*, 1234, 19–28.

99. Vane, J. R., & Botting, R. M. (2003). The mechanism of action of aspirin. *Thrombosis Research*, 110, 255–258.

100. Verschuur, G. L. (1993). *Hidden Attraction: The History and Mystery of Magnetism*. Oxford University Press.

101. Tressoldi, P. E. (2011). Extraordinary claims require extraordinary evidence: The case of non-local perception, a classical and Bayesian review of evidences. *Frontiers in Psychology*, 2.

102. Kastrup, B. (March 29, 2017). Transcending the brain. *Scientific American*. Kastrup, B. (2017). Self-transcendence correlates with brain function impairment. *Journal of Cognition and Neuroethics,* 4(3), 33–42.

103. Parnia, P., et al. (2014). AWARE—AWAreness During REsuscitation—a prospective study. *Resuscitation*, 85(12), 1799–1805.

104. Kean, L. (2017). *Surviving Death: A Journalist Investigates Evidence for an Afterlife*. Penguin Random House.

105. Hagan, J. C. (2017). *The Science of Near-Death Experiences*. University of Missouri Press.

106. Beischel, J. (2011). Mediumship research. *Journal of Nervous and Mental Disease*, 199(6), 425–426. Beischel, J., & Schwartz, G. E. (2007). Anomalous information reception by research mediums demonstrated using a novel triple-blind protocol. *Explore*, 3(1), 23–27.

107. Delorme, A., Michel, L., & Radin, D. (May 17, 2016). Prediction of mortality based on facial characteristics. *Frontiers in Human Neuroscience*.

108. Okay, that last motto was actually a favored saying of the Borg, from the *Star Trek* franchise. I imagine that the Inquisition would have gotten along quite well with the Borg.

109. Kroupa, P. (November 25, 2016). Has dogma derailed the scientific search for dark matter? *Aeon*. Bates, M., et al. (2016). Challenging

dogma and stagnation in TB research. *International Journal of Myco-bacteriology*, 5(4), 373. González-Fernández, J., et al. (2016). Allergenicity of vertebrate tropomyosins: Challenging an immunological dogma. *Allergologia et Immunopathologia*, 45(3), 297–304. Weatherall, J. O. (2014). Against dogma: On superluminal propagation in classical electromagnetism, *Studies in History and Philosophy of Science Part B: Studies in History and Philosophy of Modern Physics*, 48, Part B, 109–123.

110. To advance science we need to think about the impossible. (March 1, 2017). *New Scientist*.

111. Delorme, A., Beischel, J., Michel, L., et al. (2013). Electrocortical activity associated with subjective communication with the deceased. *Frontiers in Psychology*, 4, 834.

112. Cordina, T. (1984). *13 Steps to Mentalism*. Supreme Magic.

113. Moore, J. (2010). *The James Bond Cold Reading*. The Cold Reading Company. Kindle Edition, 56–59.

114. Delorme, A., Beischel, J., Michel, L., et al. (2013). Electrocortical activity associated with subjective communication with the deceased. *Frontiers in Psychology*, 4, 834.

115. Nothing has demonstrated the truth of this more clearly than the cantankerous 2016 presidential election in the United States, or the outcome and aftermath of that election. Committed supporters of the two main candidates found it virtually impossible to understand the other's position.

CHAPTER 7: MERLIN-CLASS MAGICIANS

1. Grosso, M. (2016). *The Man Who Could Fly: St. Joseph of Copertino and the Mystery of Levitation*. Rowman & Littlefield, 22. Thurston, H. (1952). *The Physical Phenomena of Mysticism*. Burns Oates.

2. For the five people in the world who don't get this reference, Lord Voldemort is a fictional evil magician in the Harry Potter books.

3. The odor of sanctity is a phenomenon associated with saintly people. Grosso, M. (2016). *The Man Who Could Fly: St. Joseph of Copertino and the Mystery of Levitation*. Rowman & Littlefield, 92: "Padre Giuseppe was rewarded with the gift of this mystical perfume, which everyone could smell. It penetrated his body and his clothes and his cell and everything belonging to him—a smell so pleasant that it astonished all who knew it."

4. Grosso, M. (2016). *The Man Who Could Fly: St. Joseph of Copertino and the Mystery of Levitation*. Rowman & Littlefield, 75.

5. Ibid, 86.

6. Lamont, P. (2005). *The First Psychic: The Peculiar Mystery of a Notorious Victorian Wizard*. Abacus.

7. Ibid, 260.

8. Ibid, 261.

9. Ibid, 94.

10. Ibid.

11. Ibid, 94–95.

12. Zorab, G. (1970). Test sittings with D. D. Home at Amsterdam (1858). *Journal of Parapsychology, 34,* 57.

13. Ibid, 34, 60.

14. Lamont, P. (2005). *The First Psychic: The Peculiar Mystery of a Notorious Victorian Wizard*. Abacus, 94–96.

15. Mishlove, J. (2000). *The PK Man: A True Story of Mind over Matter*. Hampton Roads Publishing. Kindle ed., 729–730.

16. Ibid, 740–743.

17. Ibid, 540–547.

18. Ibid.

19. Ibid, 574–578.

20. Ibid, 609–610.

21. Ibid, 612–616. Also Poleskie, S. (November 2015). Then and now. *Ragazine*. ragazine.cc/2015/11/stephen-poleskie-then-and-now.

22. Mishlove, J. (2000). *The PK Man: A True Story of Mind over Matter*. Hampton Roads Publishing. Kindle ed., 652–657. Also 1977: February UFO & Alien Sighting. (n.d.). *Think About It*. thinkaboutitdocs.com/2-february-march-1977-sighting.

CHAPTER 8: TOWARD A SCIENCE OF MAGIC

1. These data are reviewed in more detail in my previous books, especially Radin, D. (2013). *Supernormal*. Random House. Radin, D. (2006). *Entangled Minds*. Simon & Schuster.

2. Carpenter, J. C. (2012). *First Sight: ESP and Parapsychology in Everyday Life*. Rowman & Littlefield.

3. For future archeologists trying to understand this comment, I refer to Twitter, a smartphone texting service that began in 2006. It allowed users to broadcast text messages with a maximum of 140 characters. In 2017 it became the principal means of communication for the president of the United States.

4. Huxley, A. (1945). *The Perennial Philosophy*. Harper.

5.   Levin, J. (2008). Esoteric healing traditions: A conceptual overview. *Explore*, 4(2).

6.   Hanegraaff, W. J. (2013). *Western Esotericism: A Guide for the Perplexed*. Bloomsbury. Kindle ed., 5.

7.   There are entire books written in an attempt to define consciousness. I'm keeping it simple.

8.   Currivan, J. (2017). *The Cosmic Holograph: Information at the Center of Creation*. Inner Traditions, 178.

9.   Kastrup, B. (2014). *Why Materialism Is Baloney: How True Skeptics Know There Is No Death and Fathom Answers to Life, the Universe, and Everything*. John Hunt. Kindle ed., 5.

10.   Radin, D., Michel, L., & Delorme, A. (2016). Psychophysical modulation of fringe visibility in a distant double-slit optical system. *Physics Essays*, 29(1), 14–22. Radin, D., Michel, L., & Delorme, A. (2015). Reassessment of an independent verification of psychophysical interactions with a double-slit interference pattern. *Physics Essays*, 28(4), 415–416. Radin, D. I., Delorme, A., Michel, L., & Johnston, J. (2013). Psychophysical interactions with a double-slit interference pattern: Experiments and a model. *Physics Essays*, 26(4), 553–566. Radin, D. I., Michel, L., Wendland, P., Rickenbach, R., Delorme, A., & Galdamez, K. (2012). Consciousness and the double-slit interference pattern: Six experiments. *Physics Essays*, 25(2), 157–171.

11.   Groblacher, S., Paterek, T., Kaltenbaek, R., et al. (2007). An experimental test of non-local realism. *Nature*, 446, 871–875.

12.   Stapp, H. (2007). *Mindful Universe: Quantum Mechanics and the Participating Observer*. Springer.

13.   Harman, W., & Clark, J. (1994). *New Metaphysical Foundations of Modern Science*. Institute of Noetic Sciences.

14.   Tart, C. T., Puthoff, H. E., & Targ, R. (1980). Information transmission in remote viewing experiments. *Nature*, 284, 191.

15.   Sheldrake, R. (n.d.). Sir John Maddox—books for burning. sheldrake.org/reactions/sir-john-maddox-book-for-burning.

16.   Merriam-Webster.com. (July 19, 2017). Heresy. merriam-webster.com/dictionary/heresy.

17.   Kastrup, B. (2014). *Why Materialism Is Baloney: How True Skeptics Know There Is No Death and Fathom Answers to Life, the Universe, and Everything*. John Hunt. Kindle ed., 58.

18.   Grosso, M., & Kelly, E. F. (2007). *Irreducible Mind: Toward a Psychology for the 21st Century*. Rowman & Littlefield.

19. Dossey, L. (2013). *One Mind: How Our Individual Mind Is Part of a Greater Consciousness and Why It Matters*. Hay House. Kindle ed.

20. Kelly, E. F., Crabtree, A., & Marshall, P. (eds.). (2015). *Beyond Physicalism: Toward Reconciliation of Science and Spirituality*. Rowman & Littlefield.

21. Paulson, S. (April 6, 2017). The spiritual, reductionist consciousness of Christof Koch. *Nautilus*.

22. Bohm, D. (2002). *Wholeness and the Implicate Order*. Routledge.

23. Dawes, G. W. (2013). The rationality of Renaissance magic. *Parergon* 30(2), 37.

24. Landau, E. (May 17, 2010). Awake during surgery: "I'm in hell." CNN.

25. Sperry, R. W. (September 1966). Mind, brain and humanist values. *Bulletin of the Atomic Scientists*, 22(7). Sperry, R. W. (1969). A modified concept of consciousness. *Psychological Review*, 76(6), 532–536.

26. Nader, T. (2015). Consciousness is all there is: A mathematical approach with applications. *International Journal of Mathematics and Consciousness*, 1(1).

27. Skinner, B. F. (1976). *About Behaviorism*. Vintage Books.

28. Currivan, J. (2017). *The Cosmic Holograph: Information at the Center of Creation*. Inner Traditions.

29. Ball, P. (September 5, 2016). We might live in a computer program, but it may not matter. BBC.

30. Dunn, P. (2005). *Postmodern Magic: The Art of Magic in the Information Age*. Llewellyn. Kindle ed., 380–384.

31. The FQXi mission: "To expand the purview of scientific inquiry to include scientific disciplines fundamental to a deep understanding of reality, but which are currently largely unsupported by conventional grant sources." fqxi.org/community/forum/category/31419.

32. Tegmark, M. (2014). *Our Mathematical Universe: My Quest for the Ultimate Nature of Reality*. Knopf.

33. Penrose, R. (September 1, 2009). What is reality? *New Scientist*.

34. Ibid.

35. Radin, D. (June–August 2007). Intention and reality: The ghost in the machine returns. *Shift: At the Frontiers of Consciousness*, 15, 22–26.

36. Jarlett, H. K. (October 6, 2016). In theory: Is theoretical physics in crisis? CERN. home.cern/about/updates/2016/05/theory-theoretical-physics-crisis. (Emphasis added.)

37. Walker, S. I., & Davies, P. C. W. (June 23, 2016). The "hard problem" of life. arXiv:1606.07184v1 [q-bio.OT] (Emphasis added.), 2, 11.

38. Cardeña, E. (January 27, 2014). A call for an open, informed study of all aspects of consciousness. *Frontiers in Human Neuroscience.*

39. Tononi, G., & Koch, C. (2015). Consciousness: Here, there and everywhere? *Philosophical Transactions of the Royal Society, B,* 370, 20140167.

40. Koch, C. (January 1, 2014). Is consciousness universal? *Scientific American.* (Emphasis added.)

41. Zeilinger, A. (2005). [Response to the *Edge* 2005 annual question: What do you believe is true even though you cannot prove it?] https://www.edge.org/response-detail/10380.

42. Seife, C. (2007). *Decoding the Universe: How the New Science of Information Is Explaining Everything in the Cosmos, from Our Brains to Black Holes.* Penguin. Kindle ed., 176.

43. Vedral, V. (2012). *Decoding Reality: The Universe as Quantum Information.* Oxford University Press. Kindle ed., 205–208, 212.

44. For example, a 2014 special issue of *Cosmos and History: The Journal of Natural and Social Philosophy,* 10(1), titled "Foundations of Mind I: Cognition & Consciousness."

45. For example, *Psychology of Consciousness: Theory, Research and Practice.*

46. Baruss, I., & Mossbridge, J. (2016). *Transcendent Mind: Rethinking the Science of Consciousness.* American Psychological Association, 3.

47. Theise, N. D., & Kafatos, M. C. (2016). Fundamental awareness: A framework for integrating science, philosophy and metaphysics. *Communicative & Integrative Biology,* 9:3, e1155010.

48. Kauffman, S. A. (2016). *Humanity in a Creative Universe.* Oxford University Press. Kindle ed., xii–xiv, 7–8.

49. Goff, P. (March 1, 2017). Panpsychism is crazy, but it's also most probably true. *Aeon.*

50. Koons, R. C., & Bealer, G. (2010). Introduction. In Koons, R. C., & Bealer, G. (eds.), *The Waning of Materialism.* Oxford University Press. Kindle ed., 68–74.

51. Quoted in Koons, R. C., & Bealer, G. (2010). Introduction. In Koons, R. C., & Bealer, G. (eds.), *The Waning of Materialism.* Oxford University Press. Kindle ed., 300–302.

52. Laszlo, E. (2006). *Science and the Reenchantment of the Cosmos: The Rise of the Integral Vision of Reality.* Inner Traditions, 53.

53. Nagel, T. (2012). *Mind and Cosmos: Why the Materialist Neo-Darwinian Conception of Nature Is Almost Certainly False.* Oxford University Press. Kindle ed., 116–117, 131, 136–138.

CHAPTER 9: CONCLUDING THOUGHTS

1. Radin, D. I. (1993). Environmental modulation and statistical equilibrium in mind-matter interaction. *Subtle Energies and Energy Medicine*, 4(1), 1–30.

2. Shead, S., & Mercer, C. (October 20, 2016). Nine times tech leaders warned us that robots will kill us all: Stephen Hawking, Elon Musk, Bill Gates and more. *Techworld*.

3. Kurzweil, R. (2000). *The Age of Spiritual Machines: When Computers Exceed Human Intelligence*. Penguin.

4. Carroll, P. J. (1987). *Liber Null & Psychonaut: An Introduction to Chaos Magic*. Red Wheel Weiser. Kindle ed., 199.

5. No offense to real cowboys.

6. Lyons, A., & Truzzi, M. (1991). *The Blue Sense: Psychic Detectives and Crime*. Mysterious Press. Also Roland, P. (2007). *Nazis and the Occult*. Arcturus.

7. May, E. C., Rubel, V., McMoneagle, J. W., & Auerbach, L. (2015). *ESP Wars: East & West: An Account of the Military Use of Psychic Espionage as Narrated by the Key Russian and American Players*. Crossroad Press.

8. Gale, M. (December 1979). The Grill Flame Scientific Evaluation Committee report. Department of the Army.

9. General Defense Intelligence Program memorandum of March 15, 1995, approved for release by the CIA March 24, 2005.

10. Young, S. (2016). *The Science of Enlightenment: How Meditation Works*. Sounds True. Kindle ed., 236–237.

11. Rees, M. (2009). *Our Final Hour: A Scientist's Warning*. Basic Books.

ACKNOWLEDGMENTS

I am grateful to many individuals and foundations that have supported my work. They include the Emerald Gate Charitable Foundation, the Federico and Elvia Faggin Foundation, the Fetzer Institute, the Mental Insight Foundation, Interval Research Corporation, the Samueli Institute, the Parapsychological Foundation, the Bigelow Foundation, the Richard Hodgson Memorial Fund at Harvard University, the Bial Foundation (Portugal), the Swedish Society for Psychical Research, the Norwegian Parapsychological Society, the Society for Psychical Research (England), the Institut für Grenzgebiete der Psychologie und Psychohygiene (Germany), Ramakrishna Rao and the Indian Council for Philosophical Research (India), Liz Huntington and the John B. Huntington Foundation, Jeff Parrett, Richard and Connie Adams, Klee Irwin, and Claire Russell.

I am also grateful to my colleagues at the Institute of Noetic Sciences for their valuable comments on an early draft of this book, especially Leena Michel, Lorraine Walter, Garret Yount, Arnaud Delorme, Helané Wahbeh, Kerstin Sjoquist, and Julia Mossbridge, with a special tip of the hat to our president, Cassandra Vieten, and CEO, Claire Lachance. I thank Dennis Hauck for lending me the secret key to his extensive library on alchemy; Brad Stewart of the Sacred Science Institute for advice about navigating the endless literature on esotericism; Jeffrey Kripal and Claire Fanger of Rice University for revealing the vast scope of the scholarly literature on magic; David Luke of the University of Greenwich for his guidance on the anthropological literature on magic; Serena Roney-Dougal for blazing the trail; Stanley Krippner of Saybrook University for recommending author Luc Sala's comprehensive work on ritual magic, and Luc for kindly reviewing this manuscript; Rick Stack for his generous assistance with the Seth material; and finally Gary Jansen, master wizard—I mean, editor—at Penguin Random House.

INDEX

About the Author

DEAN RADIN, PHD, is chief scientist at the Institute of Noetic Sciences (IONS) and associated distinguished professor of integral and transpersonal psychology at the California Institute of Integral Studies. His original career as a concert violinist shifted into science after he earned a BSEE degree in electrical engineering, *magna cum laude* with honors in physics, from the University of Massachusetts, Amherst, and then an MS in electrical engineering and a PhD in psychology from the University of Illinois, Urbana-Champaign. Prior to joining the IONS research department in 2001 he worked at Bell Laboratories, Princeton University, University of Edinburgh, University of Nevada, and SRI International.

He is author or coauthor of hundreds of scientific, technical, and popular articles, dozens of book chapters, and the award-winning and bestselling books *The Conscious Universe*, *Entangled Minds*, and *Supernormal*. His scientific articles have appeared in a broad range of academic journals, including *Foundations of Physics*, *Psychological Bulletin*, and *Frontiers in Human Neuroscience*. He was profiled in the *New York Times Magazine*, and he has participated in hundreds of podcasts, television programs, radio shows, and independent documentary and feature films. He has given invited presentations at universities including Harvard, Stanford, Princeton, Cambridge, the Sorbonne, and the University of Allahabad; for companies including Google, Johnson & Johnson, and Rabobank; for U.S. government organizations including the Navy, the Defense Advanced Research Projects Agency (DARPA), and the National Academy of Sciences; and for foreign organizations including the Indian Council of Philosophical Research (India), the International Center for Leadership and Governance (Malaysia), and the ADC Forum (Australian Davos Connection, Australia).

ALSO BY DEAN RADIN